Hitting a Straight Lick with a Crooked Stick

Hitting a Straight Lick with a Crooked Stick

Race and Gender in the Work of Zora Neale Hurston

Susan Edwards Meisenhelder

THE UNIVERSITY OF ALABAMA PRESS

Tuscaloosa and London

First Paperbound Printing 2001

9 8 7 6 5 4 3 2 1
09 08 07 06 05 04 03 02 01

∞

The paper on which this book is printed meets the minimum
requirements of American National Standard for Information
Science-Permanence of Paper for Printed Library Materials, ANSI
Z39.48-1984.

Cover design by Shari DeGraw

Library of Congress Cataloging-in-Publication Data

Meisenhelder, Susan Edwards, 1951–
    Hitting a straight lick with a crooked stick : race and
gender in the work of Zora Neale Hurston / Susan Edwards
Meisenhelder.
        p. cm.
    Includes bibliographical references (p.) and index.

    ISBN 0-8173-1131-9 (alk. paper)
    1. Hurston, Zora Neale—Criticism and interpretation.
2. Women and literature—United States—History—20th
century. 3. Afro-American women in literature. 4. Afro-
Americans in literature. 5. Race relations in literature.
6. Sex role in literature. I. Title.
    PS3515.U789 Z785   1999
    813'.52—ddc21 98-58023

For my parents
Ralph Donald Edwards
Virginia Hefner Edwards
and
In loving memory of my grandparents
Virginia Austin Hefner
Atlas Roland Edwards
Katie Griffin Edwards

Contents

Acknowledgments

FOR PERMISSION to quote from the works of Zora Neale Hurston and from other selected correspondence and materials, I would like to make grateful acknowledgment to the following: the estate of Zora Neale Hurston; the Archives of Charles Scribner's Sons in the Manuscripts Division of the Princeton University Library (excerpts published with permission of the Princeton University Library); the collections of the Chicago Historical Society; the American Philosophical Society; The Yale Collection of American Literature, Beinecke Rare Book and Manuscript Library, Yale University; University of Florida Libraries, Department of Special Collections; Fisk University Library Special Collections; and Moorland-Spingarn Research Center, Howard University. For permission to use the photograph of Hurston taken by Carl Van Vechten, I thank the Van Vechten Trust.

My sincere thanks also go to Margaret Doane, Harry Hellenbrand, and Susan Willis for their helpful comments on earlier versions of this manuscript and to Tom for his good-humored and unflagging support.

Abbreviations

AL   Alain Locke Papers, Moorland-Springarn Research Center, Howard University Library

APS   American Philosophical Society Library

CHS   Chicago Historical Society

CSJ   Charles S. Johnson Papers, Special Collections, Fisk University Library

HC   Zora Neale Hurston Collection, University of Florida Library

JWJ   James Weldon Johnson Memorial Collection, Collection of American Literature, Beinecke Rare Book and Manuscript Library, Yale University

SC   Charles Scribner Collection, Princeton University Library

Hitting a Straight Lick with a Crooked Stick

Introduction

THE PICTURES OF Zora Neale Hurston drawn by Wallace Thurman in *Infants of the Spring* and Langston Hughes in *The Big Sea* have influenced much critical response to her work. In the thinly veiled character of Sweetie May Carr, Thurman depicted Hurston as popular with white people "because she lived up to their conception of what a typical Negro should be" (229), creating black characters who fulfilled their stereotypes: "Given a paleface audience, Sweetie May would launch forth into a tale of the little all-colored Mississippi town where she claimed to have been born. Her repertoire of tales was earthy, vulgar and funny. Her darkies always smiled through their tears, sang spirituals on the slightest provocation and performed buck dances when they should have been working" (230). Hughes's description stresses this idea with a similar tone of condescension:

> Of this "niggerati," Zora Neale Hurston was certainly the most amusing. Only to reach a wider audience, need she ever write books—because she is a perfect book of entertainment in herself. In her youth she was always getting scholarships and things from wealthy white people, some of whom simply paid her just to sit around and represent the Negro race for them, she did it in such a racy fashion. She was full of side-splitting anecdotes, humorous tales, and tragicomic stories, remembered out of her life in the south as a daughter of a travelling minister of God. She could make you laugh one minute and cry the next. To many of her white friends, no doubt, she was a perfect "darkie," in the nice meaning they give the term—that is a naive, childlike, sweetly humorous, and highly colored Negro. (238–39)

Seeing a similar persona in Hurston's writings, a number of her contemporaries, formidable figures including Ralph Ellison, Richard

Wright, Sterling Brown, and Alain Locke, attacked her work in extremely harsh and often dismissive terms that still find adherents today.[1]
Even more damaging, perhaps, is the way this image has often influenced the study of Hurston's work by more sympathetic critics. Even
though *Their Eyes Were Watching God* is almost universally esteemed as a
classic (and given the critical attention one deserves), *Dust Tracks on a
Road* is still often read as a document of racial confusion even by her
admirers while *Moses, Man of the Mountain* and *Seraph on the Suwanee*
are generally overlooked altogether. Furthermore, the persistent view of
Hurston as a "natural" raconteur—a flamboyant rather than a meticulous writer, a scribe of cultural traditions rather than a social critic—has
often, with the exception of *Their Eyes Were Watching God,* resulted in a
failure to appreciate her broad thematic scope and sophisticated literary
craft.

Interestingly enough, both Thurman's and Hughes's descriptions,
hinting at a self-conscious attitude on Hurston's part in her relationships with whites, suggest a more complex portrait. Whereas Hughes
concludes his description of the "perfect darky" with the cryptic comment, "But Miss Hurston was clever, too—" (239), Thurman explicitly
points to Hurston's image as one self-consciously created by a woman
who "knew her white folks" (229) and who performed her minstrel
shows "tongue in cheek" (229). Nathan Huggins, interviewing other of
Hurston's contemporaries, has also contributed to a more complicated
picture of Hurston's relationships with whites: "Her negro contemporaries saw her as 'playing a game,' using white folks to get what she
wanted. Langston Hughes said as much in *The Big Sea.* Louise
Thompson remembered her talking on the phone: 'Here's your little
darky' and telling 'darky' stories, only to wink when she was through,
so as to show that she had tricked them again" (130). This more paradoxical view of Hurston's relationships with whites complicates the
portrait of her as their misguided, helpless pawn and points to an issue
central for understanding the complexity of her writing. An appreciation of Hurston's strategies as a writer—a black female writer in a literary world controlled by whites—demands recognizing the complex
truth contained in these portraits, seeing in them not only the pressure
of the social context in which she was writing but also the seeds of her
response to it.

The difficult position of black writers during the Harlem Renaissance was addressed by many of them. James Weldon Johnson in "The Dilemma of the Negro Author" pointed to the problems that arise because of the "double audience"—white America and black America—that black authors faced. The dilemma of black authors is particularly complicated because the choice of either audience raises problems: if they choose to address white America, they face "a whole row of hardset stereotypes which are not easily broken up" (478). Should the black author choose a black audience, another set of difficulties arises: "He has no more absolute freedom to speak as he pleases addressing black America than he has in addressing white America. There are certain phases of life that he dare not touch, certain subjects that he dare not critically discuss, certain manners of treatment that he dare not use except at the risk of rousing bitter resentment" (480).[2]

Although Hurston's position as a black woman writer was even more complicated than that described by Johnson, one that made impossible the "fusion" of two readerships he advocated, she too was keenly aware of race as a problematic aspect of audience. One strategy she tried early in her career to escape the constraints of both a white audience and a conservative black one is explained in Langston Hughes's discussion of the literary experiment he, Hurston, Bruce Nugent, and Wallace Thurman attempted with the publication of *Fire!!*. The magazine's purpose, Hughes says in *The Big Sea,* was to destroy stereotypes of blacks, to "burn up a lot of the old, dead conventional, Negro-white ideas of the past" (235), a project that required circumventing the established literary world and financing the publication themselves. The lesson Hughes learned from that short-lived experiment—the difficulty of financially independent black expression—was also Hurston's: the magazine's failure, he says, "taught me a lesson about little magazines. But since white folks had them, we Negros thought we could have one, too. But we didn't have the money" (238).

Forced by economic realities back into mainstream publishing early in her career, Hurston recognized the constraints placed on black writers in such a context. With definite opinions about the "literary" values held by publishers (they will, she argued in "What White Publishers Won't Print," "sponsor anything that they believe will sell" [168]), she decried the narrow range of black life accepted by them. To emphasize, however, only Hurston's powerlessness in the face of these constraints is to miss the "bodaciousness" of her personality and the complexity of her art.

Whereas some of her contemporaries and later critics have argued that Hurston merely capitulated to the demands of her white readership, she actually developed a much more subversive approach to the problem of audience, one based on a shrewd assessment of complex power relations. Arguing that "tomming," while "not an aggressive act . . . has its uses like feinting in the prize ring" (*Dust Tracks,* 295), and that "the pet Negro system" is "an important thing to know if [blacks] have any plans for racial manipulations in Dixie" ("The Pet Negro," 162), Hurston repeatedly pointed out how the appearance of subservience can be a self-conscious mask blacks use to their advantage. Often treated by whites as a "pet Negro" in her personal and literary life, Hurston exploited such a persona in much of her writing. Planning her own "racial manipulations" in her books, she rarely addressed race in ways that might offend white readers; instead, she adopted a more subversive strategy, often donning the mask of "the colorful darky" to gain entry into mainstream publishing circles while submerging treatment of controversial themes.

As Hurston did with many of the values she held most strongly, she drew this persona and discursive strategy from black folklore. In fact, many of the folktales she relates demonstrate self-conscious "racial manipulation" by black people and the personal rewards to be won by exploiting stereotypes. For instance, Daddy Mention in "Characteristics of Negro Expression" cleverly uses the mask to escape from prison. "Cut[ing] capers" and creating a mindlessly subservient persona for the guards, he becomes their "pet Negro" and is finally able to walk out of prison while they watch. Hurston's most detailed description of the mask as a strategy of manipulation occurs in her essay, "High John de Conquer." Recognizing the power of the John figure and his parallel in Brer Rabbit to offer symbolic assault and psychic victory to African Americans, Hurston emphasized the significance of such models in slavery and contemporary times.[3] In addition to offering examples of spiritual resistance to domination, a central theme in Hurston's own work, John tales provided her with a strategy for addressing her own divided audience. Slaves, she suggests, could tell John stories in the presence of whites, confident that they would miss their import:

> It is no accident that High John de Conquer has evaded the ears of
> white people. They were not supposed to know. You can't know what
> folks won't tell you. If they, the white people, heard some scraps, they
> could not understand because they had nothing to hear things like that
> with. They were not looking for any hope in those days, and it was not

much of a strain for them to find something to laugh over. Old John
would have been out of place for them. (70)

Like Old Massa and Old Miss, white readers could hear Hurston's stories, enjoy them (and pay for them), without ever realizing that they
were often being manipulated and ultimately lampooned in them:

> So Old Massa and Old Miss and their young ones laughed with and at
> Brer Rabbit and wished him well. And all the time, there was High
> John de Conquer playing his tricks or making a way out of no-way.
> Hitting a straight lick with a crooked stick. Winning the jack pot with
> no other stake but a laugh. Fighting a mighty battle without outside
> showing force, and winning his way from within. Really winning in a
> permanent way, for he was winning with the soul of the black man
> whole and free. So he could use it afterwards. (70)

To address her own fractured audience, Hurston drew on the rich
trickster tradition (and its related strategies of masking and "signifying") that many critics including Houston Baker, Lawrence Levine,
Nathan Huggins, Henry Louis Gates, Jr., John Roberts, and Michael
Cooke have demonstrated is central to African American culture and
literature.[4] Despite her image often as a writer whose work was shaped
by a white world, she actually grounded her literary craft in traditions
of black expressivity, using the trickster figure as a flexible discursive
strategy to confront *both* the racial and the gendered aspects of black
women's oppression. Like many other black women writers, including
her own contemporaries Nella Larsen and Jessie Redmond Fauset, who
disguised their subversive treatment of gender issues, Hurston developed
her themes from a position of racial and sexual subordination that required indirection, masking, and ambiguity too often seen simply as
conventionality and conservatism.[5]

One of Hurston's first published stories reveals her use of such trickster strategies and the more complicated interpretation of her work such
an approach invites. On the surface, "Isis," originally titled "Drenched
in Light," seems a rather shallow story about the innocent joyousness
of a black girl and the appreciation she receives from white people.
Viewed simply through the lens of "race," it can be read as one of
Hurston's early works to present a discomfittingly idealized and naive
picture of relationships between black and white people. In many ways,
Isis seems the stereotypical "primitive," the perpetual dancer, to whom
"music . . . meant motion" (14). Although some critics have argued that

Isis's adoption by whites and her apparent affection for them reflect Hurston's own false consciousness, the story is both a subtle self-portrait of Hurston as a black female artist and early evidence of her concern with the complex interaction of race and gender in the lives of black women.

Central to the story is the white couple's condescending response to Isis. Blind to her internal aspirations and frustration, they see her only as "Isis the Joyful" (10), the carefree and ever-dancing black they finally "adopt," not out of genuine concern for her but to fill a spiritual void in their own lives. Although the man and woman in the story only see (and reward) carefree spontaneity in Isis, Hurston stresses that her life is fraught with conflict. Whereas her crying only signifies childish melodrama to her white audience (they laugh at her anguish and dub her "Madame Tragedy" [16]), the gendered aspect of Isis's suffering is central in her experience: like Hurston in her autobiography and Janie in *Their Eyes Were Watching God,* Isis stands at the gate yearning for a trip down the shell road toward the horizon, for broader possibilities of self-definition than she is offered as a young black girl. Throughout the story, Isis struggles not just with whites but within her own community, in pitched battle—one in which race and gender interlock—with Grandma over her future as a black woman. Grandma's model of black womanhood involves neither dancing nor "romping," but "women's work": while her brother goes fishing, Isis must rake the yards and ("being the only girl in the family" [11]), wash the dishes. Grandma's anger and violence are direct responses to Isis's refusal to accept a model of womanhood defined by subordination, restriction, and dehumanization. Significantly, Grandma responds most violently to Isis's perching on the gate-post, as if she recognizes the dangerous threat to her plans for Isis this action symbolizes.

Usurping traditional male prerogatives in the shaving episode and in her wanderlust, resisting the role of "mule" Grandma assigns her and throwing down her rake in defiance at every opportunity, Isis dreams of other possible identities, imagining herself as "various personages," "wearing robes, golden slippers with blue bottoms" and riding "white horses with flaring pink nostrils to the horizon" (12).[6] She "romps" whenever Grandma's back is turned and manages momentarily to become one of these more exciting figures when she steals Grandma's tablecloth and becomes a gypsy dancer. For Isis, her dancing and even her "joyousness" are no expression of simple primitivism as the white people believe, but acts of racial *and* sexual rebellion against the strangling restraints placed upon her as a black female.

Unless one recognizes the intraracial, gendered aspects of Isis's struggle and the unwitting role the white woman plays in Isis's battle for self-determination as a black female, she may seem sold into a kind of slavery at the end of the story. Her benefactor does, after all, buy her for five dollars, the inflated price of Grandma's soiled tablecloth. The ending of the story is, however, as complicated and paradoxical as the portraits drawn by Hughes and Thurman. Contrary to the white people's own racially paternalistic understanding of their role, they represent for Isis a critical opportunity for power and freedom. What Isis stands to gain is prefigured in her relationship with the white cattlemen, who offer her both a brief ride on the shell road and escape from oppressive gender constraints when they "take her almost out of the danger zone" (10) of Grandma's wrath. This seemingly insignificant vignette is important for understanding Isis's response to the white woman, for she has already learned from these men the potential benefits white patronage offers a black girl.

Although, like John, Isis is misunderstood by her benefactors and undeniably treated as a racial stereotype, the story's conclusion strongly suggests aspects of her triumph. She has, through the woman's intervention, not merely escaped a brutal whipping for her transgressions; but, leaving her rake and dirty dishes behind, she heads down the shell road as the exotic personage she had dreamed of, now the proud owner of Grandma's tablecloth. Having earlier dreamed of riding "white horses . . . to the horizon" (12), Isis, spirited away by white horsepower here at the story's end, journeys toward wider definitions of black female self.[7] Seated in between the two white people, she usurps their power for her own purposes and exercises subtle control, despite the apparent surface inequality that exists between her and her patrons and that is ironically highlighted in the man's satirical comment to the woman: "There, Helen, *you've* been adopted" (18, emphasis added). She emerges from the story finally, not as a racial dupe, but as a figure (like her African goddess namesake) of formidable power and magical words.

As the complexity of this story suggests, the strategy Hurston adopted to survive in a publishing world controlled by whites and a few black men necessarily became a flexible one, a give and take affair in which she constantly had to weigh what she censored (or submerged) in order to get published and what she could openly express. Despite the humor and cultural celebration Hurston foregrounded in much of what she wrote for mainstream publications, her work (as "Drenched in Light" so richly forecasts) is fraught with obliquely expressed racial and sexual conflict. No essentialist about either race *or* gender (she finds Janie and Mrs. Turner, Tea Cake and Joe Starks, with their radically different senses of themselves as black women and men, in the same world), Hurston viewed both as socially constructed and culturally influenced aspects of identity. Although skin color "tells nothing about the insides of people" (325), as she says in *Dust Tracks on a Road* and set out to demonstrate in her original version of "My People! My People," Hurston did often emphasize differences in black and white cultural values and invariably saw in the dominant white world a set of racial and sexual hierarchies she rejected.[8] In works as diverse in subject matter as *Mules and Men, Their Eyes Were Watching God,* and *Seraph on the Suwanee,* she critiqued that world—its denigration of blackness and its model of oppressive gender identities—and detailed the costs for black people who strove to emulate it. Those characters who embrace the values and worship the gods of that world—the "pink Jamaicans" ridiculed in *Tell My Horse,* the black American middle-class lampooned in *Dust Tracks on a Road,* or the many fictional characters who recreate the dynamics of the dominant white world in a black one—are invariably stunted and unfulfilled in critical ways. Hurston's healthy black characters—male or female—neither internalize nor acquiesce to racial and sexual dominance; rather, like Isis, they resist such power imbalances either through subversion or more overt defiance to create an alternative world of radically different, more egalitarian racial and gender relationships.

Hurston glimpses the outlines of that world most often where white influence is least—on the Muck of *Their Eyes Were Watching God* rather than in the towns of *Seraph on the Suwanee,* in the lives of poor black Americans and the marroons of the Caribbean rather than in those of the black American middle-class or the "pink Jamaicans." She sees in these more autonomous worlds the possibility of what she throughout her career posited as the ideal world for black people—one of vigorous racial and sexual identity where power and strength are not synonymous with dominance and control. The "gods" she holds up, in stark contrast to the ideals she sees in the dominant white world, are black ones that image both racial health and gender equality. The gods of the Voodoo pantheon, for instance, are not imitation Christian figures, as Hurston decribes them in *Tell My Horse,* but gods that reflect both racial autonomy and gender equality. In contrast to the patriarchal bias of Christianity, she emphasizes the "bi-sexual concept of the Creator" (142) in Voodoo, its recognition of the creative powers of both male and female, and its images of male and female gods not defined in the power/weakness, active/passive terms characterizing European culture. Damballah, the main male deity, markedly different from both Jehovah of the Judeo-Christian tradition and male Greek gods, is no stern punisher of human beings but a "sweeter" god around whom centers the worship of the beautiful in Nature. Just as Damballah is a feminized male deity, Er-zulie, his female counterpart, is no passive female, but a very dynamic goddess of love. Unrelated (Hurston claims) to either Venus of Greek mythology (144) or the Virgin Mary of the Christian one, "Erzulie is not the passive queen of heaven and mother of anybody. She is the ideal of the love bed" (144), as awesomely powerful as male gods traditionally are.

Isis and Osiris (as Hurston's frequent use of the name "Isis" for her characters suggests) offer another model of identity important throughout Hurston's canon. In these African gods, Hurston sees a model of female and male identity and relationships between black women and men to replace the imbalanced, invariably oppressive models of masculinity and femininity she sees in the dominant culture. In subtle ways, she weaves this myth throughout her work to suggest further the kind of social rebirth possible when reciprocal relationships between equally powerful women and men are taken as the model for other relationships in a black world. Whereas Hurston's work most often chronicles the difficulty of achieving her ideal, as Isis's experience suggests, she examines the interaction of race and gender in the lives of black people by focusing on the question whether black people will draw their racial and sexual identities from a white world or from the positive models within a black one; whether they will live as imitation white women and men, merely recreating the oppressive hierarchies of Jim Meserve's world, or, worshiping gods like Damballah and Erzulie, Isis and Osiris, create a healthy black world in their image.

The discursive dilemmas that arise for a black woman writer with these themes are complex. Hurston's difficulty in critiquing a white world perhaps became most obvious when she attempted to address Western imperialism in her autobiography, but it certainly was significant earlier in her career as well in, for instance, Mrs. Mason's insistence that she focus solely on the "primitivism" of black culture. To critique a white world in overt Big Sweet fashion (as Hurston often did in black periodicals and in letters to black contemporaries) risked alienating not only powerful white figures on whom she depended for publication but also middle-class black people whom she consistently criticized for simply imitating whites. When Hurston critiqued relationships between black women and men, yet another fracture in her audience presented itself. For her, as for black women writers since her day, the treatment of intragroup conflict between black women and men presented real problems of reception not only with black men but also with a potentially racist white audience.

The spyglass I have directed on Hurston's writing to examine how she dealt with these difficulties is indebted to the work of many black feminist critics who have answered Barbara Smith's 1977 call in "Toward a Black Feminist Criticism" for an examination of the interlocking politics of race and gender in the works of black women writers. Although race and gender have certainly been examined in Hurston's work, they have often been looked at in isolation from one another; in fact, "race" was the lens through which Hurston was most often viewed by her contemporaries and "gender" (especially in much of the writing on *Their Eyes Were Watching God*) has often been the focus of our own. As Mae Henderson has pointed out (and as "Drenched in Light" suggests), such an approach to the writing of black women writers oversimplifies and even falsifies the experience of black women as characters and writers who must negotiate a complex set of overlapping power structures. In examining the interrelationships of race and gender in Hurston's work, both as a theme in her writing and as an issue of representation that shaped it, I have been influenced by Henderson's notion of the "simultaneity of discourse" in the writing of black women writers and consequently have attempted to employ a mode of reading that examines how the interrelations of race and gender structure her discourse.

I have also been influenced by black women critics, especially Hazel Carby (*Reconstructing Womanhood*) and Deborah McDowell ("New Directions"), who have emphasized the importance of examining the work of black women writers in their historical and social context. This approach is, in my view, especially important with Hurston. Like the trickster tales she was influenced by, Hurston's work (as "Drenched in Light" so richly forecasts) is often radically and self-consciously ambiguous. Just as the "inside meaning" of John tales depends on an awareness of the context in which the tales are narrated (the needs of the slave narrator and the predilections of the slaveowning audience), understanding the context in which Hurston wrote is often critical for appreciating specific aspects of her writing. Although the basic power dynamics involved for a black woman writing in a predominantly white publishing milieu spanned her career, specific features of that context— the individual people whose support she sought or whose control she wrestled with, the dominant literary tastes during the time she wrote individual books—changed considerably over the decades during which she wrote. When the influence of specific context is taken into consideration, the radically different subject matters and approaches she took in *Jonah's Gourd Vine* and *Seraph on the Suwanee*, for instance, are explained less by positing major changes in Hurston's views or values (as has usually been done) and more by recognizing the profound changes that took place in her writing context. In my reading of Hurston, the fact that one was written during the Harlem Renaissance at a time when she hoped to win support from James Weldon Johnson and the other during the 1940s when she was trying to establish a relationship with Marjorie Kennan Rawlings explains more about the seeming disparaties between the two works than does the common assumption of Hurston's growing conservatism. Letters, reviews, and manuscripts, which taken together provide a record of Hurston's career-long struggle with powerful literary figures—usually white ones, sometimes black men—have often been important keys in my understanding of the specific contexts in which Hurston shaped her writing. Especially in the case of *Mules and Men* and *Seraph on the Suwanee*, her correspondence often sheds light on Hurston's relationships with mentors and the ways she responded to their influence in her writing. Contemporary reviews of her work have been another important piece in my understanding of Hurston's context. Representing not only stark evidence of the divided audience Hurston was saddled with and the misreadings she often endured, they also often provide insight into the ways Hurston tried to exploit literary tastes for her own purposes.

Hurston's own canon is often another context important in interpreting individual passages or works. Whereas much criticism on Hurston has focused on individual works in isolation—most often, of course, *Their Eyes Were Watching God*—I have often found a kind of cross-reading through her works both a helpful tool for individual interpretive problems and for appreciating the rich unity of all her work. *Their Eyes Were Watching God* and *Seraph on the Suwanee,* for instance, echo and contrast with one another in ways that Hurston intended, that enrich both, and that illuminate other works. Characters who superficially have little in common—Joe Starks, John Pearson, Jim Meserve, and Moses, for instance—often echo (sometimes virtually verbatim) one another in telling ways that provide keys for understanding them. Certain metaphors—plants and gods, horses and mules, dogs and snakes—that are central to her treatment of race and gender resonate through her anthropology and her fiction with thematic force and complexity equal to those discussed by Karla Holloway in *Moorings and Metaphors.*

While trying to provide this kind of cross-reading in my discussion, I have chosen to organize my discussion around individual works for several reasons. In addition to allowing examination of the unique contextual story behind each of Hurston's works, each one a complex tale of patronage, revision, publication, and reception, focusing on individual books also facilitates the kind of close textual analysis that Deborah McDowell ("New Directions") and others have argued is important in the study of African American women writers. For a writer as significant as Hurston is, she has—with the notable exception of *Their Eyes Were Watching God*—not been the subject of the kind of close reading other major authors have benefited from, a fact that has led sometimes to ungrounded generalizations about her views and at others to premature assumptions of artistic carelessness or decline. Despite her claims to have dashed some books off in a matter of weeks, the picture of Hurston as a writer that emerges from such close readings is not that of an inner-conflicted, thoughtless, or even "natural" storyteller, but of a meticulous writer of more than one major book, each with an internal integrity and sophisticated discursive strategy. Finally, examining specific veiling techniques Hurston adopted in individual works has led me to reexamination of anomalous passages or problematic features of Hurston's works (her use of folk language in *Jonah's Gourd Vine,* her narrative technique in *Their Eyes Were Watching God,* and her apparent contradictions in *Dust Tracks on a Road,* for instance), to different interpretive angles on some works, and to increased appreciation of some that have been neglected or dismissed as marginal.

Turning the spyglass around to examine the sum total of these individual readings reveals a writer whose oeuvre coheres, despite wide variety of subject matter, genre, and style, in its consistent treatment of the complex interaction of race and gender in the lives of black people. Buried in each of the books dealt with in the following chapters, beneath the often lighthearted surfaces and the "charming" characters often praised by Hurston's reviewers, lie stories of power and dominance, acquiesence and resistance to the racial and gender hierarchies Hurston saw in the dominant world. As the tone of some of her letters suggests, Hurston might certainly have preferred to engage readers in more direct ways—"specifying" rather than "signifying," lambasting rather than lampooning—but in the social context she found herself, she most often adopted John de Conquer's way of wrestling with her heterogenous audience: "Hitting a straight lick with a crooked stick. Winning the jack pot with no other stake but a laugh. Fighting a mighty battle without outside showing force, and winning his way from within."

1 "Fractious" Mules and Covert Resistance in *Mules and Men*

IN AN OFT-QUOTED PASSAGE from her introduction to *Mules and Men,* Hurston stresses the difference between her childhood unreflective immersion in black folklife and her later understanding of it:

> When I pitched headforemost into the world I landed in the crib of negroism. From the earliest rocking of my cradle, I had known about the capers Brer Rabbit is apt to cut and what the Squinch Owl says from the house top. But it was fitting me like a tight chemise. I couldn't see it for wearing it. It was only when I was off in college, away from my native surroundings, that I could see myself like somebody else and stand off and look at my garment. Then I had to have the spy-glass of Anthropology to look through at that. (3)

As Hurston suggests here, she is more than a passive transcriber of folktales in *Mules and Men.* Distanced from the culture she depicts, trained as an anthropologist to analyze it, she shapes her material in order to reveal the warp and woof of the fabric she saw. Whereas *Mules and Men* seems (and was, in fact, seen by most reviewers as) a straightforward, nonthreatening depiction of the humorous and exotic side of black culture in the rural South, Hurston offers in veiled form a complex analysis of race and gender in black life.[1] Detailing the effects of white domination on the racial and gender identities of black people, Hurston examines the price paid for internalizing the values of the dominant culture, the avenues available for resisting its hierarchies, and the possibility of a radically different, autonomous alternative.

Part of the reason Hurston takes an indirect approach to this critique stems from her dependence on white figures who exerted considerable control over her work. Charlotte Osgood Mason, for instance, literally owned Hurston's material and consistently pushed Hurston to express only the "primitivism" she saw in black culture. Hurston's struggle with Franz Boas in her research and writing of *Mules and Men* is less well known, but as the correspondence between him and Hurston indicates, his control over her field work at this time in her career was just as intrusive as that exerted by Mason. In addition to dictating the focus of her research and treating her as an aid or informant rather than a researcher in her own right, Boas also clearly pressed Hurston to accept his interpretation of her material.[2] Aware of Boas's power to validate or dismiss the significance of her research, Hurston addresses him not by directly asserting her views but by posturing as a deferential disciple, requesting permission to express her own conclusions. As she looks over her material, she writes to him on April 21, 1929:

> Is it safe for me to say that baptism is an extension of water worship
> as a part of pantheism just as the sacrament is an extension of cannibal-
> ism? Isn't the use of candles in the Catholic church a relic of fire wor-
> ship? Are not all the uses of fire upon the altars the same thing? Is not
> the christian ritual rather one attenuated nature-worship, in the fire,
> water, and blood? Might not the frequently mentioned fire of the Holy
> Ghost not be an unconscious fire worship? May it not be a deification
> of fire?
>
> May I say that the decoration in clothing is an extension of the primi-
> tive application of paint (coloring) to the body?
>
> May I say that all primitive music originated about the drum and
> that singing was an attenuation of the drum-beat? (APS)

The tentative tone of Hurston's correspondence reflects her awareness of Boas's power but not her acquiescence to it. That it represents the mask she donned to deal with a powerful mentor rather than her own uncertainty is clear from a letter she wrote Langston Hughes nine days after her letter to Boas. Despite Boas's unsupportive response (April 24, 1929, APS), she unequivocally and enthusiastically expressed to Hughes her view of Christianity as rooted in nature worship (April 30, 1929, Yale, JWJ).[3] Hurston had her own anthropological views to express in *Mules and Men* as well. What she discovered when she looked at her culture through the spyglass of anthropology was that the folktales she had al-ways heard were not merely amusing stories, nor even relics of slavery, but living forces, strategies used in her own day for dealing with racial and sexual inequities. As she emphasized in "Characteristics of Negro Expression," "Negro folklore is not a thing of the past" (56) but testi-mony to the power of her own contemporaries to do battle in a world of inequality.

Faced with the dilemma of how to present her analysis in a way that could bypass the censoring eye of her mentors and potentially unsympathetic white readers, Hurston adopted a strategy of masking social conflict and critical commentary with humor. The persona she creates is crucial to this project. By presenting herself as a lovable "darky," one who thanks white folks for "allowing" her to collect folklore and who praises the magnanimity of her patron, Mrs. Mason, she appears a narrator with no racial complaints or even awareness. Pouring on "the charm of a lovable personality," commented on by Boas in his Preface (x) and by reviewers, Hurston paints herself as an Uncle Remus figure pleased to entertain the white world with her tales.[4] Making no controversial statements and, in fact, offering little explicit analysis, she plays a role eminently acceptable to whites: lovable, entertaining, and intellectually mute.

Hurston reminds us in *Mules and Men,* however, that black humor is richly multifaceted, reflecting a wide range of emotions: "The brother in black puts a laugh in every vacant place in his mind. His laugh has a hundred meanings. It may mean amusement, anger, grief, bewilderment, chagrin, curiosity, simple pleasure or any other of the known or undefined emotions" (67–68). Much of the humor in *Mules and Men* reflects this complexity rather than the primitive simplicity and carefree gaiety seen by reviewers. Hurston also hints at the complex ambiguity of folktales themselves in discussing the black person's strategy for deflecting the probe of white cultural analysis:

> . . . the Negro, in spite of his open-faced laughter, his seeming acquiescence, is particularly evasive. You see we are a polite people and we do not say to our questioner, "Get out of here!" We smile and tell him or her something that satisfies the white person because, knowing so little about us, he doesn't know what he is missing. The Indian resists curiosity by a stony silence. The Negro offers a feather-bed resistance. That is, we let the probe enter, but it never comes out. It gets smothered under a lot of laughter and pleasantries.
>
> The theory behind our tactics: "The white man is always trying to know into somebody else's business. All right, I'll set something outside the door of my mind for him to play with and handle. He can read my writing but he sho' can't read my mind. I'll put this play toy in his hand, and he will seize it and go away. Then I'll say my say and sing my song." (4–5)

While Hurston makes these comments to convince readers that they are reading the unvarnished truth in *Mules and Men,* that she is initiating them into the black world, her remarks provide an interesting comment on her strategy in the work.[5] She uses "feather-bed tactics" in her rendition of folktales, placing her "lovable personality" and the seemingly simple, humorous stories of her informants as a "play toy" in the hands of her white readers.

As Hemenway suggests in his introduction, Hurston's "cultural messages" in *Mules and Men* are "coded" ones (xxiii), similar to black proverbial expressions or "by-words," which as one man explains, "'all got a hidden meanin'" (134). Conveying her cultural messages not by explicitly analyzing folktales but by embedding them in a social context, Hurston uses that context and careful juxtaposition of tales to underscore controversial issues of race and gender.[6] Undoubtedly aware that the context of Joel Chandler Harris's tales had defused the conflict and resistance in them, Hurston embeds her tales in situations that highlight this function of black folklore. Her mode of presentation in *Mules and Men* is thus crucial. As Boas notes in his Preface, it was a novel one; "by giving the Negro's reaction to every day events," by placing tales in "the intimate setting in the social life of the Negro" (x), Hurston is able to convey her commentary without asking permission or offending her mentors.

Whereas Boas rather dimly praises this aspect of *Mules and Men* in his Preface, his correspondence with Hurston reveals her trials in getting him to write it. Fully aware what his stamp of approval would mean for her work's acceptance, she pleads with him to write an introduction: "I am full of terrors, lest you decide that you do not want to write the introduction to my 'Mules and Men.' I want you to do it so very much" (August 20, 1934, APS). From her extensive experience with Boas's scientific "rigor," Hurston was clearly aware that the novelistic frame for her tales might present a potential problem for Boas. She was, therefore, extremely careful to explain the conversations and incidents between tales as required by the publisher's desire for a readable book aimed at the general public (August 20, 1934, APS). Foisting responsibility for "unnecessary" elements in her work onto her publishers and further implying they are anthropologically insignificant, Hurston ends this letter with her familiar strategy of ingratiation:

> So *please* consider all this and do not refuse Mr. Lippincott's request to write the introduction to *Mules and Men*. And then in addition, I feel that the persons who have the most information on a subject should teach the public. Who knows more about folk-lore than you and Dr. Benedict? Therefore the stuff published in America should pass under your eye. *You* see some of the preposterous stuff put out by various per-

sons on various folk-subjects. This is not said merely to get you to write
the introduction to my book. No. (August 20, 1934, APS)

Hurston's strategy of deferential humility, of course, worked. She was
able to publish her work with this crucial contextual material and to get
Boas's (albeit brief and rather condescending) approval in the Preface.[7]

The "between-story conversations and business," the contexts in
which tales are narrated, are central in *Mules and Men,* for they highlight
the realities of racial and sexual oppression in the lives of the characters
who relate them. One set of tales, for instance, those told in the context of the sawmill in Polk County (Chapters IV and V), provides an
important commentary on the situation of black workers in the South.
Hurston sets up this work scene to emphasize white domination and
control of these men's lives: arriving at work to find no straw boss, the
men think they will be given a day off but are disappointed when the
foreman orders them on to the mill to see if they are needed there (74).
Telling tales all the way, they walk the long distance to the mill, only
to be summarily dismissed by the mill boss (100). Moved from one
work location to the next, never informed of the white boss's plans, the
workers use traditional tales throughout this section to defy the white
world's definition of them as mules and to assert their humanity. For
instance, after general speculation that the swamp-boss is absent due to
illness, one man sneers, " 'Man, he's too ugly. If a spell of sickness ever
tried to slip up on him, he'd skeer it into a three weeks' spasm' " (73).
This last comment leads into a series of exaggeration stories, in which
the workers try to top one another's stories about men who are "so
ugly." As a later series of exaggeration stories told while fishing shows
(106), this traditional form is often a form of fun-filled verbal play engaged in for its own sake. In a dehumanizing work context, however, the
form is used specifically to lampoon a white power figure. Similarly, the
men deal with their frustration and anger when the foreman announces
that they must report to the mill through another series of exaggeration tales about mean men, initiated by one man's comment, " 'Ain't dat
a mean man? No work in the swamp and still he won't let us knock
off.' " The tales that follow detail one straw boss " 'so mean dat when the
boiler burst and blowed some of the men up in the air, he docked 'em
for de time they was off de job' " and a road boss so mean " 'till he laid
off de hands of his watch' " (75).

Significantly, stories about "slavery days" are most common in this
section of *Mules and Men.* Often focusing on the trickster figure, John,

and the slave's strategies for dealing with apparent powerlessness, many of them graphically demonstrate the impossibility of open defiance and the need for indirection in battling oppressive whites.[8] In "Big Talk," for instance, one slave foolishly speaks out against his master (and is nearly killed) after having heard another slave brag that he "cussed" him without punishment. The braggart later explains the crucial difference in their defiance: "'Ah didn't say Ah cussed 'im tuh his face. You sho is crazy. Ah thought you had mo' sense than dat. When Ah cussed Old Massa he wuz settin' on de front porch an' Ah wuz down at de big gate'" (83–84). As this tale suggests, overt resistance, with death as the price, is the strategy of fools; indirection, on the other hand, is a crucial strategy for survival and for victory. As one listener remarks, such foolhardiness is not the hallmark of the black folk hero, John: "'dat wasn't John de white folks was foolin' wid. John was too smart for Ole Massa. He never got no beatin'!'" (85).

The slavery stories in these two chapters, the bulk of the ones told in *Mules and Men,* function as a model for these men in psychologically resisting their own oppression. Unable to openly defy their bosses, they too "talk at the big gate" in the tales they narrate, reliving the slave's symbolic victory. Tales related in this section also solidify the group, uniting the men, who at least twice respond to stories by moving "closer together" (73, 74) in spiritual opposition to their bosses. By placing most John stories in this section, by having them told against a backdrop of economic slavery, Hurston reinforces the contemporary subversive import of these tales. As she suggests in her essay, "High John de Conquer," in which she analyzes the dynamics of these stories, a John story "was an inside thing to live by. It was sure to be heard when and where the work was the hardest, and the lot most cruel. It helped the slaves endure" (69). In the Polk County section of *Mules and Men,* Hurston demonstrates that John did not die with Emancipation, but "retire[d] with his secret smile into the soil of the South and wait[ed]" (*Sanctified Church,* 78), reemerging—even in the 1920s—when needed to help black people deal with oppression. By not analyzing in *Mules and Men* how these tales work, by inserting her extremely brief description of John only in her glossary, and by giving tales innocuous titles that mask their thematic import, Hurston hoped to recreate the plantation dynamics of the John tales. Like Massa and Old Miss, her contemporary "masters" could hear the tales without understanding their subversive import.

The complex ambiguity of these tales is evident in one John story narrated in this section, "Ole Massa and John Who Wanted to Go to

Heaven," a favorite of Hurston's told elsewhere as "The Fiery Chariot." Although the tale seems to poke fun at the black man through a series of racist stereotypes, a different kind of humor derives from the depiction of John as a trickster who not only outruns the Lord but also verbally outwits him. Whereas escape is obviously uppermost in his mind, he engineers it by feigning concern for the Lord's interests. He begins with a short appeal to decorum: "'O, Lawd, Ah can't go to Heben wid you in yo' fiery chariot in dese old dirty britches; gimme time to put on my Sunday pants'" (77). When this strategy is exhausted because "John didn't had nothin' else to change" (77), he lays the groundwork for his escape by appealing to "facts" God cannot possibly deny, His superiority (77) and the black man's inferiority (77–78). John's last plea is a rhetorical flourish, demonstrating that what Hurston has called in "Characteristics of Negro Expression" the black person's "will to adorn" often derived not just from love of the poetic possibilities of words but from an awareness of their strategic rhetorical value. Here John calls on metaphor, double descriptive, and parallelism for perhaps the most serious persuasive motive—to save his own life: "'O, Lawd, Heben is so high and wese so low; youse so great and Ah'm so weak and yo' strength is too much for us poor sufferin' sinners. So once mo' and agin yo' humber servant is knee-bent and body-bowed askin' you one mo' favor befo' Ah step into yo' fiery chariot to go to Heben wid you and wash in yo' glory—be so pleased in yo' tender mercy as to stand back jus' a li'l bit further'" (78). Just who in this scene is "brighter" becomes quite complicated when "Ole Massa stepped back a step or two mo' and out dat door John come like a streak of lightnin'" (78).[9]

Whereas Hurston deliberately leaves unstated the meaning of everybody's "Kah, Kah, Kah," their "laughing with their mouths wide open" (78), the context of their own feelings of impotence in this section strongly suggests their delight in the black man's wiliness and the white's gullible vanity.[10] Many of the tales that follow repeat this theme and function psychologically to remind men of their humanity, no matter how mulish their existence. Roused to self-respect by this tale, they next tell "Massa and the Bear," a story in which black and white roles are starkly reversed. Ordered by his master to catch a corn thief, John spends a whole night fighting the guilty bear. When the master takes over so that John can go for help, John staggers off and sits down to rest. John responds to the master's threat to turn the bear loose: "'Turn 'im loose, then. Dat's whut Ah tried to do all night long but Ah couldn't'"

(80). The men again all laugh (80) not in careless joy, of course, as an outsider might assume, but in delight at John's victory as a trickster.

In the social context Hurston so carefully details before stories are narrated, tales often acquire more subversive import than their amusing (and sometimes even racist) surface might at first suggest. One such tale is "Deer Hunting Story," told at the end of Chapter IV. In this tale, Massa instructs the black man to shoot the deer when he "skeer[s]" him up, but when the deer runs by, the black man does nothing (82). When questioned by Massa, the slave claims to have seen no deer: "'All Ah seen was a white man come along here wid a pack of chairs on his head and Ah tipped my hat to him and waited for de deer'" (82). While one listener finds this tale proof that "'Some colored folks ain't got no sense'" (82), the context in which this tale arises, one that highlights the men's awareness of the economic oppression blacks suffer at the hands of whites, points to another reason for the slave's inaction.[11] First of all, the tale follows Jim Presley's suggestion that they should not worry about work since "de white folks made work" (80) and two tales, "Why the Sister in Black Always Works the Hardest" (80–81) and "De Reason Niggers Is Working So Hard" (81), that pinpoint the role of whites in black oppression. As Jim Presley's comment immediately before the story suggests, in a world of harsh racial and economic inequalities, one in which "'ought's a ought, figger's a figger; all for de white man, none for de nigger'" (81), the black man who works diligently only serves the white man's interests rather than his own. With the literal context of the men's own slow walking to avoid work borne in mind, the story emerges as one extolling the subversive virtues of laziness, an indication of the slave's clever strategies for avoiding work through the appearance of stupidity.[12]

The many stories lampooning whites and showing the superior wit of blacks allow the sawmill workers to fight emotionally against their own masters while they listen to stories of John "'wearin' [out] Ole Massa's southern can'" (92). But Hurston is careful not simply to romanticize black response to white oppression. As she demonstrates, the conflict between the desire to see oneself as human and the pressures to accept white definitions of oneself as a mule is an intense one. She highlights this struggle several times in the men's conversations between tales, casting Jim Allen as the mouthpiece for white psychological control. In contrast to men like Jim Presley, who argues for the virtues of "laziness"—"'Don't never worry about work. . . . There's more work in de world than there is anything else. God made de world and de white folks made work'" (80)—Jim Allen repeatedly urges the men to hurry to work (80, 91, 95). The other men's disdain for Allen's acquiescence to authority finds voice in Lonnie Barnes's telling insult: "'Aw naw—you sho is worrysome. You bad as white folks'" (95).

The conflicting reactions of black people to white power—clever defiance or defeated acceptance—evident in these conversations is also reflected in the tales told in this section. Significantly, in addition to John stories, the section of *Mules and Men* set in the work context of Polk County also has the harshest examples of self-denigrating tales narrated in the entire work.[13] Through her careful attention to context, Hurston suggests that these tales constitute another black response to oppression. For instance, as the men approach the mill and the stark reminder of their situation that it represents, an abrupt change of mood occurs (86). In her descriptive "between-story business," Hurston highlights the harsh reality that engenders the hopelessness and self-hatred characterizing some of the later tales: "Well, we were at the mill at last, as slow as we had walked. Old Hannah was climbing the road of the sky, heating up sand beds and sweating peoples. No wonder nobody wanted to work. Three fried men are not equal to one good cool one. The men stood around the door for a minute or two, then dropped down on the shady side of the building. Work was too discouraging to think about. Phew! Sun and sawdust, sweat and sand" (90–91). Even John tales cannot immediately erase this stark reminder of oppression. Instead, what follows this recognition of the mill's reality are self-degrading tales, the most bitter, "From Pine to Pine Mr. Pinkney," showing the destructive psychological effects of white oppression. The story of an escaped slave, Jack, caught because another slave helps the master, the tale ends with a depressing reminder of the men's own slavery symbolized by the mill: he is caught, sentenced to one hundred lashes, and put back to work.

Although these stories reveal harsh economic realities, the power of white definitions of blackness, and the divisiveness of oppression, Hurston refuses to let these stories stand as the last word. By embedding them in the context of John tales, she highlights the power of black people to withstand psychological oppression even in the face of racist definitions. Chapter V closes not with a self-denigrating tale but with a John story, "'Member Youse a Nigger,'" in which John wins his freedom by saving Massa's children. As Massa calls farewell, he repeatedly reminds John of his status in the eyes of whites:

Well, Ole John started on down de road. Well, Old Massa said, "John
de children love yuh."
"Yassuh."
"John, I love yuh."
"Yassuh."
"And Missy *like* yuh!"
"Yassuh."
"But 'member, John youse a nigger."
"Yassuh."
Fur as John could hear 'im down de road he wuz hollerin', "John, Oh
John! De children loves you. And I love you. De Missy *like* you." (98)

Although John mouths acceptance of the white man's denigrating view
of him, the tale emphasizes the freedom possible even in the face of
such racism: yelling "Yassuh," he nevertheless "kept right on steppin' to
Canada. He answered Old Massa every time he called 'im, but he consumed on wid his bag" (98). For Hurston, this tale reveals the slave's
ability to render racism psychologically impotent. Instead of outwardly
defying white definitions (and risking death), the slave simply dons the
mask of subservience to further his own ends. The strategy underlying
many of the John and Massa stories, it represents for the men hearing
these tales not deluded wish-fulfillment but graphic demonstration that
black men can enjoy psychic freedom even when defined by whites as
mules. As Hurston suggests in her essay, "High John de Conquer," the
spiritual freedom depicted and experienced in hearing these stories is
extremely important: these tales of John "Fighting a mighty battle
without outside-showing force, and winning his war from within" are
meaningful victories showing a black hero "Really winning in a permanent way, for he was winning with the soul of the black man whole
and free. So he could use it afterwards" (*Sanctified Church,* 70–71). While
the mill and its definitions of black men still await them, such stories
allow the workers to enter inured from the most devastating effects of
spiritual enslavement.

Although Hurston's treatment of the work context in Polk County
examines the contemporary realities of oppression and the variety of response—acquiesence or resistance—to it, Hurston also suggests in *Mules
and Men* aspects of a more autonomous alternative, one in which black
people's sense of themselves differs radically. When the workers in Polk
County finally do get their day off to go fishing and the realities of
racial oppression are no longer their focus, they tell tales quite different

from those narrated at work, not John tales but light-hearted fish tales (103–4) and exaggeration stories (123–25) that demonstrate their delight in verbal play for its own sake. They also engage in traditional verbal contests, vying with one another for the best tales about the hottest weather (106), the biggest mosquito (108–9), the richest and poorest land (109–10). Hurston also places in this fishing context etiological tales (104–6, 111–16) that reveal a freed imagination tackling profound philosophical issues and a different kind of black cultural creativity that flourishes outside the range of white control.

When the figure John (or Jack) does appear in this fishing section, he is a quite different hero than the "doubleteened" trickster focused on at work. In the last tale narrated before the men return home, "How the Lion Met the King of the World," John, who brags that he is "King of de World," must fight both the bear and the lion to prove his boast. Tackling them in cosmic warfare, he easily emerges the victor, not through cunning but through brute strength. Even the mighty lion affirms the god-like power of this black figure: he knows he has met the King " ' 'Cause he made lightnin' in my face and thunder in my hips' " (143). A similar kind of tale, "Strength Test Between Jack and the Devil," the only one told at the Jook that night and the last one narrated in the Polk County section, paints a similar picture of the black hero created outside the psychic perimeter of white oppression. In a decidedly black milieu (which Hurston carefully details), this formidable figure, who matches the devil's strength picking up trees and a mule under each arm, is depicted finally as even stronger than the devil.

The effects of freedom from white control on the story-telling imagination of black people are also evident in Chapter X when Hurston goes to Mulberry, Pierce, and Lakeland. In her "between-story business" Hurston contrasts this environment with the oppressive one at the saw-mill camps: "The company operating the mines at Pierce maintains very excellent living conditions in their quarters. The cottages are on clean, tree-lined streets. There is a good hospital and a nine-months school. They will not employ a boy under seventeen so that the parents are not tempted to put minors to work. There is a cheerful community center with a large green-covered table for crap games under a shady oak" (166). In this comparatively benign context, the stories told are not ones such as the John stories, in which blacks must use indirect ways to maintain power against whites. When whites are again on the periphery, the story-tellers focus instead on etiological tales that evoke "blow-out laughs" (167) and on tales of supernatural power. Black figures focused on in this section include ones of mythic proportions and strength like Big Sixteen (172) as well as mythic hoodoo doctors like High Walker and Raw Head. Out of range of white control, in a world as characterized by Nanny, " 'where de black man is in power' " (29), black people feel their power not just to understand the cosmos but to control it.

Battles between blacks and whites are not the only ones waged in *Mules and Men,* for Hurston pays equal attention to power struggles between black men and women, showing not only how men oppress women (and use folktales to legitimate it) but also how women fight against their subservient role.[14] As she suggests in her discussion of the black woman's status in the jook ("Characteristics of Negro Expression"), black women often suffer the consequences when white racist attitudes spill over into their community. When black men internalize the dominant cultural definitions of blackness and womanhood, they often stereotype the black woman as hateful and violent, valuing instead the light-skinned one as loving and sweetly passive. This "scornful attitude toward black women" ("Characteristics," 64) is also expressed by black men in *Mules and Men.* Mr. Pitts, for instance, uses a derogatory comment about black women as the basis of his flirtatious "woofing" with Hurston: " 'Dese mens don't even know how to talk to nobody lak you. . . . Now, if you wuz some gator-black 'oman dey'd be tellin' you jus' right. But dat ain't de way tuh talk tuh *you*' " (69).

Part of Hurston's purpose in both her essay and in *Mules and Men* is to celebrate the power of black women to fight the sexism undeniably present in the black communities Hurston visits. An important theme developed both in the tales and in the "between-story conversation and business" is the various ways, both direct and more subversive, that they do so. Immediately noticeable is the sheer number of arguments between men and women that Hurston describes (31–33, 40, 58, 100, 133, 170). Whereas conflicts between males are often innocuous and playful, the ones between men and women are "red hot" (58), waged vigorously and heatedly. Although Hurston never explicitly analyzes the gender battles underlying most of the arguments, the sexist stereotypes and oppressive double standards that often spark them are highlighted through her juxtaposition and contextualization of tales. One such instance is the argument that takes place between Good Bread and Mack Ford over Good Bread's size. Rather than straightforwardly exposing the sexism in Mack Ford's attitudes, Hurston simply chronicles the series of jokes told at Good Bread's expense and the laughter they elicit. That this scene reflects sexist attitudes rather than good-natured fun is revealed in the next folktale narrated. The story of Big Sixteen (172–73), who is so "big and strong" (172) that he can carry a mule under each arm and is feared even by the devil, it shows a mythic admiration for male strength and power. As the preceding "between-story conversation and business" reveals, however, a "big and strong" woman is often a source of scorn: the men not only hate her size, but the equality with men she also asserts in her overalls (171), "'bull woofin' '" (171), and "loud talk[ing]" (171).

Hurston uses her folk material in other ways to dramatize and covertly analyze the gender battles waged in the community. Given the different social positions of women and men, it is not surprising that they often know and tell different stories. Generally, men tell ones that reflect and reinforce their power over women while women tell ones that "strain against" it. Even when men and women hear the same tales, they often draw different meanings from them that reflect their contrasting interests in much the same way that blacks and whites may see different significances in many of the John tales.[15]

Hurston uses both of these techniques to deal with two major areas of conflict between women and men: work and love. The tale that most starkly delineates a masculinist perspective on work is "Why the Sister in Black Works Hardest," told by Jim Allen in Polk County. According to his rendition of the tale, God originally put work in a box. Unaware of its contents, Ole Massa orders the black man to carry it, who then orders his wife to do so. When the black woman gets the box, she opens it eagerly. The tale ends with its moral: "So she run and grabbed a-hold of de box and opened it up and it was full of hard work. Dat's de reason de sister in black works harder than anybody else in de world. De white man tells de nigger to work and he takes and tells his wife" (81). Although this tale (accurately, for Hurston) places black sexual inequality in a larger context of racial oppression, a comparison between this rendition of the tale and the one Nanny gives in *Their Eyes Were Watching God* reveals the gendered bias in Allen's version. Explaining to Janie why she must marry Logan Killicks, Nanny tells another version of this tale: "'Honey, de white man is de ruler of everything as fur as Ah been able tuh find out. Maybe it's some place way off in de ocean where de black man is in power, but we don't know nothin' but what we see. So de white man throw down de load and tell de nigger man tuh pick it up.

He pick it up because he have to, but he don't tote it. He hand it to his women-folks. De nigger woman is de mule uh de world so fur as Ah can see'" (29). Whereas Nanny's version paints the black woman as a victimized mule, Allen's version, with its parallels to the story of Pandora's box, legitimates the black woman's oppression by making her, through her own curiosity, responsible for it. Told in the context of the workers' racial oppression in Polk County, the tale ironically reveals another way in which black men assert their own humanity: they can see themselves as men by making black women mules. Told by Jim Allen, the most psychologically oppressed black man in the group, the tale in context finally exposes racial inequality and insecurity as the foundation of black male oppression of black women.

In her depiction of the men's return to the quarters after having been sent home by the straw boss, Hurston reveals how this male point of view is played out in the social life of the community:

> When Mrs. Bertha Allen saw us coming from the mill she began to hunt up the hoe and the rake. She looked under the porch and behind the house until she got them both and placed them handy. As soon as Jim Allen hit the step she said:
>
> "Ah'm mighty proud y'all got a day off. Maybe Ah kin git dis yard all clean today. Jus' look at de trash and dirt! And it's so many weeds in dis yard, Ah'm liable to git snake bit at my own door."
>
> "Tain't no use in you gittin' yo' mouf all primped up for no hoein' and rakin' out of me, Bertha. Call yo' grandson and let him do it. Ah'm too ole for dat," said Jim testily.
>
> "Ah'm standin' in my tracks and steppin' back on my abstract—Ah ain't gointer rake up no yard. Ah'm goin' fishin'," Cliffert Ulmer snapped back. "Grandma, you worries mo' 'bout dis place than de man dat owns it. You ain't de Everglades Cypress Lumber Comp'ny sho nuff. Youse shacking on one of their shanties. Leave de weeds go. Somebody'll come chop 'em some day."
>
> "Naw, Ah ain't gointer leave 'em go! You and Jim would wallow in dirt right up to yo' necks if it wasn't for me."
>
> Jim threw down his jumper and his dinner bucket. "Now, *Ah'm* goin' fishin' too. When Bertha starts her jawin' Ah can't stay on de place. Her tongue is hung in de middle and works both ways. Come on Cliff, less git de poles!" (100–101)

Unlike Tea Cake, secure enough in his racial and sexual identity to labor beside Janie both in the field and in the home, Jim Allen refuses any task resembling "women's work." Clifford's sneering reminder that the

Everglades Cypress Company owns the place further demonstrates that the men see this work, like their own at the mill, in racial terms—as toil for white men. They fail, however, to acknowledge the female needs this labor serves, emphasized in Bertha's comment, "'Ah'm liable to git snake bit at my own door.'" Thus, the "laziness" that functioned as a subversive racial strategy against white power at the mill actually furthers female oppression at home. The dynamics of male oppression are also highlighted here in Jim's changed behavior. Unable to feel "like a man" at work, he becomes one at home by imperiously tossing his load to a black woman. While he takes off fishing, his wife, left behind as a mule alone in her work, pays the price for his psychological freedom.

As Big Sweet's fighting over Joe Willard's infidelity demonstrates, love is also a major struggle between men and women. In the several courting conversations she narrates, Hurston demonstrates how male and female perspectives differ: for men, love is often characterized as no more than a game with women as the dehumanized sexual prize. One story told by a man, in fact, reveals much about male attitudes toward love and their strategies for winning women. In this courtship story, a man woos a woman by pointing to a farm, cattle, sheep, and hogs and telling her, "All of these are mine" (179). When she goes home with him, only to find it a "dirty li'l shack" (179) and berates him for his lies, he responds, "'I didn't tell you a story. Everytime I showed you those things I said "all of these were mine" and Ah wuz talkin' bout my whiskers'" (179). Whereas such insincerity is a source of humor for men, several episodes in *Mules and Men* reveal it as the traditional norm in courting. As Hurston's own experience demonstrates (68–70), a woman's ability to protect her own interests often depends on recognizing such "woofing" for the "aimless talking" (253) that it is.

Men's view of love as a game and fidelity as a trap is clear in Willie Sewell's boast: "'Ya'll lady people ain't smarter *than* all men folks. You got plow lines on some of us, but some of us is too smart for you. We go past you jus' like lightnin' thru de trees. . . . And what mek it so cool, we close enough to you to have a scronchous time, but never no halter on our necks. Ah know they won't git none on dis last neck of mine'" (38). The conflict between men's and women's interests is highlighted in Gold's retort, "'Oh, you kin be had. . . . Ah mean dat abstifically'" (38) and Willie's rejoinder, "'Yeah? But not wid de trace chains. Never no shack up. Ah want dis tip-in love and tip yo' hat and walk out. Ah don't want nobody to have dis dyin' love for me'" (38). The disagreement does not end with the conversation between this man and woman. Jack Oscar Jones reinforces the male perspective with his "speech about love" (38), actually a poem about a man having concurrent love affairs with three women. Like other black women who use their tongues as "weapon[s]" (33), marshaling folktales to counter sexism and to further their own interests, Shug responds to Jack's paean to philandering with the comment, "'Well, de way Ah know de story, there was three mens after de same girl'" (40). She then proceeds with the story of the heroic feats three men perform to win the hand of a girl in marriage, a tale, which narrated in another context, might seem simply another mythic story of heroic black deeds, similar to those told in Chapter X. In the male/ female battle out of which it grows, it more accurately demonstrates the women's use of folktales to elevate their status. Reversing the numbers and the roles here, showing men eager for marriage, Shug paints the men in her tale delivering on their promises, performing heroic labors and even "female" tasks to prove their love.

The men's frequent use of folktales to counter women's assertions of equality and to reinforce the status quo is evident in three tales told at the end of Chapter VII, "The Son Who Went to College," "Sis Snail," and "Why the Waves Have Whitecaps," all narrated in the context of heated arguments between men and women that infuse them with gender-specific meanings.[16] The scene begins with one of the battles between Big Sweet and Joe Willard over his infidelity. Introducing his contribution to a series of stories about dogs, Gene Oliver comments, "'Talkin' 'bout dogs, . . . they got plenty sense. Nobody can't fool dogs much'" (133).[17] Recognizing Gene's "by-word" reference to men, Big Sweet changes the direction of the conversation with her own "'signify[ing]'" (133) comment: "'And speakin' 'bout hams, . . . if Joe Willard don't stay out of dat bunk he was in last night, Ah'm gointer sprinkle some salt down his back and sugar-cure *his* hams'" (133). The interchange between her and Joe Willard that follows highlights Big Sweet's verbal skill in asserting her own sexual interests:

> Joe snatched his pole out of the water with a jerk and glared at Big Sweet, who stood sidewise looking at him most pointedly.
> "Aw, woman, quit tryin' to signify."
> "Ah kin signify all Ah please, Mr. Nappy-chin, so long as Ah know what Ah'm talkin' about."
> "See dat?" Joe appealed to the other men. "We git a day off and

figger we kin ketch some fish and enjoy ourselves, but naw, some wim-
mins got to drag behind us, even to the lake."

"You didn't figger Ah was draggin' behind you when you was
bringin' dat Sears and Roebuck catalogue over to my house and beggin'
me to choose my ruthers. Lemme tell *you* something, *any* time Ah shack
up wid any man Ah gives myself de privilege to go wherever he might
be, night or day. Ah got de law in my mouth."

"Lawd, ain't she specifyin'!" sniggered Wiley. (133–34)

Joe's "appeal" to the men does not go unheeded, for they immediately launch into a series of stories told specifically to denigrate women.
Jim Allen introduces the first with the telling comment, "'Well, you
know what they say—a man can cakerlate his life till he git mixed up
wid a woman or git straddle of a cow'" (134). As astute in interpreting
words as she is in speaking them, Big Sweet decodes the gender equation
thinly veiled in Allen's signifying comment: "'Who you callin' a cow,
fool? Ah know you ain't namin' *my* mama's daughter no cow'" (134). In
this specific context, the story of a man riding a cow to tame her functions as a thinly veiled tale of male sexual and emotional domination of
women. Told by Jim Allen, it mirrors his relationship with his burdened
wife and again dramatizes the racial component in black women's oppression. As the man who feels most heavily the weight of white oppression, Allen must "ride" a woman to feel himself less like a mule.[18]

The men immediately launch into another tale commenting on relationships between men and women. The story of Sis Snail (also told
in *Dust Tracks on a Road*) in another context might function simply as an
innocuous animal tale. Here, however, the gender dynamics of the preceding arguments highlight the male attitudes toward women evident
in the tale:

> "You know de snail's wife took sick and sent him for de doctor. She
> was real low ill-sick and rolled from one side of de bed to de other. She
> was groanin', 'Lawd knows Ah got so much misery Ah hope de Doc-
> tor'll soon git here to me.'
>
> After seben years she heard a scufflin' at de door. She was real happy
> so she ast, 'Is dat you baby, done come back wid de doctor? Ah'm so
> glad!'
>
> He says, 'Don't try to rush me—Ah ain't gone yet.'
> He had been seben years gettin' to de door." (137)

While men's failure to support women is humorously rationalized and
legitimated in this tale, it is an ironically accurate reflection on the level
of support Jim Allen and other men offer their wives.

The last tale, innocently cast as an etiological tale with the title, "Why the Waves Have Whitecaps," is firmly grounded in stereotypes of women. The wind and the water are both cast as women who, "jus' like all lady people," spend much time "talk[ing] about their chillun and brag[ging] on 'em" (138). The tale, significantly narrated by Jim Allen's grandson and protégé, is much more than a parable of women's vanity, however; for their maternal devotion takes a most sinister turn—when Mrs. Wind's children ask Mrs. Water for a drink, she drowns them. The tale ends with an explanation of the origin of white caps:

> Mrs. Wind knew her chillun had come down to Mrs. Water's house, so she passed over de ocean callin' her chillun, and every time she call de white feathers would come up on top of de water. And dat's how come we got white caps on waves. It's de feathers comin' up when de wind woman calls her lost babies.
> When you see a storm on de water, it's de wind and de water fightin' over dem chillun. (139)

Although Hurston will rework this metaphorical treatment of the storm, embracing it as an image of black women's powers of resistance in several later works, the men here, as in much European folklore, locate the roots of human and cosmic discord in women's actions.

Although Hurston relentlessly exposes the sexism in the black world described in *Mules and Men,* she holds firmly to an ideal of equality between men and women. As Cheryl Wall ("Zora Neale Hurston," 377–78) has pointed out, Hurston smuggles in a religious affirmation of this theme by inserting the sermon, "Behold the Rib." Ostensibly just another happenstance revelation of the richness of black pulpit oratory, the sermon repeats the story of Adam and Eve, but with a radically revised interpretation:

> Behold de rib!
> A bone out of a man's side.
> He put de man to sleep and made wo-man,
> And men and women been sleeping together ever since.
> Behold de rib!
> Brothers, if God
> Had taken dat bone out of man's head
> He would have meant for woman to rule, hah
> If he had taken a bone out of his foot,
> He would have meant for us to dominize and rule.
> He could have made her out of back-bone
> And then she would have been behind us.

But, no, God Almighty, he took de bone out of his side
So dat places de woman beside us. (150–51)

Although spoken to an unenthusiastic audience who do not even comment on the preacher's message or respond to his good "strainin' voice,"
this speech represents the ideal against which relationships between men
and women are measured in *Mules and Men*.

The character who comes closest to achieving this ideal even in the
face of male efforts at domination is, of course, Big Sweet, a woman
who "didn't mind fighting; didn't mind killing and didn't too much
mind dying" (159) to protect what she sees as hers. In one conversation
Hurston highlights her affinities with the black woman of men's nightmares described in "Characteristics of Negro Expression." One man,
alluding to the fight brewing between Big Sweet and Joe Willard, reveals his hatred of male and female equality: "'If a man kin whip his
woman and whip her good; all right, but when they don't do nothin'
but fight, it makes my stomach turn'" (147). Undeterred by such sentiments, Big Sweet vows to cut "' 'round de hambone'" (147) to force Joe
Willard's fidelity. The feared black woman with the physical power and
the weapons to promote her interests, she is, significantly, the only black
person who stands up to white people in overt defiance that even Joe
Willard acknowledges is the "noble" act of "uh whole woman and half
uh man" (162).

Hurston is careful not to paint Big Sweet as simply racially defiant
and dangerously violent. Rather, she stresses in the character of Big
Sweet a fusion, suggested even in her name, of traditional male tough-
ness and female tenderness. The value Big Sweet places on generous support for another—her use of power not to dominate but to liberate—is
first indicated in the tale she narrates about the mockingbird. Telling
about the death and damnation of an evil man who was only good to
birds, Big Sweet stresses the selfless devotion evident in the birds' hercu-
lean labor: "De birds all hated it mighty bad when they seen him in hell,
so they tried to git him out. But the fire was too hot so they give up—
all but de mockin' birds. They come together and decided to tote sand
until they squenched de fire in hell. So they set a day and they all agreed
on it. Every Friday they totes sand to hell. And that's how come nobody
don't never see no mockin' bird on Friday" (103). Hurston associates this
value on selfless devotion and supportive friendship with black women
by detailing male response to this tale and by suggesting (as she often

does to highlight gender issues) that the men do not know this story. When Big Sweet (before telling her tale) explains the absence of birds by the fact that "It's Friday and de mocking bird ain't here" (102), Eugene reveals his ignorance of the tale with the comment, "What's Friday got to do with the mockin' bird?"—an attitude reiterated by Joe Wiley: "Dat's exactly what Ah want to know" (102). Hurston also suggests that the men do not understand the tale's significance after they hear it. Joe Wiley's "chuckl[ing]" comment, "If them mockin' birds ever speck to do dat man any good they better git some box-cars to haul dat sand. Dat one li'l grain they totin' in their bill ain't helpin' none" (103), reveals how totally he has missed the tale's emotional point. Sensitive only to the tale's personification, he can make just the weakest of interpretive stabs at the tale's meaning: "But anyhow it goes to show you dat animals got sense as well as peoples" (103). He then launches into a tale, jarring with the empathy and pathos of Big Sweet's, about a catfish that drags a fisherman into deep water and drowns him (103).

Just as men act out the dynamics of their tales in daily life, Big Sweet demonstrates her selfless devotion in her behavior toward Hurston. She protects her, not for the pragmatic reason that she represents an ally, for Hurston is honest in depicting her own inefficacy in the fighting. Rather, Big Sweet selflessly supports Hurston's purposes, even if they must have seemed inexplicable ones: "You come here tuh see and lissen and Ah means fuh yuh tuh do it" (186). She is willing to fight for Hurston even though this support only creates for herself more enemies. Big Sweet, thus, represents the ideal black woman for Hurston—tender and supportive with those she loves, ruthless when necessary for her own survival or that of her loved ones.[19]

Big Sweet is, nevertheless, an ideal. She herself suggests that not every black woman can be so direct in asserting her rights when she warns Hurston not to " 'let yuh head start more than yo' rump kin stand' " (187). For women of less titanic proportions, the strategies necessary to battle sexual inequality are often more indirect ones. Oppressed by men within their own communities, they must often act in ways that echo those used by blacks in battling racial oppression. These parallels are emphasized in the story Mathilda Moseley tells early in the book, "Why Women Always Take Advantage of Men." Again, Hurston highlights the role women's stories play in attacking sexism by detailing the discussion that prompts Mathilda to tell this tale, a conversation peppered with derogatory comments about women and male bragging about their superiority. To counter these comments, Mathilda launches into a story that, first of all, reinforces the message of the "Behold de Rib!" sermon. Women are not "naturally" inferior to men, she points out, because originally " 'de woman was just as strong as de man and both of 'em did de same things. They useter get to fussin' 'bout who gointer do this and that and sometime they'd fight, but they was even balanced and neither one could whip de other one' " (33–34). In yet another radical revision of the creation myth, Eden is destroyed by male perfidy when the man asks God for more strength so he can " 'whip' " the woman and " 'make her mind' " (34).

When the man swaggers home to announce, " 'Ah'm yo' boss' " (35), the woman, as feisty as Big Sweet, heroically fights back. Now physically "double-teened," however, she finds herself a mule in relation to her husband. " 'Long as you obey me,' " he warns, " 'Ah'll be good to yuh, but every time yuh rear up Ah'm gointer put plenty wood on yo' back and plenty water in yo' eyes' " (35). Determined to regain her strength, the woman (after God refuses her request) finally goes to the Devil, "a powerful trickster" (254) who helps women in their battles with black men just as he often helps black men in their struggles with whites. Teaching her to be a cunning trickster herself, counseling her to ask God for his keys, he promises that in an indirect fashion, she can " 'come out mo' than conqueror' " (35). Hitting a straight lick with her crooked stick, she gets the keys to the kitchen, the bedroom, and the cradle and returns to the devil who instructs her not to " 'unlock nothin' until [her husband] use his strength for yo' benefit and yo' desires' " (36). Unable to "rear up" (35) in open defiance of her rider, the woman, like High John, nevertheless wins without "outside show of force," as Mathilda's self-satisfied conclusion suggests: " 'de man had to mortgage his strength to her to live. And dat's why de man makes and de woman takes. You men is still braggin' 'bout yo' strength and de women is sittin' on de keys and lettin' you blow off till she git ready to put de bridle on you' " (38). With the woman holding the bridle now rather than wearing it, the mule and rider motif shifts starkly at this point in the tale. As the last sentence suggests, this female trickster, despite apparent inequality, exercises considerable control in her relationship with men. So do the women in *Mules and Men*. That they use similar strategies for survival and victory over their oppressors can be seen in Mrs. Allen's response to her husband's refusal to clean the yard: instead of foolishly confronting her husband physically, she uses one of her keys. When the men return from fishing, "The fishermen began scraping fish and hot grease began to pop in happy houses. All but the Allen's. Mrs. Allen wouldn't have a thing to do with our fish because Mr. Allen and Cliffert had made her mad about the yard" (147).

As this tale suggests, Hurston treats race and gender as complexly interrelated issues in the black world she describes. Gender inequality not only grows out of racial inequality (the black woman's burden can, after all, be traced back to the white man who originally orders the black man to pick it up); it operates in strikingly parallel ways in *Mules and Men* and in Hurston's fiction. Her ambiguous title captures the richness of her analysis. A world controlled by whites, one (like that of the sawmill) in which black men are economically oppressed and socially defined by them, is a world of mules and men. Tragically, for Hurston, when black men like Jim Allen, John Pearson, or Joe Starks draw their self-concepts from white people and make themselves feel like men by slipping their halters onto black women, the black community becomes another. Hurston's analysis of power relations between black and white or between black men and women is, however, even more complex, one that involves not just grimly detailing oppression but also enthusiastically depicting resistance to it. As many of her folktales and fictional characters demonstrate, any world of mules and men is potentially unstable. As black men in their relationships with whites and black women in their relationsips with black men repeatedly show throughout Hurston's oeuvre, mules are not simply brutalized beasts of burden who silently endure their slavish existence; they can often be "fractious" beasts who throw off their burdens and their riders or subtle tricksters who more slyly slip their halters.[20]

2 "Natural Men" and "Pagan Poesy" in *Jonah's Gourd Vine*

As Deborah McDowell argues in "Reading Family Matters," the treatment of conflicts between black women and men is a discursive project fraught with difficulties for African American women writers. Hurston's interest in the oppression of black women by black men, both the notion of masculinity from which it arises and black women's means of resisting it, was evident in her earliest fiction. In one of her first short stories, "Magnolia Flower," published in *The Spokesman* in 1925, she suggests the interaction of race and gender in models of masculinity played out in domination of black women through the character, Bentley, a freed slave so spiritually enslaved to the values of his former slave owners that he recreates master/slave relationships with his wife and his community. Whereas Hurston's early development of this theme is unsuccessful because the pastoralism she uses in the story as a masking technique seems contrived and hackneyed, she returned to the theme in both *Jonah's Gourd Vine* and *Their Eyes Were Watching God,* finding more successful ways to veil her treatment of models of black masculinity and of female resistance to male oppression. Aware of the complexities of treating intragroup conflict before a heterogenous audience (the precise difficulty both John and Janie encounter at their trials), Hurston used elements of African American folk culture not merely to celebrate it but to mask treatment of the interlocking nature of race and gender in relationships between black women and men.

In writing *Jonah's Gourd Vine,* Hurston crafted a story with immense potential for popular success. Focusing on black folk life, drenched in rich dialect and poetic black preaching, it foregrounded aspects of black experience popularized by other black writers during the Harlem Renaissance. Its central character, John, possessed two traits necessary to make him a black hero at the time. The master of "pagan poesy" (141), he was, like the black preachers extolled in James Weldon Johnson's *God's Trombones,* gifted with a "bold and unfettered" imagination and "the power to sweep his hearers before him" (*God's Trombones,* 5).[1] In many ways a "primitive" like those created by other writers of the period, John Pearson is a "natural man," sexually vigorous and verbally power-ful. In writing the novel Hurston gauged white literary tastes well: re-views of her book, almost universally warm, nearly always praised its flamboyant language and its lusty main character.[2] Hurston's evalua-tion of both, however, is much more complex. Just as *Mules and Men* provides a subtle analysis of race and gender beneath its celebration of the "primitive" vitality of rural black culture, *Jonah's Gourd Vine,* at the same time that it glorifies a black world, also focuses on conflicts within it. Through John, Hurston critiques a notion of black masculin-ity that arises out of racial insecurity and plays itself out in oppres-sion of women.[3] The elements of a rich black folk culture, largely re-sponsible for the book's popularity, are both mask and vehicle for that critique.

Hurston used elements of black culture popular during the Har-lem Renaissance to deal with a gender theme in another early work, "Muttsy," a seemingly lighthearted tale of Harlem nightlife. In this story, the main male character, a wealthy rake named Muttsy, briefly falls into the throes of respectability, giving up gambling, taking a foreman's job, and marrying an innocent young woman, Pinkie. The story ends, however, with his return to a more vibrant and raucous life of gambling, a conclusion easily read during the Harlem Renaissance as a rejection of respectable but insipid white middle-class values. Focusing on the blues and gambling in the story, Hurston reinforces this ethnic reading by seeming to glorify in a straightforward manner the features of black life popular with whites at the time. A tale about black people "liv[ing] on hotly their intense lives" (21) in a variety of ways, it opens on a note quite familiar to readers of many black works of the 1920s: "The piano in Ma Turner's back parlor stuttered and wailed. The pianist kept time with his heel and informed an imaginary deserter that 'she might leave and go to Halimufack, but his slow-drag would bring her back,' mourn-fully, with a memory of tom-toms running rhythm through the plaint" (19). Blues music played in the background throughout the story and dance, characters "shaking shimmies to music, rolling eyes heavenward as they picked imaginary grapes out of the air" (24), are details Hurston

used to evoke an exuberant, vibrant existence, the "primitivism" whites
had come to expect in descriptions of black life. This joyous and, for a
white audience, exotic setting is, however, a diversionary tactic, a mask
behind which lies a complex account of the interaction of race and gender in the lives of black people. In fact, the raucously carefree ethnic setting symbolized by the blues music is finally extremely ironic in terms
of gender. The refrain repeated throughout the story, "'Ahm gointer
make me a graveyard of mah own'" is a telling one: this is exactly what
the woman of the story, Pinkie, does.[4]

Despite Muttsy's association with a black gambling world, Hurston
actually paints him, much like Joe Starks of *Their Eyes Were Watching
God,* as a product of the white world. Dressed not in overalls but "in
sartorial splendor" (30), Muttsy uses his wealth not for his community
but to become its overlord, achieving his ends often by "squinching the
spirit" of those around him. The narrator's comments that he is "king uh
de bones" (36) and possessed with a "lordly stride" (35) are not straightforward compliments but rather are comments on his desire to be above
other blacks, his respect for hierarchy and his demands for deference. He
is, finally, a surrogate white oppressor, a modern-day slave overseer, perfectly qualified (as white men recognize) to be "a boss stevedore" (29)
and "manage the [black] men" (29) for them.

Muttsy's dependence on white models of identity is further displayed in his relationship with Pinkie. Like Joe Starks, who imitates
white notions of male and female relationships in his own with Janie,
Muttsy simultaneously places Pinkie on a pedestal and strangles her
selfhood. His vow to Ma, "'Ah'm gointer treat [Pinkie] white'" (34), is
thus an honest statement filled with irony: he pampers her, showers her
with wealth, and "respectably" marries her, but destroys her in the process. Even though Pinkie seems to win the respectable life so important to her—marriage and economic security—she pays a high price
for this reward. The antithesis of characters like Janie and Big Sweet,
women who are strong, independent, and equal to their men, Pinkie
becomes Muttsy's "doll baby" (33, 34) and consequently faces a life as
spiritually deadening as Janie's with Joe Starks. Hurston depicts the self-
annihilation Pinkie will suffer, not by showing us her life after marriage
(we, in fact, never see her after that point) but more obliquely through
the images she associates with Pinkie and Muttsy before their marriage.
The dehumanization and spiritual death she faces are foreshadowed, first
of all, in Muttsy's courting: he proposes while she is unconscious—

in fact, "sleepin' lak she's buried'" (31)—without ever asking her her wishes. In this scene, Hurston also reveals the spiritual violence lurking in Muttsy's love and the mortal threat to her selfhood marriage to him promises: "He tipped up to the bed again and knelt there holding her hands so fiercely that she groaned without waking. He watched her and he wanted her so that he wished to crush her in his love; crush and crush and hurt her against himself, but somehow he resisted the impulse and merely kissed her lips again, kissed her hands back and front, removed the largest diamond ring from his hand and slipped it on her engagement finger" (32).

Aware of how popular black vernacular was with whites during this period, Hurston also carefully uses black slang not simply for local color or cultural celebration but to underscore subtly the imbalance in Muttsy and Pinkie's relationship, one in which Muttsy plays the predatory role of dog (as his name and the images associated with him suggest) and Pinkie that of his hapless prey, a helpless victim with no more defences than the "'li'l biddy'" (19, 22), "'li'l chicken'" (19, 28), and "'real li'l pullet'" (26) she is described as.[5] While Muttsy chivalrously claims to protect Pinkie from being devoured by other men—"'Come on befo' some uh dese niggers sprinkle some salt on yuh and eat yuh clean up lak uh raddish'" (27)—he does so only to save her for himself, the voracious "hunger" (32) in his own kisses as well as his brag that he "'eats fried chicken when the rest of [the] niggers is drinking rain-water" (27), both ominous indicators of the emotional dynamics in their relationship. The self-annihilation that awaits Pinkie is foreshadowed in the engagement celebration—"'fried chicken fuh breakfus'" (33)—and reinforced in the story's ending. She does not "live happily ever after," for when Muttsy cavalierly returns to the dice, she must suffer what she tried so hard to avoid, the disrepute of being married to a gambler. Even worse, she must also endure psychologically (if not legally) what she most feared. As Muttsy's last comment, "'What man can't keep one li'l wife an' two li'l bones?'" (37), suggests, Pinkie faces the life of a "kept woman," dependent and dehumanized despite her marriage and affluence. The lighthearted humor at the story's end may unproblematically conclude the story if one reads it only through the lens of "race," but behind the carefree mood and the black men "'laughin' all the time'" lies a tragedy for the black woman in the story.[6]

Although John is a more complex character than Muttsy, Hurston could count on her readers viewing John as a heroic folk figure. Nevertheless, *Jonah's Gourd Vine,* read from Lucy's point of view, paints a very different portrait of his spontaneity and exuberance. Even the title, a richly ambiguous one, highlights two very different ways events and the relationship between John and Lucy can be read. Hurston points out the biblical allusion in a letter to Carl Van Vechten: "Oh yes, the title you didn't understand (Jonah 4:6–10). You see the prophet of God sat up under a gourd vine that had grown up in one night. But a cut worm came along and cut it down. Great and sudden growth. One act of malice and it is withered and gone" (Feb. 28, 1934, JWJ). The passage she points to elucidates another important symbolic aspect of this gourd vine: God made the vine grow "that it might be a shade over [Jonah's] head, to save him from his discomfort" (Jonah 4:6). Although Lucy never openly tells her anguished story and is often silent in her suffering, reviewing events from her perspective highlights the fact that John, despite his eloquent promises, is never a support to Lucy. Contrary to the assumptions of most commentators and of men in the book (146, 154) that John is the gourd vine, Lucy is actually the real protecting power throughout the novel.[7] The cut worm (one of several ominous phallic symbols in the novel) that destroys her is John himself.[8]

When the events of the novel are stripped of John's grand promises and eloquent apologies, the humiliations Lucy has to endure in her marriage because of his irresponsibility stand out in stark relief. One of the earliest is the visit of her brother when she is pregnant. Embarrassed by Bud's knowledge of John's infidelity, she is further humiliated when she cannot repay the three dollars they owe him (even though John is off, at that moment, spending money on Delphine [89]). It is painfully appropriate for Bud to take their marriage bed that "Lucy loved . . . above all else" (81), for John consistently betrays the spiritual and physical commitment it represents. Her pain from John's actions is not over, for Lucy must still give birth that evening—alone on the floor—while John is off philandering. When John returns home, ashamed to see his family cared for by someone else, he seems genuinely contrite. He reacts, however, by stealing a shoat to feed them and by beating Bud in retaliation. Even though John feels more "like a man" for these acts, they bring only further suffering to his family when he is jailed and must flee from the law. Both the emptiness of John's vows and the reality of his manliness are clear when he brags to Lucy after the theft: "You got uh *man* tuh fend fuh yuh" (95), "gimme uh chance tuh show mah spunk" (95). His manliness is immediately evident: he has to run away in the dark of night, chased by the "patter rollers," having been rescued from prison by Lucy and the white judge. Bud speaks the bitter truth about this series of events when he tells John, "'If you wuz any kind of man, all dis wouldn't come tuh pass'" (94). Even though John brags about his manliness repeatedly and acts to prove it, Hurston ironically undercuts John's claims; he often acts, not like a man but like an irresponsible child, albeit a charming and articulate one.

That John's promises to support Lucy, even those he makes to himself, mean nothing is a truth reiterated throughout the novel. After leaving Lucy to escape the law, he vows to send for her as soon as he is settled (103–4), but "one thing and another delayed him" (108). Although Hurston mimics John's evasion of responsibility in the phrase, "one thing and another," the details of that sequence make it clear that other women make John forget his devotion to Lucy. John's plans to go to Eatonville to make a new start are deferred for similar reasons: "There were many weeks between John and the little Negro village. He would resolve to move there on next pay-day, but trips to town, and visitors to camp defeated his plans" (107–8). Even without intrusive authorial comment by Hurston, the narrative reveals the purpose of the trips and the gender of the visitors. His selfish abandonment of Lucy is no momentary weakness either; as Lucy points out, it is "'might nigh uh yeah'" before he actually sends for her (108).

When Lucy finally arrives in Eatonville, John, seemingly happy to have her there, showers her with love talk that ironically contrasts with his actions: "'Ah'd send fuh you, if Ah didn't have bread tuh eat'" (108). All of his promises to Lucy are as meaningful as his "sweet talk" when she arrives. Like many of the courting rituals in *Mules and Men,* his traditional, hyperbolic words—"'Ah'd sweat in hell fuh yuh. Ah'd take uh job cleaning out de Atlantic Ocean jus' fuh yuh'" (111)—are beautiful to hear but dangerous to believe. What John's devotion really means is ironically revealed in a statement he makes to one of his many lovers: "'Some women you wouldn't mind tearin' up de pavements uh hell tuh built 'em uh house, but some you don't give 'em nothin'. You jes' consolate 'em by word uh mouf and fill 'em full uh melody'" (155–56). John seems here to contrast his love for Lucy with his lust for (and deception of) other women, but throughout their marriage he gives Lucy only eloquent words.

He gives his children little more. When the family steps off the train, John brags to the children, "'Yo' papa lookin' out fuh yuh'" (108), but it is Lucy who does all the planning for the family. Immediately securing a house (108–9) and pointing out carpentry as a viable job for John (109), she makes plans for them to own their own home. Just what it means to have John as the papa "lookin' out for yuh" becomes clear when Isis contracts typhoid. Unable to bear the pain of his daughter's possible death, John leaves Lucy to worry over the sick child alone: "He was gutted with grief, but when Hattie Tyson found out his whereabouts and joined him, he suffered it, and for some of his hours he forgot about the dying Isis, but when he returned a week later and found his daughter feebly recovering, he was glad. He brought Lucy a new dress and a pineapple" (117). The convoluted syntax here mirrors John's twisted rationalizations: he may feel "a new dress and a pineapple" an appropriate offering, but it is ludicrously small payment on his emotional debt to Lucy.

John's weakness—the gulf between his words and actions—is confirmed after Lucy's death. As his betrayal of Sally (even when forewarned by Hambo [196]) shows, his personal "conversions" mean as little as some he stimulates in church. Even though the suffering John endures and his expressions of self-pity invite one to sympathize with him in his plight with Hattie and to excuse his behavior, his irresponsible way of dealing with difficulties remains unchanged. His conscience pricked in his relationship with her, he denies any responsibility for it and, foisting all the "sin" onto her shoulders, sees himself as a victim caught in the snares of a conniving woman. As if his children were Hattie's responsibility, he blames her for the fact that they no longer live with him. When he turns a self-righteous eye to the liquor bottles littering the house, Hattie makes the obvious point that he drinks too. Undaunted and dogged in his denial of responsibility, John replies that Lucy "'never brought none in de house tuh tempt me'" (144). John ultimately hates Hattie not because she is sinful but because she does not protect him as Lucy had. When John slings the ultimate insult, "'You sho ain't no Lucy Ann,'" one has to admit the truth in Hattie's rejoinder: "'Naw, Ah ain't no Miss Lucy, 'cause Ah ain't goin' tuh cloak yo' dirt fuh yuh. Ah ain't goin' tuh take offa yuh whut she took so you kin set up and be uh big nigger over mah bones'" (145).

While Hattie adamantly refuses to protect and unquestioningly adore John (and is therefore spurned), John finds another mother figure in Sally. Confessing his sins to her, John recreates that earlier relationship: he becomes a child, "lay[ing] with his head in her lap sobbing like a boy of four" (189), with Sally playing the role of mother, "run[ing] her fingers soothingly thru John's hair" (189) just as Lucy had (93). Confident of unqualified devotion from Sally, he runs to her after his brief liaison with the Ora Patton like a wayward child to his doting mother: "Soon he would be in the shelter of Sally's presence. Faith and no questions asked" (200).

Through John, Hurston thus critiques a kind of masculinity that is fundamentally childlike in its emotional dependency and irresponsibility. Through him she goes even further to examine the source of this male identity. As in *Mules and Men,* in which she traces the black woman's burden back to a white source, Hurston in *Jonah's Gourd Vine* suggests a racial component in the gender relations of black life. As if to highlight the relationship between racial insecurity and sexual oppression in the lives of black people, Hurston raises this theme in the opening argument between Amy and Ned, one which delineates the basic conflicting values of the novel. Ned is clearly a tragic victim for Hurston, a " 'mule' " (40), as Amy astutely perceives, who nevertheless emulates his own oppressor in his relationships with and in his views of black people. Accepting the white world's divisive, false characterizations of black people as "house niggers" and "field niggers," light-skinned and dark-skinned, he consistently echoes the slave owner's attitudes, labeling John " 'de house-nigger' " (4) and arguing that " 'niggers wuz made tuh work' " (5). Condemning John as " 'biggity' " (44), irritated that he " 'ought to be humble, but he ain't' " (44–45), Ned takes it upon himself to "crumple his feathers," symbolically selling John back into slavery under the employ of Mimms. John inadvertently exposes the bitter parallels between Ned and a white oppressor when he consoles his family, " 'Sometimes Ah jes' as soon be under Mimms ez pappy. One 'bout ez bad as tother' " (8).

The tragic toll of these attitudes on a black person's self-concept is clearest in one interchange between Ned and Amy. When Amy argues that they should seek a better life for their children than they have had, Ned again expresses attitudes toward blacks rooted in his belief that " 'Dese white folks orta know' " (9): " 'How come dey's diffunt? We'se all niggers tuhgether, ain't us? White men don't keer no mo' 'bout one dan he do de other' " (5). In her response, Amy articulates Hurston's view on the importance of black pride and cultural independence:

"Course dey don't, but we ain't got tuh let de white folks love our chillun fuh us, is us? Dass jest de pint. We black folks don't love our chillun.
We couldn't do it when we wuz in slavery. We borned 'em but dat
didn't make 'em ourn. Dey b'longed tuh old Massa. 'Twan't no use in
treasurin' other folkses property. It wuz liable tuh be took uhway any
day. But we's free folks now. De big bell done rung! Us chillun is ourn.
Ah doan know, mebbe hit'll take some of us generations, but us got tuh
'gin tuh practice on treasurin' our younguns." (16)

Unlike Amy, Ned sees no black identity beyond that assigned by whites
and can imagine "manliness" only in the white terms he has known.
Demanding silence and subservience at home to convince himself of
manhood denied outside, Ned resorts to trace chains and the overseer's
whip when he feels threatened. Reenacting the dynamics of the plantation, he whips Amy and orders John to "'Drop dem britches below yo'
hocks, and git down on yo' knees'" (46). Here, as in "Sweat," Hurston
uses phallic imagery of the whip to suggest a notion of masculinity
expressed in soul-crushing force and rooted in racial oppression.

Ultimately, Ned (like Jim Allen in *Mules and Men*) is a tragic figure
for Hurston, a pitifully weak man despite his big talk and violence toward others. Although Ned tries to make himself feel less like a mule
and more like a man by treating his family and his race as animals, when
faced with power greater than his own (for instance, when John threatens to beat him), he can only skulk off. One of our final images of
Ned captures the pathetic and paradoxical situation of such a man: Ned
"limped behind his plow, stumbling now and then, slashing the mule
and swearing incessantly" (43).

Although on the surface John seems a very different character, the
novel chronicles his development into a distressingly similar one. Attrib-
uting John's behavior and demise to more than individual weakness,
Hurston makes a much broader social critique by underscoring John's
acceptance of white notions of blackness. Despite his association with
rich black folk culture, John repeatedly reveals his racial insecurity. He
cannot, for instance, imagine a black world independent of a white one;
when he comes to Eatonville, he is (like Joe Starks) puzzled as to who
"bosses" the town in the absence of whites (107). John cannot imagine
a black world equal to a white one either; when Lucy urges them to buy
their own home, he (echoing Ned) responds, "'Dat's uh bigger job than
Ah wants tuh tackle, Lucy. You so big-eyed. Wese colored folks. Don't be

so much-knowin'"" (109). That John's attitudes about black possibilities are dependent on white definitions is highlighted by a comparison of his and Lucy's views. They have very different notions, for instance, of what power and freedom mean. For Lucy "being a man" means display-ing independence and shouldering responsibility while for John it sim-ply means having license to do what one wishes. As she tells John, "'be uh *man*. Cover de ground you stand on. Jump at de sun and eben if you miss it, yuh can't help grabbin' holt uh de moon'" (95). When they see a chance for John to become mayor of Eatonville, John is eager for per-sonal power and status, whereas Lucy sees an opportunity for her chil-dren to grow up with self-respect in a world protected from whites and racism: "'Dey won't be seein' no other kind of folks actin' top-superior over 'em, and dat'll give 'em spunk tuh be bell cows theyselves'" (109). For John being an important person—"'uh big nigger'" (116), as he says—means aping the finery and values of whites, parading in his "dark blue broadcloth, his hand-made alligator shoes, and his black Stetson" (116).

Like Ned, John gets his notion both of blackness and of maleness from a white world. Even his sexuality, which (in the terms of the Har-lem Renaissance) seems such an exuberant and vital contrast to the in-sipidity seen in white culture, is treated as quite complicated. Immedi-ately noticeable is John's belief in a double standard of sexual behavior for black women and men. At the same time that he defines his own sexual freedom in terms of the right to numerous affairs, he can (armed with a rifle to reinforce his point) announce to Lucy, "'Ahm de first wid you, and Ah means tuh be de last. Ain't never no man tuh breathe in yo' face but me'" (110). Furthermore, although John's sexuality is lusty and uninhibited, Hurston often symbolically portrays it as oppres-sive, repeatedly associated with ominous phallic imagery to suggest spiritual violence. Despite their seeming exuberance and spontaneity (from John's point of view), his sexual relations are, Hurston subtly suggests, often unequal and dehumanizing. Even though John treats Mehaley and Big 'Oman, for instance, as mere sexual beings (in the same way that Alf Pearson defines John as a "walking orgasm"), Hurston ac-tually describes relationships that are more emotionally complex. The scene of Mehaley's marriage on the rebound—her piteous weeping for John on her wedding night (84)—bespeaks an emotional sensitivity that John never acknowledges and a relationship deeper for her than sexual liaison.[9] Similarly, John's behavior toward Big 'Oman makes her seem the embodiment of female lust; but when he leaves her, she is a "weeping girl," pleading to know when he will return (86).[10]

Although John's relationships with Mehaley and Big 'Oman recapitulate Alf Pearson's with his slaves, even he recognizes the possibility of a more meaningful relationship; as he tells Mehaley, "'Ah tastes her [Lucy] wid mah soul, but if Ah didn't take holt uh you Ah'd might soon fuhgit all 'bout yuh'" (81). What makes John's relationship with Lucy special, as even he knows, is the fusion of the physical and spiritual in their love, expressed in a sexual relationship that denies neither the body nor the soul. Theirs is potentially the kind of marriage suggested in Hurston's image of the pear tree in *Their Eyes Were Watching God,* a true communion based in equality and reciprocity, one only threatened by John's notion of the "natural man" and the imbalanced relationships between men and women it legitimates.

The threat posed to their relationship by an oppressive notion of masculinity is graphically symbolized in Hurston's description of the snake-killing scene early in their courtship. After ritualistically killing the snake as a commitment that he will be a different man with Lucy, John carries her over the bridge, crossing a threshold into a new kind of relationship. Nevertheless, as the rest of the novel reveals (and as Lucy's worry about the presence of other snakes in the creek ominously foreshadows [34]), the symbolic snake in their relationship is not destroyed. As John's own excuse to Lucy for his adultery suggests, the "'brute beast'" (88) still lurks within him and is, he claims, a legitimate and adequate explanation for his behavior.[11] Although he sees himself as a "'natchel man'" (122), one whose sexual nature is compelling and overpowering, Hurston critiques John's notion as a mask for oppression and an excuse for black men's betrayal of black women. As she suggests through Alf Pearson and his role in John's life, there is nothing "natural" about this notion of black male sexuality, for it is the animalistic one assigned black men by whites, by men such as Pearson, who sees John as "'a fine stud'" (17), a "'splendid specimen'" (18), and a "'walking orgasm'" (50).

Hurston further critiques John's conception of masculinity through her use of train imagery in the novel.[12] Like the snake, the train is a rather obvious and ominous phallic symbol, a "panting" (15), "dangerous lookin'" (16) "monster" (15) that John, displaying his intuitive wisdom early in the novel, initially finds "'frightenin''" (16). Despite its demonic qualities, however, John is attracted to the power—both sexual and material—represented by the train:

> The rhythmic stroke of the engine, the shiny-buttoned porters bawling out the stations, the even more begilded conductor, who looked more imposing even than Judge Pearson, and then the red plush splendor, the gaudy ceiling hung with glinting lamps, the long mournful howl of the whistle. John forgot the misery of his parting with Lucy in the aura of it all. That is, he only remembered his misery in short snatches, while the glory lay all over him for hours at a time. He marvelled that just anybody could come along and be allowed to get on such a glorified thing. It ought to be extra special. He got off the train at every stop so that he could stand off a piece and feast his eyes on the engine. The greatest accumulation of power that he had ever seen. (104)

In *Jonah's Gourd Vine,* Hurston uses the train as a broad symbol of power, wealth, and manhood as defined not in black but in white terms. A mechanistic symbol (like those so often used to describe a white world during the Harlem Renaissance) rather than the plant imagery Hurston associates with black identity, the train represents the kind of gaudy— and spiritually empty—splendor embodied in the gold watch in "The Gilded Six-Bits."[13] It also represents, Hurston suggests, a kind of false freedom for blacks. While John escapes his legal problems on the train, he also leaves behind the one real support in his life, Lucy. Hurston further unmasks this aspect of the train's glitter in a somewhat anomalous section of the novel describing the black migration from the South during and after World War I. Although blacks escape by train the oppression of the South to what seems a Northern "land of promise" (151), an exodus Hurston explicitly compares to that of the Hebrews out of Egypt [151]), they face only new forms of exploitation: they are the first to be "shove[d] in front" (148) in the white man's wars, and they work in his factories only as "muscled hands" (149).

John's fascination with all these aspects of the train mirrors his adoration of values that prevent his development of an autonomous black male identity. As is hinted in the above passage, the train and Lucy (as representatives of two sets of very different cultural values) do ultimately compete for John's allegiance, with Lucy invariably the loser: he runs to say farewell to the train rather than to Lucy the first time he leaves (41) and later, seduced by its "aura" (104), forgets about her when he flees from the law. John also promises to keep coming back to find out what it says (16), a vow he carries through more diligently than he does for those he makes to Lucy. In a subtly ironic touch, Hurston gives words to the train revealing how misguided John's allegiance to it is. The train's messages, " 'Opelika black and dirty' " and " 'Wolf coming' " (41), are both accurate indicators of what the train symbolizes. John's reverence for it inevitably leads to Opelika and Do-dirty's tricks, the lengthiest and one of the most threatening breaks with Lucy. The saying "Wolf coming" ominously foreshadows John's situation late in the novel when the congregation turns against him: his church members mill around him "like a wolf pack about a tired old bull—looking for a throat-hold, but he had still enough of the former John to be formidable as an animal and enough of his Pagan poesy to thrill. The pack waited" (141). Unfortunately, John hears but cannot interpret the words of the train, just as he does not understand what it represents. Seduced by the appearance of unrestricted freedom and awesome power, he keeps returning to the train, in the end literally and spiritually destroyed by it.[14]

Many of these issues and symbols of identity converge in John's final *tour de force,* his sermon on "The Wounds of Jesus" (175–81). Just as Hurston could, in *Mules and Men,* use a folktale to celebrate rich black oral traditions and, at the same time, to reveal a character's racial insecurity or sexism, she uses this sermon—as she does folk saying and courtship ritual in *Jonah's Gourd Vine*—not simply as cultural showpiece but as the stuff of fiction to be shaped into ironic reflection of character and symbolic development of theme. While she rides on the popular wave of fascination with black pulpit oratory, she finally reveals much about John's character beneath his most eloquent and passionate performance of "pagan poesy."[15] Whereas Hurston apparently transcribed the sermon from one she heard delivered (she had earlier published it in Cunard's *Negro: An Anthology* and in *Mules and Men*), she incorporates it artfully and ironically into the themes and image patterns of the novel to function as a final indictment of John. When we only know that C. C. Lovelace delivered the sermon at Eau Gallie in Florida, on May 3, 1929 (Cunard, 35), we are led simply to appreciate its artistic value and poetic elegance. When we know, however, that John delivers the sermon to a congregation on the verge of expelling him for his illicit behavior, its significance is much more complex.[16]

John's motive in delivering the sermon is clear in a conversation with Hambo after the unsuccessful move by dissidents to fire him. Even though this first attempt has failed for lack of leadership, his problems with his congregation are unresolved. After hearing of John's concern,

Hambo clarifies the dynamics of John's situation: " 'But dey ain't got no guts. Dey wants tuh do dey work under cover. Dey got tuh fight war if dey wants tuh win dis battle, and dey needs cannon-guns. You can't fight war wid a brick' " (173). As Hambo's metaphors suggest, John is now engaged in battle with his congregation. When this purpose is borne in mind, the sermon becomes not an example of pure poetic creativity or speaking "from the heart" but a dazzling piece of persuasive rhetoric.

As John suggests, his sermon is a "parable": ostensibly about the wounds of Jesus, it is really an allegory about John himself, the real meaning of which is not lost on his congregation. Part of his strategy involves an equation of himself and Christ—both have been cruelly wounded, not by strangers but by their friends. His depiction of Christ is designed to emphasize the "injustice" of his own situation:

> I see Jesus
> Leaving heben with all of His grandeur
> Dis-robin' Hisself of His matchless honor
> Yielding up de scepter of revolvin' worlds
> Clothing Hisself in de garment of humanity,
> Coming into de world to rescue His friends. (177)

The dramatic immediacy he evokes in describing the betrayal of such self-sacrifice functions as a stern finger pointed directly at his congregation:

> Look into dat upper chamber, ha!
> We notice at de supper table
> As He gazed upon His friends, ha!
> His eyes flowin' wid tears, ha! He said
> "My soul is exceedingly sorrowful unto death, ha!
> For this night, ha!
> One of you shall betray me, ha!
> It were not a Roman officer, ha!
> It were not a centurion
> But one of you
> Who I have chosen my bosom friend
> That sops in the dish with me shall betray me." (177)

Masterfully, John erases the issue of his own sins by making the congregation the guilty party. This speech, thus, is his most adept use of the "loud-talkin'," defined by Hurston in her glossary as "making your side appear right by making more noise than the others" (205). It underlies his use of language with his church members, with Hattie, and with Lucy.

In this war with his congregation, John has more than one weapon in his arsenal. The Jesus he creates and identifies himself with is not a meek, suffering servant, but the wielder of raw power, able to muscle even the cosmic elements into submission. The spectacularly violent images evoked in the last half of the sermon, no mere poetic embellishment, are missiles aimed squarely at his audience. The price for betrayal of this awesomely fearful Jesus is much more severe than a guilty conscience. When Jesus cried,

> "My God, my God! Why hast Thou forsaken me?"
> The mountains fell to their rocky knees and trembled like a beast
> From the stroke of the master's axe
> One angel took the flinches of God's eternal power
> And bled the veins of the earth
> One angel that stood at the gate with a flaming sword
> Was so well pleased with his power
> Until he pierced the moon with his sword
> And she ran down in blood. (179)

The ending of John's sermon offers his congregation an option: they may foolishly pit themselves against such power or, by submitting and "prais[ing] His name forever," be protected by it:

> For in dat mor-ornin', ha!
> When we shall all be delegates, ha!
> To dat Judgment Convention
> When de two trains of Time shall meet on de trestle
> And wreck de burning axles of de unformed ether
> And de mountains shall skip like lambs
> When Jesus shall place one foot on de neck of de sea, ha!
> One foot on dry land, ah
> When His chariot wheels shall be running hub-deep in fire
> He shall take His friends thru the open bosom of an unclouded
>   sky
> And place in their hands de "hosanna" fan
> And they shall stand 'round and 'round his beatific throne
> And praise His name forever, Amen. (181)

Although John wins this battle with his congregation by overwhelming his opposition verbally and psychologically, he has also unwittingly revealed his values. In context, the sermon, like many of his professions, is a hypocritical and self-aggrandizing denial of his own shortcomings. Immediately noticeable is his characteristic hubris in comparing himself with Christ, an equation Hurston does not allow to go unchallenged. Jesus may have stepped down "with all of His grandeur / Dis robin' Hisself of His matchless honor" to minister to humankind, but John's move up from abject poverty to a lucrative ministry can hardly be described in such terms. Hurston also undercuts the parallels John tries to draw between the injustice of Christ's betrayal and his own: "'Jesus was not unthoughtful. He was not overbearing. He was never a bully. . . . and yet he was wounded'" (175). By his own logic, John, who has consistently been all three, deserves the ill will he reaps. Hurston also subtly exposes John's moral hypocrisy. Given our detailed knowledge of the suffering John has caused, his moralizing rebuke of his congregation—"'every sin we commit is a wound to Jesus. The blues we play in our home is a club to beat up Jesus, and these social card parties'" (175)—bespeaks a self-righteous denial of his much graver sins. Hurston also underscores John's culpability and the mortal wounds he has delivered in suggesting parallels between John and one angel who "'Was so well pleased with power / Until he pierced the moon with his sword / And she ran down in blood.'" Echoing the light imagery associated with Lucy throughout the novel, Hurston reminds us once again of John's role in Lucy's death.

John's misguided worship of power is also revealed in his use of train imagery. By developing its symbolic significance early in the novel, Hurston makes even these traditional allusions in the sermon ironic comments on John's character. John still worships the train and all it represents, picturing himself as Christ "grab[bing] de throttle / Of de well ordered train of mercy" (178). He intends his depiction of the "damnation train" to suggest his own martyrdom for his congregation:

> I heard de whistle of de damnation train
> Dat pulled out from Garden of Eden loaded wid cargo goin' to
>   hell
> Ran at break-neck speed all de way thru de law
> All de way thru de prophetic age
> All de way thru de reign of kings and judges—
> Plowed her way thru de Jurdan
> And on her way to Calvary, when she blew for de switch
> Jesus stood out on her track like a rough-backed mountain

And she threw her cow-catcher in His side and His blood
   ditched de train
He died for our sins. (180–81)

Out of context this passage is an exquisite image of self-sacrifice. In-
credible irony results when it is juxtaposed with the scene of John's
death: "The engine struck the car squarely and hurled it about like a toy.
John was thrown out and lay perfectly still. Only his foot twitched a
little" (200). The harsh reality of his insignificant car tossed "like a toy"
and the indignity of "his foot twitch[ing] a little" explodes John's false
grandiose and mythic visions of heroic martyrdom. The "damnation
train" that kills him is the set of values displayed in this sermon and in
the entire novel.

    Although Hurston's contemporary reviewers often focused on John
and overlooked Lucy's importance, Hurston works as artfully in creating
her character, using folk material to treat problems of black womanhood
that at the time would be more difficult to address directly. Charting the
development of a woman as spunky as Janie or Big Sweet, Hurston follows this woman in her struggles for a relationship with her husband
grounded in emotional reciprocity and mutual support. This thematic
thread leads to a bitter conclusion potentially unpopular with many of
Hurston's readers, both white and black; for Lucy, blinded by adoration
of a man who gives nothing in return for her selflessness, love is finally
" 'de prong [she] git[s] hung on' " (*Their Eyes Were Watching God,* 41).
    Her route to this end is quite complicated, however, for Lucy in wits
and emotional strength is at least John's equal. Aware both of his past
sexual behavior and its signficance for their future, she wrestles with
him throughout their courtship to define their relationship not as a bru-
tishly physical one but as a fusion of physical and spiritual devotion.
Through an ingenious rendition of courtship rituals, Hurston is able
(while appearing merely culturally celebratory) not only to foreshadow
potential problems in their relationship but also to show Lucy's astute
maneuvering to elicit emotional commitment from him.
    In describing their courtship, Hurston goes to great lengths to stress
that although Lucy is quite young, she is extremely proficient verbally
and particularly conversant in folk language, using traditional sayings
to communicate her spunky self-confidence (" 'Ah'm uh li'l piece uh
leather, but well put t'gether' " [35]) and to challenge others. Throughout

their courtship, Lucy draws on this verbal facility to negotiate the relationship with John she desires. When, in one of their first encounters, he thoughtlessly comments, "'When youse thru wid yo' work. Don't you do nothin' but warm uh chair bottom'" (32), Lucy adeptly refuses to let their relationship develop on this ground: "'Oooh, John Buddy! You talkin' nasty. . . . You didn't hafta say 'bottom'" (32). John immediately knows that another approach will be required: "John shriveled up inside. He had intended to recite the rhymes to Lucy that the girls on the plantation thought so witty, but he realized that 'Some love collard, some love kale, / But I loves uh gal wid uh short skirt tail' would drive Lucy from him in disgust" (32–33). John fails again to strike the proper note when he indecorously blurts out his desire to "'smack [her] lips'" (74). To let John know that such love talk and the relationship it portends is unacceptable to her, Lucy adeptly responds to this announcement by pretending she does not hear it: "'Whut's dat you say, John?'" (74). Lucy is not naively or prudishly trying to avoid kissing John (she, in fact, willingly does so shortly thereafter); rather, she is disturbed at the suggestion of a relationship no different from John's trysts with Mehaley and Big 'Oman.

The way Lucy maneuvers for a commitment from John, for a love more lasting than lust, is delightfully revealed in the conversation leading up to John's proposal. In this verbal joust, we see the spunk and resourcefulness that characterize Lucy throughout the novel. John starts to move the conversation into the realm of his feelings by cryptically commenting, "'Lucy, something been goin' on inside uh me fuh uh long time'" (75). In response to this ambiguous statement (just what part of his anatomy is stirred?), Lucy replies, "diffidently, 'Whut, John?'" John then returns with a statement he might well have used with Mehaley, "'Ah don't know, Lucy, but it boils up lak syrup in de summer time'" (75). With this suggestion of love as physical arousal hardly the commitment Lucy is seeking, her response is thus a hilarious one: "'Maybe you needs some sassafras root tuh thin yo' blood out'" (75). As John indicates, Lucy understands more than she shows: "'You know whuss de matter wid me—but ack lak you dumb to de fack'" (75).

John's second foray involves an elliptical reference to birds: "'Lucy, you pay much 'tention tuh birds?'" (75). As Robert Hemenway has noted in "Are You a Flying Lark or a Setting Dove?" he is obviously initiating a well-known courting ritual in which the man (in order to discern the woman's feelings for him) asks if she would rather be a flying lark or a setting dove. Lucy refuses to play her formulaic role, not because she is unfamiliar with the ritual but because she wants to circumvent a commitment before John has made one himself. She responds with a reference to the jay bird who "'go to hell ev'ry Friday and totes uh grain uh sand in his mouf tuh put out de fire, and den de doves say, "Where you *been* so long?"'" (75). Lucy here alludes to a different bird story, one told by Big Sweet in *Mules and Men* (102–3) about a bird who goes to hell with a grain of sand to save a man who has been good to birds all his life. As Big Sweet hints concerning the moral of the story, they go "'with a grain of sand in they mouth to help out they friend'" (102). Lucy's allusion to this folktale is quite significant, for loyalty and mutual support characterize the relationship she seeks. With John she wants the physical side of their relationship to be an expression of mutual concern, in which each partner serves to "prop" the other "on every leaning side."[17]

John does not respond to Lucy's implicit message, however: "John cut her short. 'Ah don't mean dat way, Lucy. Whut Ah wants tuh know is, which would you ruther be, if you had yo' ruthers—uh lark uh flyin', uh uh dove uh settin'?'" (75). As she does at other times (75, 89), Lucy ignores this pointed demand by feigning naive ignorance of the convention: "'Ah don't know whut you talkin' 'bout, John. It mus' be uh new riddle'" (75). At this point John seems totally disheartened and about to give up the game altogether: "'Naw, 'tain't, Lucy. Po' me, Lucy. Ahm uh one winged bird. Don't leave me lak dat, Lucy'" (75). Aware that John needs more direct guidance, Lucy cleverly points to the love knot she has "helped" him tie throughout their conversation, deftly directing John's attention to it at a strategic moment.

Although John responds to Lucy's subliminal message as she had hoped he would—"'Yeah, Lucy iss sho pretty. We done took and tied dis knot, Miss Lucy, less tie uh 'nother one'" (75)—she, nevertheless, cautiously avoids overeagerness. Wanting to be certain of his meaning to avoid being left in the embarrassing situation of saying "yes" to a proposal that John has not really made, she replies, "'You got mo' han'kerchiefs in yo' pocket?'" (75). John now really has no choice but to continue with his words of proposal: "'Naw. Ah ain't studyin' 'bout no handkerchers neither. De knot Ah wants tuh tie wid you is de kind dat won't come uh loose 'til us rises in judgment. You know mah feelings'" (76). This allusion to "eternal love" and permanent commitment is exactly what interests Lucy, so she draws him out with "'How Ah know whut you got inside yo' mind?'" When he asks for a kiss to "'loose me so Ah kin talk'" (76), Lucy, interested in hearing more along these lines, consents even though she had been offended at his crass suggestion three pages earlier. Working in the circuitous, superficially diffident manner exploited by John in the Massa tales or the women with their keys in *Mules and Men* (but as verbally savvy as both), Lucy emerges victorious: John proposes marriage before the conversation ends.[18]

With John's vow as empty as his other promises, Lucy's victory is, however, ultimately a bitter one. As seduced by his love talk as his parishioners are by his preaching, she accepts his words at face value during their courtship and ignores ominous foreshadowings submerged in much of the folk material in this section of the novel. She misses, for instance, the truth about their future relationship anticipated early in the love notes they send to one another. Lucy is certainly true to the sheltering gourd vine role she will play: "Long as the vine grow 'round the stump / You are my dolling sugar lump" (53). Unfortunately, she does not attend to the ominous metaphor for oppression in John's promise: "Whin you pass a mule tied to a tree / Ring his tail and think of me" (52).[19] Hurston also hints at Lucy's fate in a relationship with John through the ballad she has her deliver at the school recital (36). That unnamed poem, "Lord Ullin's Daughter" by Thomas Campbell (elliptically identified in the novel by only two quoted lines), deals with the death of a young woman who elopes with her lover against her father's wishes (Johnson, *Popular English Ballads,* III: 144–46). The duet "Oh Soldier, Will You Marry Me?" she and John sing at the school recital, with John "perfect as the philandering soldier" and Lucy "just right as the over-eager maid" (37), is likewise inauspicious. The actual lyrics are even more telling in their foreshadowing of John's infidelity. When, through eight stanzas, the maid asks the soldier to marry her, the soldier replies that he could not marry "such a pretty girl" because he lacks a hat, shirt, shoes, and clothes. After the maid dutifully supplies all these, the song ends:

> "Now, soldier, won't you marry, marry me,
> With yer musket, fife an' drum?"
> "Oh, how could I marry sech a pretty gal as you,
> When I've got a little wife at home?" (Richardson and Spaeth,
>   51)

Deaf to these warnings in their courtship and often seemingly blind to the emotional imbalance in their marriage, Lucy consistently endures silently her pain from John's infidelity, accepting the most su-

perficial professions of love as sufficient atonement (119–20) and per-
ceiving even a glance from him (115) as a triumph. An astute judge of
character and savvy political strategist who more than once effectively
counsels John how to "'handle [his] members'" (112), Lucy is clear-
headed about every relationship except her own marriage. Unable to
apply the advice she gives John—"'Everybody grin in yo' face don't
love yuh'" (112)—to him, Lucy uses her powers in John's service
throughout their marriage. Unlike Amy who confronts Ned's emotional
and physical violence, defending herself and her children like a "black
lioness" (2) or a "tigress" (8), Lucy, paralyzed by her devotion to John,
protects him until that relationship emotionally destroys her. Although
too late to save herself, Lucy finally understands the price of her selflessness. As she lies on her death-bed, hoping to save Isis from a similar fate,
she warns her about the dangers of untempered love: "'Don't you love
nobody better'n you do yo'self. Do, you'll be dying befo' yo' time is out.
And Isie, uh person kin be killed 'thought being struck uh blow'" (130).

One level of *Jonah's Gourd Vine,* then, beneath the seeming racial
affirmation, involves a story of female betrayal. Even though John is a
more seductive character than Sykes of "Sweat" (he claims to love
Lucy and only beats her once), both men physically and spiritually abuse
their wives' devotion and deny their sacrifice. Although she exposes
the oppressiveness of both men and the victimization of both women,
Hurston, as *Mules and Men* highlights, was rarely content simply to
chronicle oppression, either racial or sexual. As her treatment of the
John stories and of women with their keys suggests, her persecuted
characters—even when "doubleteened"—are seldom utterly powerless.
Beyond simply portraying Lucy as female victim, Hurston (in an understandably indirect way given the volatility of the implications) allows
her more than a small measure of victory after her death.

It was one thing to show, as Hurston had in "Spunk," a black man
taking revenge for his mistreatment at the hands of an oppressive black
man. To write about black women taking action to liberate themselves
from those same oppressive men was, as Hurston well knew, a much
more explosive issue. One of her interesting early treatments of black
women's active response to male mistreatment and one that sheds light
on some aspects of *Jonah's Gourd Vine* is an unpublished narrative, "Black
Death," a story in which a mother goes to a hoodoo doctor for help
in murdering the man who has jilted her pregnant daughter. Hurston's
trickster strategies for dealing with such a controversial topic are evident

as early as the title, which directs attention away from the sexual conflict in the story, a diversion further developed by Hurston's emphasis on supernatural elements. Hurston's frame for this story, highlighting ethnic exoticism, titillates a white audience with the promise of initiation into a side of black life they never see:

> We Negroes in Eatonville know a number of things that the hustling, bustling white man never dreams of. He is a materialist with little care for overtones.
>
> For instance, if a white person were halted on the streets of Orlando and told that Old Man Morgan, the excessively black Negro hoodoo man can kill any person indicated and paid for, without ever leaving his house or even seeing his victim, he'd laugh in your face and walk away, wondering how long the Negro will continue to wallow in ignorance and superstition. But no black person in a radius of twenty miles will smile, not much. They *know.*
>
> His achievements are far too numerous to mention singly. Besides many of his cures or "conjures" are kept secret. (1, CSJ)

Hurston reinforces this mysterious and sensationalist tone in the story's conclusion:

> —The coroner's verdict was death from natural causes—heart failure. But they were mystified by what looked like a powder burn directly over the heart.
>
> But the Negroes knew instantly when they saw that mark, but everyone agreed that he got justice. . . .
>
> And the white folks never knew and would have laughed had anyone told them,—so why mention it? (7, CSJ)

Although Hurston foregrounds hoodoo in a self-consciously sensational manner, at the heart of the story lies a sexual conflict between a black woman and a rogue as callous as Muttsy. This Lothario succeeds in his sexual desires with the more innocent Docia, only to deny in the cruellest fashion that he is the father of the child she is carrying. Although Docia (as docile as her name suggests) is crushed by this betrayal and immobilized by her grief, her angered mother reacts quite differently: "Drip, drip, drip, went her daughter's tears on the old woman's heart, each drop calcifying a little the fibers till at the end of four days the petrifying process was complete. Where once had been warm, pulsing flesh was now cold heavy stone, that pulled down pressing out normal life and bowing the head of her. The woman died, and in that heavy cold stone a tiger, a female tiger—was born" (5, CSJ).[20] Visiting a "two-headed" doctor who tells her how to fire a gun into a mirror and kill Beau, an act she commits at the story's end, she is "possessed" by desire for revenge: "three hundred years of America passed like the mist of morning. Africa reached out its dark hand and claimed its own. Drums, tom, tom, tom, tom, tom, beat in her ears. Strange demons seized her. Witch doctors danced before her, laid hands upon her alternately freezing and burning her flesh" (6, CSJ). What Hurston celebrates through this vivid language describing Mrs. Boger is not the wild exoticism or "primitive" emotions of black life (even though, as Hurston well knew, that might be what white readers would have seen) but the energy and emotional power of a black woman, who like Big Sweet and Hurston herself in *Dust Tracks on a Road,* will fight to protect herself or the ones she loves. Striking back to protect her daughter, Mrs. Boger acts as a black woman sometimes must (and as Amy in *Jonah's Gourd Vine* actually does)—not as a passive victim but as a female "tiger." "Black Death" is thus a dangerous story of female vengeance cleverly masked. Mrs. Boger's violence, albeit deadly, is indirect: she defends not herself, but her daughter; she acts not alone, but in shared responsibility with the male hoodoo doctor who guides her; and she shoots the man not face-to-face, but through his reflection in a mirror. Through clever distancing devices such as these and through her apparent focus on black cultural celebration, Hurston allows a story of a black woman's retaliation to "pass" as one of unproblematic ethnic affirmation.

Hurston's treatment of Lucy's death is equally complex. Although John seems perversely triumphant when she dies, Hurston, by subtly suggesting that Hattie's spirit work is not the only supernatural force in the novel, makes Lucy more than a passive victim. Aware of her own importance in John's life and (as her comment to Isis suggests) his role in killing her, Lucy has a spiritual conversion on her deathbed that profoundly affects the power dynamics of her relationship with him. No longer satisfied with glib words and loving glances, she becomes a verbal "lioness," standing up for the rights of herself and her children, condemning his behavior in a most direct manner. Significantly, also for the first time, she sees through the magnificent rhetoric camouflaging his betrayal and mercilessly deflates it: "'Big talk ain't changin' whut you doin'. You can't clean yo'self wid yo' tongue lak uh cat'" (128–29). When John responds to this unmasking by slapping her, Lucy draws on all her spiritual and verbal strength, grimly forecasting his future with the emotional equivalent of a curse: "'De hidden wedge will come tuh light some day, John. Mark mah words. Youse in de majority now, but God sho don't love ugly'" (129).

Like the mysterious spider she watches as she dies (perhaps related to the trickster Spider Anansi of West African and Caribbean folklore) who "'Look lak he done took up uh stand'" (129), Lucy makes an emotional stand against John, cutting herself off from him by "pull[ing] her lids over her eyes" (130) and sealing herself in her room (132). Just as Janie is freed from Starks's emotional control when, after recognizing him as a false idol, she walls off her inner life from the world outside, Lucy, now safe from intrusion, is emotionally reborn. As she tells a visitor, "'Ah done died in grief and been buried in de bitter waters, and Ah done rose agin from de dead lak Lazarus. Nothin' [including John] kin touch mah soul no mo'"" (131). Engaging John in pitched battle protected by the "'armor'" (131) of her own indifference, knowing herself to be a critical force in John's life, Lucy abandons John, willing her own death by "turn[ing] her face to the wall and refus[ing] her supper" (129). She takes control of her destiny at that point, transforming her death from proof of her victimization into a self-conscious, vengeful counterblow against her enemy.

The powerful anger that Lucy directs toward John at her death is also submerged in Hurston's treatment of another aspect of black folklife, Lucy's cryptic demand that deathbed traditions not be observed (130). Although Lucy provides no reasons for her request, Hurston seems to offer an explanation of this custom in her glossary: "The pillow is removed from beneath the head of the dying because it is said to prolong the death struggle if left in place. All mirrors, and often all glass surfaces, are covered because it is believed the departing spirit will pause to look in them and if it does they will be forever clouded afterwards" (206). That Lucy's motive, however, is not to save herself suffering (or to protect the mirrors of those she leaves behind) is suggested by more extensive discussions of such rituals and their role in protecting the living from the spirits of the dead. In *Folk Beliefs of the Southern Negro,* Puckett discusses a number of these customs:

> If a person dies hard it is a bad sign; he will haunt the survivors. Thus
> the first efforts are made to enable the dying man to leave this world
> with as little suffering as possible. The bed should never be placed "cross-
> ways uh de world" (north and south), but east and west with the head

toward the west. This would make the departure less prolonged, but if not, the pillow should be taken from under the head of the dying person. (81)

Similarly, mirrors are covered (81) not only to preserve them, but more significantly, to prevent bad luck for the survivors. Hurston also emphasizes this idea in her discussion of such rituals in *Mules and Men:* "The spirit newly released from the body is likely to be destructive. This is why a cloth is thrown over the face of a clock in the death chamber and the looking glass is covered" (236). In making her requests of Isis, then, Lucy hopes to allow her spirit to torment John after her death.[21] In providing limited explanation for these requests, Hurston can control the significance seen in them by readers unfamiliar with the rituals and thus smuggle an act of female retaliation into her novel under cover of what might have appeared mere quaint superstition.

That her spirit (like that of Kanty returned to take revenge on Spunk) does still haunt John, despite community efforts to lay her to rest, is suggested in numerous references to Lucy's spirit throughout the rest of the novel (132, 142, 145). Whereas Hattie's root work can be neutralized by other rituals, Lucy's curse cannot be undone, even by John's doleful pleas. Like Delia who, strengthened by her own spiritual earthworks, impassively watches Sykes die, Lucy shows no mercy from beyond the grave, neither answering his prayers for forgiveness nor offering him spiritual support. Haunted by Lucy's spirit, doomed to live out her curse until he finally acknowledges her power, John (in stark contrast to his earlier claims not to need her as his "guardzeen" [116, 128]) finally admits her role as sheltering gourd vine:

> The world . . . was not new and shiny and full of laughter. Mouldy, maggoty, full of suck-holes—one had to watch out for one's feet. Lucy must have had good eyes. She had seen so much and told him so much it had wearied him, but she hadn't seen all this. Maybe she had, and spared him. She would. Always spreading carpets for his feet and breaking off the points of thorns. But and oh, her likes were no more on this earth. (173)

Hurston's use of folk belief in the supernatural to treat an important aspect of the battle between Lucy and John is just part of her creative shaping of black folk culture in *Jonah's Gourd Vine* to veil a complex treatment of gender conflict. Directing this message to a black audience, but forced for pragmatic reasons to appeal simultaneously to a white readership, she hoped, by pushing into the foreground those aspects of black culture in vogue with whites, to draw their attention away from the novel's treatment of intragroup conflict. She reveals something of her own dilemma in the courtroom scene surrounding Hattie's divorce from John. The response to black people's openly airing their problems before a white audience is predictably degrading and racist. When Hattie tells her "troubles" with John, the white lawyers leer,

> "So you wanta quit yo' husband, Hattie? How come? Wasn't he all right? Is *that* him? Why he looks like he oughta be okeh. Had too many women, eh? Didn't see you enough, is that it? Ha! ha! couldn't you get yo'self another man on the side? What you worrying about a divorce for? Why didn't you g'wan leave him and get yourself somebody else? You got divorce in yo' heels, ain't you? You must have the next one already picked out. Ha! ha! Bet he ain't worth the sixty dollars." (167)

In a rare taciturn moment, John refuses to offer in his defense any information about Hattie's own infidelity and conjure work. Explaining to Hambo why he did not call him as a witness, John emphasizes his awareness that such knowledge would only support racist stereotypes:

> "Dey thinks wese all ignorant as it is, and dey thinks wese all alike, and dat dey knows us inside and out, but you know better. Dey wouldn't make no great 'miration if you had uh tole 'em Hattie had all dem mens. Dey spectin' dat. Dey wouldn't zarn 'tween uh woman lak Hattie and one lak Lucy, uh yo' wife befo' she died. Dey thinks all colored folks is de same dat way. De only difference dey makes is 'tween uh nigger dat works hard and don't sass 'em, and one dat don't." (169)

His decision to keep such issues from a white audience echoes Hurston's in *Jonah's Gourd Vine*. Despite the fact that she must publish in a white world, she nevertheless manages to convey her message by hypnotizing that audience with the beat of her tom-tom and the rhythms of John's pagan Poesy. John's comment to Hambo could well be Hurston's explanation for her strategy in *Jonah's Gourd Vine*: " 'Ah didn't want de white folks tuh hear 'bout nothin' lak dat. Dey knows too much 'bout us as it is, but dey some things dey ain't tuh know. Dey's some strings on our harp fuh us tuh play on and sing all tuh ourselves' " (168–69).[22]

3 "Mink Skin or Coon Hide": The Janus-faced Narrative of *Their Eyes Were Watching God*

As in *Jonah's Gourd Vine,* Hurston also focused on "family matters" in *Their Eyes Were Watching God,* examining in greater detail models of black male and female identity and the larger social worlds they both reflect and shape. Echoing John Pearson, Bentley, and Muttsy in her depiction of Janie's husbands, she critiques a false model of masculinity drawn from a white world and the notion of black female identity it assumes. As suggested in the allusions to the two-faced Janus figure Hurston exploits in her delineation of Janie, Janie struggles between two identities in the novel, one like Pinkie's drawn from the white world and foisted upon her and a more vigorous model of black womanhood she tries to forge for herself.[1] The discursive difficulties Hurston faced in telling this story were perhaps even greater than those she faced in writing *Jonah's Gourd Vine,* for the powerful black woman Janie becomes resists oppression not merely by haunting her husband after her death as Lucy does, but much more directly, "killing" one man with words and another with a gun. In *Their Eyes Were Watching God* Hurston cloaks this more daring exposé of female resistance in lush naturalistic imagery and rich folk idiom to create a novel in which racial and sexual conflict was so carefully masked that it was read by most of her contemporaries (as she fully expected) as one merely celebrating the spontaneous primitivism of black life.[2]

The novel's rich metaphors, many of which Hurston developed in revision of the novel's manuscript, emphasize both race and gender in Janie's struggle for self-fulfillment. Certainly the most explicit reference in the novel to their interaction in the lives of black women is Nanny's speech to Janie before her first marriage:

Honey, de white man is de ruler of everything as fur as Ah been able
tuh find out. Maybe it's some place way off in de ocean where de black
man is in power, but we don't know nothin' but what we see. So de
white man throw down de load and tell de nigger man tuh pick it up.
He pick it up because he have to, but he don't tote it. He hand it to his
womenfolks. De nigger woman is de mule uh de world so fur as Ah can
see. (29)[3]

Drawing her model of black female identity from her own experience
with the harshest forms of racial and sexual oppression (slavery and
rape), Nanny is both accurate in her assessment of the world "where
the white man is the ruler" (as many incidents in *Mules and Men* suggest)
and limited in her conception of alternatives. Accepting the hierarchies
and inequalities of her world as universal and immutable, she hopes to
save Janie from becoming either a mule or a "spit-cup" (37) by placing
her under the "big protection" (41) of an economically secure husband.
Unable to imagine a world where black woman and mule are not synonymous, she embraces an ideal that from her experience seems the only
alternative, one drawn from a romanticized conception of the lives of
white women. Although Janie's first two marriages show the limitations
of Nanny's understanding, detailing both the enervating effects of "settin' on porches lak de white madam" (172) as well as the many ways
women can be spit-cups and mules *with* male protection, Nanny's mule
metaphor is, nevertheless, a very complicated piece of social commentary, more accurate in its analysis of race and gender in a world where
"de white man is de ruler" than the young Janie realizes. As the rest of
the novel will reveal, in a community ruled by whites or their black
surrogates, race and gender interact in complicated ways, creating artificial status and power differences between black men and women.[4]

Although Nanny cannot imagine a world free of hierarchy and
domination, such a vision is expressed in Janie's metaphor of the pear
tree, itself a densely complex social metaphor:

She was stretched on her back beneath the pear tree soaking in the alto
chant of the visiting bees, the gold of the sun and the panting breath of
the breeze when the inaudible voice of it all came to her. She saw a
dust-bearing bee sink into the sanctum of a bloom; the thousand sister-
calyxes arch to meet the love embrace and the ecstatic shiver of the tree
from root to tiniest branch creaming in every blossom and frothing
with delight. So this was a marriage! She had been summoned to be-

hold a revelation. Then Janie felt a pain remorseless sweet that left her
limp and languid. (24–25)

On one level, an obvious metaphor for sexual relationships, the passage is
a powerful contrast to Nanny's spit-cup and mule metaphors with their
suggestions of rape and female dehumanization. Echoing the male/
female equality extolled in the "Behold the Rib!" sermon of *Mules and
Men,* this metaphor for sexuality is one free of domination and active/
passive polarities: there is no suggestion of rapacious violence on the part
of the (male) bees who "sink into the sanctum of a bloom" or of passive
victimization on the part of the "sister-calyxes [who] arch to meet the
love embrace." The sexual relationship imaged here, one between active equals, is not only one of sexual fulfillment and "delight" but, as the
metaphor of pollination implies, one of creativity and fecundity.[5]

Casting this metaphor in naturalistic and mythic terms seemingly
unrelated to race, Hurston further masks its import by assigning it a
domestic referent, marriage. Although she does not identify her metaphor as in any way racially specific, it forms a part of a larger pattern of
tree imagery developed in the novel to describe black identity. In contrast to those characters whose lives have been largely shaped in a
white-dominated world and who are described as mutilated trees
(Nanny [26], her daughter, and Killicks [39], for instance), only Tea
Cake—with Woods for a last name—and Janie, who at the chronological
end of the novel sees her life "like a great tree in leaf" (20), experience the kind of relationship imaged in the pear tree and appear as the
racially and sexually vibrant, "undiminished human beings" (85) described by Alice Walker. As their relationship and experience on the
Muck suggests, the kind of relationship imaged here—sexual or more
broadly social—cannot flourish in a world of hierarchy and domination.
Only possible where the white man is not the ruler of black people's
lives, the pear tree images the model of relationships necessary for black
vitality—male *and* female. The novel, in large measure, chronicles the
struggle between the racial and sexual identities packed into Janie's
and Nanny's metaphors. Although the novel will reveal complications in
both, the options facing Janie are clear early in the novel: to live as the
mule or imitation white woman implied in Nanny's vision or as the
vigorous black one imaged in her own.

The difficulties Janie will experience trying to become such a
woman married to Joe Starks are clear from the very beginning of their

relationship, for Hurston is careful in almost every detail of his character to paint him as a false model of black manhood, one like John's drawn from white world. As deeply influenced as Nanny by the experience of "workin' for white folks all his life" (47) and as committed to the underlying dynamics of her social metaphor and the multilayered hierarchy on which it rests, he strives simply to usurp the white man's place at the top of the social ladder. Aware from his own experience that "de white folks had all de sayso where he come from and everywhere else" (48), he moves to the all-black community of Eatonville, where, as "a big voice" (48), he can play the white man's role, tossing his load to the black men beneath him and the black women beneath them. As Hurston shows, Starks's attempt to emulate whites—even Janie immediately notices that he looks (56) and acts (49) like white men—ultimately shapes his relationship with his community and with his wife.[6] Forfeiting the possibility of healthy black relationships imaged in the pear tree, he becomes sexually dead and socially isolated, elevated above but alienated from other black people, an observer rather than a participant in the porch-front banter and cultural life of his community. No representative of "sun-up and pollen and blooming trees" (50), his big voice takes the "bloom off things" (69), leaving him a tree as starkly denuded as Killick's stump.

Starks's desire to imitate white men and its effect on his relationship with the people in Eatonville is evident in the objects with which he surrounds himself. To go with his desk (one "like Mr. Hill or Mr. Galloway over in Maitland" [75] owns), he buys a fancy gold spittoon "just like his used-to-be bossman used to have" (75) that symbolizes for him his sophistication and status above the common people. In addition to humorously spoofing white pretensions here (this is, after all, a spit-cup despite its price tag), Hurston emphasizes the damaging effects of Starks's finery on the black people around him. Just as Starks behind his desk "weakened people" (76), his spittoon makes them question their own identity: "how could they know up-to-date folks was spitting in flowery little things like that? It sort of made the rest of them feel that they had been taken advantage of. Like things had been kept from them. Maybe more things in the world besides spitting pots had been hid from them, when they wasn't told no better than to spit in tomato cans" (76). Whereas the community members are awed and intimidated by Starks, they sense something unnatural in his actions: "It was bad enough for white people [to act like he did], but when one of your own color could

be so different it put you on a wonder. It was like seeing your sister turn
into a 'gator. A familiar strangeness. You keep seeing your sister in the
'gator and the 'gator in your sister, and you'd rather not" (76). Paradoxi-
cally, both Starks's and the community's sense of identity are damaged
with the purchase of this spittoon, for he (as the people recognize) becomes a freakish hybrid, neither black nor white.

When he comes to town, Starks also brings with him white definitions of leadership and power. He inadvertently reveals his plans when
he arrives, responding in telling astonishment to an announcement that
the town has no mayor: " 'Ain't got no Mayor! Well, who tells ya'll what
to do?' " (57). Whereas Starks sees himself as a "leader" who brings order
and progress to the community, Hurston suggests a more sinister motive:
he plans to control the town like his former "boss-men," a fact evident
when he immediately puts the men to work cutting trees. Talking like
a "section foreman" (58) with "bow-down command" (75) in his face,
Starks recreates power dynamics of the most oppressive sort, a fact recognized by the residents themselves, who, when forced by Starks to dig
ditches, "murmured hotly about slavery being over" (75). Significantly,
he builds for himself a slave owner's mansion to symbolize his power
over the community and installs the light post in imitation of the white
god he worships.[7]

Just as Starks draws his model for social relationships from the white
world, his view of the ideal relationship between a man and a woman is
similarly imported. Vowing to place Janie on "de front porch" so she can
"rock and fan [herself] and eat p'taters dat other folks plant just special
for [her]" (49), Starks promises only a modification rather than an abo-
lition of Nanny's hierarchy. While Janie will be above "the gang," she
will be subjugated and objectified in her relationship with Joe: her pedestal will place her above other black women, but decidedly beneath
him. Nanny, thus, fails to recognize the complexity of her own "mule"
metaphor, for merely replacing a white man's face with a black one does
not free Janie. Ironically, she lives a life Nanny worked so hard to avoid
for her, enduring what Nanny feared despite having attained the economic circumstances she desired. Although in more complex ways than
the literal rape Nanny feared, Janie becomes a spit-cup for Joe, her passive status exemplified in the spittoon he gives her. "A little lady-size
spitting pot" (smaller, of course, than Joe's) with "little sprigs of flowers painted all around the sides" (76) in seeming contrast to its earthy
function, the fancy spitting pot symbolizes the deceptive appearance of

Janie's relationship with Starks. Although Janie, like white women, ostensibly lives on "a flowery-bed-of-ease" (*Mules and Men* 85) with Joe, this veneer of economic affluence and elevated class status relative to other blacks only thinly covers the degradation she experiences.[8]

As other critics have pointed out, Janie also becomes a mule in her relationship with Starks, a parallel Hurston buries in the anomolous, "comic" story of Matt Bonner's mule.[9] Underneath what appears merely a playful depiction of folk life and the richness of storefront banter, Hurston reveals that Jody's "noble" (91) behavior toward the mule is very much like his "solicitous" treatment of Janie; his motivation in pampering both mules is simply to elevate himself in the community, and in both cases, his "kindness" is deadly. Just as Joe's "solicitation" spiritually strangles Janie, Hurston also ironically suggests that Starks's munificence kills the mule, for the mule dies in a way that "wasn't natural and . . . didn't look right" (93) after Jody begins the practice of piling up fodder for it (92). The suggestion that the mule dies from overfeeding is reinforced in the later anomalous section depicting the buzzards coming to feed on the mule's carcass. In their declaration that "Bare, bare fat" (97) has killed the mule, we see the double paradox in Starks's behavior: the mule dies from his cruel kindness just as surely as Janie is spiritually starved by his poor, poor wealth.

The broader treatment of the black woman as mule is further reinforced in this chapter through the story of Mrs. Tony Robbins, the woman who comes to beg food from Joe Starks. Like the yellow mule episode and many episodes in *Mules and Men,* this scene (judging from the male characters' reactions) seems also simply a lighthearted interlude with Mrs. Robbins as easy a target for scorn as Matt Bonner. Just as Jody and the town men enjoy "mule-baiting" and teasing Matt Bonner (89), Joe relishes "baiting" (113) and "jok[ing] roughly" (113) with the woman when she comes to the store. Significantly, Joe Starks responds to her hunger with the same penury Matt Bonner did to his mule's. Like Bonner who only fed his mule with a teacup (83) and "was known to buy side-meat by the slice" (88), Jody stingily cuts off a tiny slab of meat for Mrs. Robbins (115), not forgetting, of course, to charge it to her husband's account. In fact, the yellow mule is finally treated more generously than Mrs. Robbins. In a telling comment on the fate of women who do not passively accept their status as mules, the men on the porchfront respond to Mrs. Robbins's complaint that her husband does not feed her with violent wrath, one vowing "Ah'd kill her cemetery dead" (115–16) and another saying "Ah'd kill uh baby just born dis mawnin' fuh uh thing lak dat."[10]

In ways that would undoubtedly have surprised Nanny, Janie thus finds herself in a world of "mules and men" married to Joe; and for much of their relationship, she accepts her status. Like the "fractious" mules celebrated in *Mules and Men,* however, she increasingly resists his control, speaking out in Big Sweet fashion first for the yellow mule, then for Mrs. Turner, and finally for herself. In her famous rejoinder to Starks's public humiliation of her, she breaks out of Nanny's hierarchy, refusing to be the mule and deflating the pretensions of the man who has made her one: "'You big-bellies round here and put out a lot of brag, but 'tain't nothin' to it but yo' big voice. Humph! Talkin' 'bout *me* lookin' old! When you pull down yo' britches, you look lak de change uh life'" (123).[11]

Janie's equations here are significant ones reminding us how completely Jody's identity—his big belly, which makes him "Kind of portly like rich white folks" (56), and his "big voice"—is drawn from the white world. As Janie's final allusion to sexual impotence suggests, it is an empty model of male identity, for Joe's illusions of masculinity and power are immediately destroyed when Janie refuses to play her supporting role. Hurston's description of Starks's lingering illness further suggests the emptiness of white models of manhood, for Jody is almost literally deflated by Janie's comments, gradually losing weight until even his big belly is only a saggy remnant of his former grandeur, "A sack of flabby something [that] hung from his loins and rested on his thighs when he sat down" (126).

In every respect, Tea Cake Verigible Woods is portrayed as Starks's antithesis, his feminized nickname promising a "sweeter," gentler kind of masculinity and his surname a healthy black identity compared to the sterility implied in Joe's. Hurston stresses this contrast by painting Tea Cake as emphatically black and by detailing his defiance of the hierarhcical values Starks imports from the dominant white culture. He also repeatedly rejects the definition of male/female relationships that Joe had internalized and forced on Janie. In teaching Janie to play checkers, to shoot, to drive, and in inviting her to work alongside of him, Tea Cake breaks down the rigid gender definitions Joe sought to impose, bringing Janie into the cultural life of the black community and building a relationship with her grounded in reciprocity rather than hierarchy. Unlike Starks, who uses language to intimidate, dominate, and silence Janie, Tea Cake encourages her to voice her own feelings honestly, to "'Have de nerve tuh say whut you mean'" (165). His belief in the legitimacy of black women's self-expression is evident in his courting behavior, which contrasts sharply with the other male courting rituals and "mule talk" described in Chapter Six. When Jim and Dave engage in their love talk, Daisy is merely a silent and passive vehicle for them "to act out their rivalry" (107). As they vie with one another for the most hyperbolic sign of their devotion, promising to give her passenger trains and steamships, the male audience for their performance explodes in "A big burst of laughter at Daisy's discomfiture" (107).[12] Tea Cake, on the other hand, brings Janie into his game as an active participant. When Janie teases him for his generous purchase of two Coca-Colas with the comment, "'We got a rich man round here, then. Buyin' passenger trains uh battleships this week?'" (153), Tea Cake addresses his love talk to Janie rather than the other male in the store: "'Which one do *you* want? It all depends on you'" (153). That invitation initiates the first instance in the novel of a man and woman engaged in the kind of playful discourse normally reserved for males:

> "Oh, if you'se treatin' me tuh it, Ah b'lieve Ah'll take de passenger train. If it blow up Ah'll still be on land."
> "Choose de battleship if dat's whut you really want. Ah know where one is right now. Seen one round Key West de other day."
> "How you gointuh git it?"
> "Ah shucks, dem Admirals is always ole folks. Can't no ole man stop me from gittin' no ship for yuh if dat's what you want. Ah'd git dat ship out from under him so slick till he'd be walkin' de water lak ole Peter befo' he knowed it." (153–54)

As this evidence of Tea Cake's belief in linguistic reciprocity suggests, Janie is right that Tea Cake teaches her "the maiden language," for he is the first man who has not wanted to make her a spit-cup for his words.

Tea Cake's fundamental defiance of the dominant culture's notions concerning both race *and* sex and his rejection of the oppressive hierarchies that typify a world of mules and men make him "a bee to [Janie's] blossom" (161). In every aspect of their early relationship, he represents the model of masculinity imaged in the bee, encouraging Janie to express the equality and activity expressed in the blossom. Tea Cake's brand of masculinity and the kind of reciprocal relationship it makes

possible are imaged early when Janie falls asleep and wakens to find Tea
Cake combing her hair. Unlike Starks who asserts his oppressive masculinity, controlling Janie's sexuality by forcing her to bind up her hair,
Tea Cake here not only engages in a traditional female activity but also
luxuriates in the freedom her hair represents. Whereas Starks sees Janie's
hair as a symbol of his control of her, Tea Cake combs Janie's hair in the
spirit of reciprocity that characterizes their early relationship, experiencing pleasure in giving it (157). Ready to accept Janie as the person she is rather than attempting to remold her to his desires, he not
only combs her beautiful hair but also "scratch[es] the dandruff from
her scalp" (156). With such a "bee-man," Janie becomes "petal-open,"
and the union of bee and blossom that results is, as Janie realizes, the real
"beginning of things" (163), a profoundly creative moment contrasting
sharply with Starks's parody of Creation.

As Cynthia Pondrom and John Lowe have suggested (195–96),
Hurston draws heavily on the myth of Isis and Osiris in her creation of
Janie and Tea Cake to suggest their equal stature and power and to create
a mythic analogue for her pear tree vision. The same age as Osiris, associated with trees and enjoyment as the Egyptian god was and called by
his title, "Son of the Evening Sun" (264), Tea Cake represents an ideal
of masculinity in pointed contrast to Starks's oppressive, white male god
and is the fitting mythic consort for the powerful black woman that
Janie becomes. In drawing on the Isis and Osiris myth, Hurston grounds
this relationship, one characterized by reciprocity and self-affirmation
rather than oppression and hierarchy, in African rather than in European
culture. Significantly, Janie and Tea Cake's relationship flourishes not in
Nanny's or Joe Starks's world but on the Muck, a setting Hurston depicts as a black Eden free of outside cultural influence and the deadly
insipidity of the dominant white world. Stressing both the blackness of
the soil and the rich plant life it supports in her first description of the
Muck, Hurston images (as she had in the supernatural tales of *Mules and
Men*) the flowering of black people possible outside white influence:

> everything in the Everglades was big and new. Big Lake Okechobee, big
> beans, big cane, big weeds, big everything. Weeds that did well to grow
> waist high up the state were eight and often ten feet tall down there.
> Ground so rich that everything went wild. Volunteer cane just taking
> the place. Dirt roads so rich and black that a half mile of it would have
> fertilized a Kansas wheat field. Wild cane on either side of the road hid-
> ing the rest of the world. People wild too. (193)

The interpersonal relationship that Tea Cake's racial and gender identity makes possible with Janie is here translated to a larger societal level. In the soil of this black milieu grow vigorous black people, plants contrasting sharply with the ones stunted and mutilated in a white world. With the status differences and white values that Starks sought to reinforce absent on the Muck, artificial hierarchical divisions evaporate: Janie is just another person rather than Mrs. Mayor, and the Saws, instead of being ostracized, are accepted as equals. The gender hierarchies of Nanny's metaphor are also foreign to this community. With no white man tossing his load to the black man, black men do not toss it on to black women; and in the absence of oppressive sex roles that restrict women to serving men, Janie and Tea Cake "partake with everything," sharing in both paid labor and domestic work (199). On their porch, everyone takes part in the rich cultural life of the community, including Janie, who is no longer merely an outside observer or a spit-cup for men's words, but an active participant who "could tell big stories herself" (200).

The exception to the vigorous racial and sexual identities in the community (in fact, the serpent in this Eden) is Mrs. Turner, a female version of Joe Starks, who also rejects her own blackness and the cultural vitality around her. Hurston stresses the spiritual insipidity and deformed identity that result from her worship of white gods in her description of her as "a milky sort of a woman that belonged to child-bed. Her shoulders rounded a little, and she must have been conscious of her pelvis because she kept it stuck out in front of her so she could always see it" (208). Like Starks whose body looks "like bags hanging from an ironing board" (125), Mrs. Turner's "was an ironing board with things throwed at it" (208). Just as Starks's definition of maleness finally makes him impotent, Mrs. Turner is sexually insipid and symbolically uncreative. Even though she has given birth to six children, only one has lived (211), and he is, as Mr. Turner tells Tea Cake, "de last stroke of exhausted nature" (214). Her husband, an ideal mate for her, is another emphatically diminished human being: "He was a vanish-looking kind of man as if there used to be parts about him that stuck out individually but now he hadn't a thing about him that wasn't dwindled and blurred. Just like he had been sand-papered down to a long oval mass" (214).

Largely a ludicrous and pathetic figure (merely a source of gossip "when things were dull on the Muck" [217]), Mrs. Turner poses no threat to the community as long as she is met with the kind of unruffled indifference Janie displays.[13] Tea Cake's response is quite different, however. His statement that he "hates dat woman lak poison" (213), as later events will show, signals not a rejection of her cultural whiteness, but his own insecurity in the face of it. Jealousy of another man as vigorous as himself would have been understandable and benign (as Janie's of Nunkie is), but his fear that Janie will respond to Mrs. Turner's matchmaking attempts arises not from lover's passion but from his own submerged racial and sexual insecurity. The first evidence that Tea Cake has been infected with Mrs. Turner's poison and the effect this will have on his pear tree relationship with Janie arises when he beats Janie. It is not the violence of the act that Hurston pinpoints as problematic, but Tea Cake's motives for it, a fact emphasized in the contrasts between Tea Cake's beating of Janie and their earlier fight over Nunkie. When Janie feels jealous of Nunkie, she tackles both her and Tea Cake in the heat of passion, "Never th[inking] at all . . . just act[ing] on feelings" (204). That the honest expression of feelings among equals—even when acted out violently—poses no threat to the balance of their relationship is depicted in Hurston's description of their reconciliation. Their reunion, described in language that echoes the pear tree metaphor, reflects the reciprocity of their fight: "They wrestled on until they were doped with their own fumes and emanations; till their clothes had been torn away; till he hurled her to the floor and held her there melting her resistance with the heat of his body, doing things with their bodies to express the inexpressible; kissed her until she arched her body to meet him and they fell asleep in sweet exhaustion" (205). Like the bee that "sink[s] into the sanctum of a bloom" and "the thousand sister calyxes [that] arch to meet the love embrace" (24), Tea Cake and Janie here reenact the pear tree scene, fighting and loving as equals.

Tea Cake's violence toward Janie—no spontaneous expression of feeling but a premeditated "brainstorm" (218) hatched after Mrs. Turner's brother returns to the Muck—has both a very different motivation and a very different effect.[14] Fundamentally manipulative and coercive, the beating is calculated to assert his domination of Janie: Tea Cake whips her "Not because her behavior justified his jealousy, but [because] it relieved that awful fear inside him. Being able to whip her reassured him in possession. No brutal beating at all. He just slapped her around to show he was boss" (218). His target (as he admits) is not Janie, but Mrs. Turner: "'Ah didn't whup Janie 'cause *she* done nothin'. Ah

beat her tuh show dem Turners who is boss' " (220), to " 'let her see dat
Ah got control' " (220).

Equating light skin with passive female victimization and blackness
with defiance, the men on the Muck express admiration not only for Tea
Cake's assertion of dominance but also for what they fantasize as Janie's
acquiescence:

> "Uh person can see every place you hit her. Ah bet she never raised her
> hand tuh hit you back, neither. Take some uh dese ol' rusty black
> women and dey would fight yuh all night long and next day nobody
> couldn't tell you ever hit em. Dat's de reason Ah done quit beatin' mah
> woman. You can't make no mark on 'em at all. Lawd! wouldn't Ah love
> tuh whip uh tender woman lak Janie! Ah bet she don't even holler. She
> jus' cries, eh Tea Cake." (218–19)

Although it is hard to imagine the Janie who has fought on equal foot-
ing with Tea Cake over Nunkie just a few pages earlier as this simper-
ing victim, Tea Cake's satisfied response, " 'Dat's right' " (219), ominously
suggests his rejection of Janie's equality and his acceptance of an identity she has fought to reject. Tea Cake's changed view of Janie is further
emphasized in this interchange among the men. When Sop-de-Bottom
bemoans his fate of being equally matched with his woman, Tea Cake's
bragging rejoinder, bespeaking an ominous value on Janie's social status
and wealth, could well have been spoken by Joe Starks: " 'Mah Janie is
uh high time woman and useter things. Ah didn't git her outa de middle uh de road. Ah got her outa uh big fine house. Right now she got
money enough in de bank tuh buy up dese ziggaboos and give 'em
away' " (219). His final remark violates their reciprocal agreement to
"partake wid everything" and makes explicit the oppression developing
in his attitude toward Janie: " 'Janie is wherever *Ah* wants tuh be' " (219).
As these comments foreshadow, Tea Cake's behavior changes from this
point on, echoing the falsely solicitous actions of Starks who oppresses
Janie at the same time that he places her on a pedestal. To assert the
power of his masculinity by assuring himself of Janie's passive femininity, he "would not let her go with him to the field. He wanted her to
get her rest" (228).

With this set of values introduced and the "pear tree" paradise of
the Muck spiritually destroyed, it is little surprise that Janie and Tea
Cake are driven out by the hurricane that strikes in the next chapter. That this banishment is punishment for Tea Cake's "sin" is strongly

hinted at in Tea Cake's reaction to signs of the approaching storm. When a friend, Lias, stops by and urges them to leave because "De crow gahn up" (230), Tea Cake ignores this natural warning, arguing in a way that indicates both acceptance of white superiority and an uncharacteristic concern for money: "'Dat ain't nothin'. You ain't seen de bossman go up, is yuh? Well all right now. Man, de money's too good on the Muck'" (230).[15] His acceptance of Mrs. Turner's social "pecking-order" is further revealed when Lias tries to persuade Tea Cake to evacuate by pointing to the Indians leaving. Tea Cake responds with a racist comment on the Indians he clearly sees as his inferiors: "'Dey don't always know, Indians don't know much uh nothin', tuh tell de truth. Else dey'd own dis country still. De white folks ain't gone nowhere. Dey oughta know if it's dangerous'" (231). With the new set of values Tea Cake embraces, it is fitting that, when he finally does try to leave, he takes his insurance papers with him (237) and abandons his guitar (238).[16]

Hurston embellishes her racial theme in the storm episode of the novel. Beneath the surface of what seems simply dramatic action and vivid language, she carefully develops the storm as a symbolic ritual of purification, a rejection of those characters who have betrayed the sexually egalitarian and culturally autonomous values of black life on the Muck. Hurston suggests this idea in the contrasts between those who are saved and those who perish. Characters such as Lias, Stew Beef, and Motor Boat, whom Hurston paints as ethnically secure and immune to Mrs. Turner's influence, survive. The casualties are those who look to the white world for answers, placing their trust in its power and failing to appreciate the storm's:

> The folks in the quarters and the people in the big houses further
> around the shore heard the big lake and wondered. The people felt un-
> comfortable but safe because there were the seawalls to chain the sense-
> less monster in his bed. The folks let the people do the thinking. If the
> castles thought themselves secure, the cabins needn't worry. Their deci-
> sion was already made as always. Chink up your cracks, shiver in your
> wet beds and wait on the mercy of the Lord. The bossman might have
> the thing stopped by morning anyway. (234)

The function of the storm as the symbolic destroyer of white power is also revealed in the language Hurston uses to depict the storm's aftermath. The apparent chaos it brings is actually described as the break-down of artificial hierarchies; for instance, the storm dissolves boundaries between the human and the natural as the lake's waters enter the houses and a terror-stricken baby rabbit seeks refuge in the house with Janie, Tea Cake, and Motor Boat (235). Even the lines between water and land become blurred when stray fish are found "swimming in the yard" (236) and the "water full of things living and dead. Things that didn't belong in water" (244). Significantly, when these boundaries are erased, so are racial distinctions. Unable to distinguish white corpses from black, white officials are stymied in their ludicrous attempt to ensure that white corpses get coffins and black ones quick-lime (253).

The destruction wreaked by the storm is also described as an act of liberation. Destroying the dike, a futile human attempt to control Nature's power, the storm loosens the lake's "chains" (239) and turns it into "a road crusher on a cosmic scale" (239), rushing "after his supposed-to-be conquerors, rolling the people in the houses along with other timbers" (239). Tea Cake and Janie sense a new order in the bizarre scenes they encounter while trying to escape: "They passed a dead man in a sitting position on a hummock, entirely surrounded by wild animals and snakes. Common danger made common friends. Nothing sought conquest over the other" (243). Even the rattlesnakes do not bite during the storm (244) in this world momentarily purged of violence and oppression.[17]

In addition to depicting the storm as the cultural equivalent of the biblical flood, Hurston also buries in the novel an implicit definition of its identity. Its fury compared to the sound of African drums (233–34), it is subtly identified as a black power, striking at night and bringing darkness in its wake. A "God" (235, 236) at war with and finally more powerful than the false white god, it literally "put[s] out the light" (236), symbolically the white principles of hierarchy and oppression embraced by Starks and rekindled by Tea Cake. Hurston also implies a gendered identity for this power. Whereas the lake is repeatedly identified as "he" (234, 235, 239), the storm—"Havoc there with her mouth wide open" (246)—is, through Hurston's symbolic use of folk saying, labeled "she." Hurston repeats this gender identification and a reminder of the storm's power to destroy white men's creations; as Janie and Tea Cake survey the ravaged city of Palm Beach, they see "the hand of horror on everything. Houses without roofs, and roofs without houses. Steel and stone all crushed and crumbled like wood. The mother of malice had trifled with men (250–51). This black, female power cleanses the world through its flood, freeing even its male counterpart in Hurston's ironic and subversive revision of the biblical myth.

Given the changes that have occurred in Tea Cake's sense of racial and gender identity, it is not surprising that he, too, is killed as a result of events surrounding the storm. Numerous details woven into this episode suggest that his death is not merely a tragic ending to a love story but rather the symbolic expurgation of the false values he has come to represent. Hurston dramatizes these changes in Tea Cake in her description of his illness. Although he seems selfless and noble, sacrificing himself to save Janie, Hurston very subtly but carefully suggests his symbolic identity with the mad dog that bites him. Walking with a "queer loping gait, swinging his head from side to side and his jaws clenched in a funny way" (271), "snarl[ing]" and giving Janie a "look of ferocity" (269), he is no longer the bee-man Osiris but the oppressive male dog of black folk culture alluded to by Big Sweet in *Mules and Men* and critiqued in Hurston's short story, "Muttsy."[18] As these details and the fact that Janie survives even though bitten by Tea Cake suggest, the illness that kills Tea Cake is a spiritual one—symbolically, he is the mad dog and not its noble victim.

Tea Cake now presents a mortal threat to Janie, as his increasing similarity to Starks suggests. For instance, Tea Cake's first thoughts about why he might feel sick echo Starks's criticism of Janie in the store: "He was not accusing Janie of malice and design. He was accusing her of carelessness. She ought to realize that water buckets needed washing like everything else. He'd tell her about it good and proper when she got back. What was she thinking about nohow? He found himself very angry about it" (259). Whereas Janie desperately tries to "partake wid everything," pleading with Tea Cake to let her share his pain (258), the reciprocity characterizing their early relationship is glaringly absent. Like Killicks and Starks, who both hid from Janie any signs of vulnerability, Tea Cake tries to hide his illness from Janie (264), hoping his symptoms "would stop before Janie noticed anything. He wanted to try to drink water again but he didn't want her to see him fail" (264). Although Tea Cake wants to let Janie comfort him as they have done for one another repeatedly, his obsession with making her realize "'it's uh man heah'" (248) makes him fearful of appearing weak and keeps him silent (266). As he moves to control her voice (271) and her movements (268, 270), his attempt to kill Janie merely images the mortal spiritual danger he poses to her. No passive victim of an uncontrollable physical disease, "even in his delirium he took good aim" (272), his three misfired shots signaling the gravity of his betrayal.[19] The events leading up to his death, thus, demonstrate the partial truth in Nanny's comments on love. In a world of "mules and men," in which relationships between men and women are not reciprocal ones, love can be—and in Janie's relationship with Tea Cake nearly is—"de very prong . . . black women gits hung on" (41).

Although Hurston's critique is necessarily veiled, Janie's character at the end of the novel is, in some ways, even more elusive and has led to vast disagreement among critics concerning her. Whereas most have argued that she emerges from the Muck as an independent female, some have concluded at the other extreme that the novel is far from feminist, one that finally paints Janie as a devoted wife who adores a husband who beats and finally tries to kill her. Jennifer Jordan provides a strong critique of the novel that highlights some of its ambiguities. Tea Cake's death, she argues is "a typical resolution of the tale of courtly love in which the young troubadour or knight engages in an all-consuming passion with a lady of high rank. Tea Cake, the young bluesman and Janie's social inferior, falls in love with a lady, dedicates himself to making her happy, and sacrifices his life fighting a dragon, a kind of mad cow/dog/monster. Hurston creates an alliance of pure romance, a life of adventure and sexual union in a kind of Eden" (110).[20] Key to such readings of Janie as no autonomous woman is the fact that we see no reaction from Janie to Tea Cake's beating (in contrast to her realization about Joe when he slaps her [112]) and hear no comments but loving ones expressed to him as his behavior becomes more threatening. Even after his death, Janie never verbalizes any defiance of Tea Cake or understanding of the changes in him that she had expressed after Joe's death. Focusing on these silences, some critics have concluded that Janie emerges from *Their Eyes Were Watching God* not as a liberated woman but as a dependent one blinded by love.

Whereas these critics point to an important issue in our evaluation of Janie, it is not adequate to see her as simply self-deluded or her silence as Hurston's own ideological blindness. She does actually kill Tea Cake when his threat to her is a mortal one—no insignificant symbolic act—as a number of readers since Alice Walker have pointed out. With a focus on this action and the less explosive narrative possibilities open to Hurston for ending the book, Hurston's novel could just as easily be read as an inversion of the canonical story Jordan finds. To have "the lady" save herself at the novel's end stretches the seams of the genre; to have "the monster" she slays be her lover and the traditional story's hero rips them apart.

The frames at the beginning and end of the novel further suggest neither a broken nor a deluded woman. Physically powerful, "her firm butttocks like . . . grape fruits in her hip pocket; the great rope of black hair swinging to her waist and unraveling in the wind like a plume; [and] her pugnacious breasts trying to bore holes in her shirt" (11), she strides into Eatonville, Hurston suggests, a strong and vigorous woman committed to life and experience despite the death of her lover. She looks over her past, not with wistful nostalgia but with a sober, philosophical eye, seeing "her life like a great tree in leaf with things suffered, things enjoyed, things done and undone" with "dawn and doom . . . in the branches" (20). No stump or mere leaf, hers is not the mutilated identity of other characters in the novel who have sold themselves to dreams that destroyed them. Rather, the beginning and ending frame for the novel suggest, she has become the kind of active female imaged in her pear tree vision, one who has experienced much in her relationship with a "bee-man" but who is not defined by that relationship. In fact, when she first talks with Pheoby, she speaks not of romance and adoration of Tea Cake but of experiences much wider than love or even Tea Cake as an individual: "'Ah been a delegate to de big 'ssociation of life,'" she tells her; "'Yessuh! De Grand Lodge, de big convention of livin' is just where Ah been dis year and a half y'all ain't seen me'" (18). In contrast to some readers' focus on romance and Janie's relationship with Tea Cake, living—not just loving—is what Janie stresses in reviewing her own experience. Such a focus is also the omniscient narrator's. When in the book's final images, Janie pulls in her horizon "like a great fish-net," it is "life" (286)—including, but certainly not limited to love—that she finds in its meshes. When Janie does speak to Pheoby about love, it is not to depict her relationship with Tea Cake as perfect or necessarily even the sole love of her life but to describe love as many-faceted and ever-changing. Love, for a woman who is supremely confident and self-affirming, "'ain't somethin' lak uh grindstone dat's de same thing everywhere and do de same thing tuh everything it touch. Love is lak de sea. It's uh movin' thing, but still and all, it takes its shape from de shore it meets, and it's different with every shore'" (284). As Janie here suggests, she emerges from the novel as no conventional romantic heroine searching to duplicate her relationship with Tea Cake or turning away from life because of the futility of doing so but as an autonomous black woman who faces the future in a spirit of engagement and openness to the flux of experience, "the dawn and doom" she has learned make up love and life.

The frames at the beginning and end of the novel presenting Janie back in Eatonville are thus critical in any evaluation of her character, for they show a woman who has gained the self-affirmation and self-expression she had sought before ever meeting Tea Cake. Having found years earlier "a jewel down inside herself" that she yearned to "gleam . . . around" (138) and having first done so in her relationship with him, the Janie of these frames is not a woman who "glow[s]" (146), "beam[s]" (153), and "lights up" only in the presence of her lover. At the novel's end, she walks with her own lamp, its light "like a spark of sun-stuff washing her face in fire" (285), fully able, even with her lover now dead, "to show her shine" (139).

Janie's wisdom and strength—even her regal, almost haughty indifference toward the gossip of the porch-talkers—indicate a woman, like Isis, not destroyed by the tragedy of her life but able to transform it. Just as Isis collected the parts of Osiris's body after his death and reanimated him, Janie re-members Tea Cake, not as the mad dog or even the "man" who needed assurance that he was one, but as a "bee-man," an Osirian figure her spiritual equal and appropriate counterpart. Burying him with his guitar and imagining him "prancing" through her room, she embraces the ideal of full reciprocity that characterized the best of their relationship. She brings home the symbol of that equality imaged in the pear blossom and bee—some seeds from the Muck, evidence not only of the creativity resulting from such healthy relationships between black women and men but also of her own unfinished life and future growth. The reconstituted masculinity and femininity that Hurston imagines are beautifully depicted in our final images of Tea Cake and Janie. Using the kind of androgynous images she had used earlier in the novel to suggest Janie and Tea Cake's healthy versions of male and female identity—Janie shooting a gun and Tea Cake combing her hair, for instance—Hurston closes the novel by cloaking Tea Cake with a feminine image, "with the sun for a shawl" (286), and Janie with a masculine one, her horizon draped over her shoulder "like a great fish-net" (286). As Janie's final thoughts, they show her embracing a conception of male and female identity that, transcending polarities of active/passive, strong/weak, replaces the gender hierarchies of Jim and Arvey Meserve's world.

As the fish-net image suggests, Janie's memory of Tea Cake is avowedly selective, not the self-deluded inability to distinguish among Tea Cake's different selves, as some critics have argued, but an active remembering. In collecting the "bee-man" parts of Tea Cake, she displays Isis's power to refashion a vibrant black man, one not dwarfed, mutilated, or dehumanized (as so many characters in the novel are) by submission to the dominant white world or its values. Just as Isis's act is responsible for the rebirth of spring, Janie's is not merely that of an adoring lover who saves and serves her love but one with much broader social significance. In imagining the possibility of black manhood different from Joe Starks or the "mad dog," Janie plants the seeds of a world purged of oppressive hierarchies, a world neither sexually nor racially one of mules and men.

Although the beginning and ending frames for the novel are an unequivocal tribute to Janie's stature and power—in a profound sense, the townspeople whose eyes are glued on Janie as she walks through her gate are also "watching God"—the narrative of Janie's relationship with Tea Cake is more ambiguous in its treatment of her experience and awareness. Whereas most critics who disagree about Janie tend to be selective, focusing either on Janie's silence and Tea Cake's beating or on the image of Janie at the beginning of the book, the complex relationship between both must be addressed. To smooth out the narrative wrinkles in the novel is both to simplify the tale of race and sex Hurston tells and to miss an important element of the strategy she fashioned to tell such a story.

That Janie's story should be subject to so many divergent interpretations among critics should not be surprising, for (as Hurston is careful to illustrate) the same is true for reactions to her story within the novel itself. The porch-talkers of Eatonville, for instance, who as Pheoby points out, "'done "heard" 'bout [Janie] just what they hope done happened'" (16), see in Janie's solitary return evidence of an older woman used and spurned by a young rake while the black men at her trial tell a story of a loving Tea Cake betrayed by her. The white jury and audience at Janie's trial have yet another interpretation of Janie's experience, one that Hurston carefully but quite subtly suggests is equally suspect.[21]

Even though they find her innocent of murder, Hurston emphasizes their lack of real knowledge about Janie or Tea Cake (274–75) and the limited version of Janie and Tea Cake's experience that they hear. We do not know exactly what Janie tells them (details Hurston quite strategically omits), but Dr. Simmons, who sets the stage and the tone for white reaction to Janie, focuses understandably on what he knows—Tea Cake's illness and death: Dr Simmons "told about Tea Cake's sickness and how dangerous it was to Janie and the whole town, and how he was scared for her and thought to have Tea Cake locked up in the jail, but seeing Janie's care he neglected to do it. And how he found Janie all bit in the arm, sitting on the floor and petting Tea Cake's head when he got there. And the pistol right by his hand on the floor" (276–77). This scene, as powerful for the judge and jury as it is for Dr. Simmons, is nevertheless limited and partial as "the whole truth and nothing but the truth" (278) about Janie and Tea Cake, for it erases both the vigorous equality of their relationship and the threats to it the changes in Tea Cake constitute.

The terms in which the judge presents the case to the jury, indebted to Simmons's testimony, similarly obscure the complexities of Janie and Tea Cake's relationship. He tells them to decide " 'whether the defendant has committed a cold blooded murder or whether she is a poor broken creature, a devoted wife trapped by unfortunate circumstance who really in firing a rifle bullet into the heart of her late husband did a great act of mercy' " (279). With the first speakers setting the tone, it is no surprise that the jury sees in Janie's story not "a wanton killer" (279) but an adoring wife who took her loving husband out of his misery. It is an interpretation that wins her her freedom and the goodwill of the white women in the room who "cried and stood around her like a protecting wall" (280), but in its view of "Janie Woods the relic of Tea Cake's Janie" (275), it falsifies Janie's experience, diminishes her stature, and transforms the self-preservation in her shooting of Tea Cake into selfless female devotion. Like the porch-talkers, the members of the white audience at the trial have heard the tale "they hoped to hear"—in this case, a story of traditional romance with characters more nearly resembling Arvey and Jim Meserve than Janie and Tea Cake.

Constantly expressing worry about being misunderstood, Janie too seems to recognize the ambiguity of her own story. As she informs Pheoby, she wants not only to tell her her story but also to help her see its significance—" 'ain't no use in me telling you somethin' unless Ah give you de understanding to go 'long wid it. Unless you see de fur, a mink skin ain't no different from a coon hide' " (19). Janie's comment indicates not only her view of Pheoby as ideal listener for her tale but also the vast difference of interpretation to which it can be subject. Without having "see[n] the fur," the white people, the porch-talkers, and the black men at the end of the novel hear what they want to hear in Janie's experience, reaching interpretations that say more about their racial and sexual identities than about Janie's.

In each of these cases, Hurston is careful to suggest that race and gender play a central role in the interpretation of Janie's story. The townspeople, the narrator explicitly announces, are not simply mean-spirited gossipers but black people who "had been tongueless, earless, eyeless conveniences all day long. Mules and other brutes had occupied their skins. But now, the sun and the bossman were gone, so the skins felt powerful and human. They became lords of sounds and lesser things. They passed nations through their mouths. They sat in judgment" (9–10). Their animosity toward a black woman grows out of a context of racial oppression as does that of Sop and his friends during Janie's trial, "there with their tongues cocked and loaded, the only real weapon left to weak folks. The only killing tool they are allowed to use in the presence of white folks" (275). Echoing the reaction of Jim Allen, Joe Starks, Mrs. Turner, and others, these "mules" have made themselves feel human by dominating and dehumanizing other victims. In the hierarchical world of race and gender described by Nanny, the black woman is "the mule of the world," the bottom where not only work but also frustrated anger and misdirected aggression ultimately land.

Although the white people's reaction is very different, Hurston emphasizes that their apparent empathy and concern for Janie is as grounded in the politics of race and gender as the black men's antipathy. Hearing a different story from the one Janie tells Pheoby (before speaking, she recognizes that she "was not at home" [278]), the white audience at the trial, Hurston suggests, supports Janie for reasons having as much to do with the context in which Janie tells her story as with whatever details she provided. Undoubtedly influenced by the support of the two powerful white men, the doctor and the sheriff, the white audience is insulated from the threat the killing of a black man by a black woman poses. As the rhetorical question in the narrative—"What need had *they* to leave their richness to come look on Janie in her overalls" (274–75)—suggests, they are untouched by the intragroup struggles between black women and men that have led to Janie's trial or that are evident at it. Rather, like Joe Starks, who owned an entire town and

Hurston actually goes to some lengths to emphasize that the narrative is much more complicated than a simple record of what Janie told her "bosom friend" as they sat on her back porch in the darkness. In addition to the movements between first and third persons, which signal voices other than Janie's, Janie expressly refuses to tell her own story. Her comment to Pheoby, "'You can tell 'em what Ah say if you wants to. Dat's just de same as me 'cause mah tongue is in mah friend's mouf'" (17), confirms that we hear Janie's story in someone else's words, someone like Pheoby, on whom Janie can depend "'for a good thought'" (19). The character of Pheoby is thus central to discerning both the "understanding" Hurston attaches to Janie's story as well as the narrative technique she devises to convey it; for through the delineation of Pheoby's character, Hurston cleverly hints at the motives of the novel's narrator and the ways that the narrator selects details to shape the intimate version of her story for a more public heterogenous audience.

A devoted friend to Janie, Pheoby at every appearance both supports and defends her friend from the "killing tools" of the community, trying at the very beginning of the novel, for instance, to fend off malicious gossip about her and vowing at the end that "'Nobody better not criticize yuh in mah hearin'"" (284). As supportive of Janie as Big Sweet and Hurston's mother were of her, Pheoby is, indeed, someone Janie can count on "for a good thought," both in real life and in her public rendering of Janie's story. Like other of Hurston's strong black women, Pheoby is also depicted as a very savvy person who knows her community and how to negotiate power within it. When she goes to warn Janie about the community gossip, she does not go by the direct route that would draw attention to her mission and elicit inquiries about Janie's business; instead, she "picked her way over to Janie's house like a hen to a neighbor's garden. Stopped and talked a little with everyone she met, turned aside momentarily to pause at a porch or two—going straight by walking crooked. So her firm intention looked like an accident and she didn't have to give her opinion to folks along the way" (168–69). Adopting the familiar posture of Hurston's other trickster figures, Pheoby's behavior exhibits the indirection and conscious use of ambiguity that characterize the novel's narration. She also demonstrates her astute awareness of audience in the counsel she gives Janie, repeatedly advising her to be silent, not to speak about her feelings to an unsympathetic audience who could not possibly understand (127, 143, 173). Practicing what she preaches, she is careful (as Janie knows [173]) about what she reveals about Janie to others and proud to acknowledge this sign of their intimacy. As she assures Janie, "'Ah jus lak uh chicken. Chicken drink water, but he don't pee-pee'" (173).

The picture that emerges of the narrator Janie chooses to have relate her story is, thus, a surprisingly full one of someone who has heard the story in Janie's own words and whose response suggests that she represents Janie's ideal listener. Supportive of Janie and astute enough to see problems in uncritically telling her story, such a narrator can hit a straight lick with a crooked stick, narrating Janie's story to be true to its volatile themes but sensitive to the context in which they will be relayed. The novel itself is told by such a circumspect narrator. The story given to the reader is in "a friend's mouth," a "kissing friend" who tells a veiled version of her story, who keeps the full "understanding" implicit in the images and symbols to protect Janie from yet more killing tools and loaded guns.

One strategy Hurston employs is Pheoby's use of silence, keeping Janie silent at the most revealing and incendiary moments in her struggle with Tea Cake. Like Pheoby, who knows when Janie's words would be misunderstood or used against her, Hurston also frequently omits Janie's reactions to and assessments of Tea Cake's abusive behavior not necessarily because she had none but because to present them would subject her story to the same dynamics of audience seen in John's and Janie's trials. For instance, whereas many critics have assumed that Janie passively accepted Tea Cake's beating of her, the narrative itself provides no such certainty. Having shown Janie's willingness to confront Tea Cake both verbally and physically in the fight over Nunkie, such a reaction seems unlikely; but for Hurston to present it directly in the narrative would be quite problematic. Hurston's narrative solution is not only to omit whatever words and actions constitute Janie's response but also to keep her off-stage for the description of it.[24] We learn about this fight after the fact through the biased version Tea Cake braggingly conveys to an envious Sop. Significantly, we also never hear in direct address what Janie thought about Tea Cake's illness and death. The rhetorical power of Hurston's narrative strategy, her decision to put Janie's story not in first person but in her friend's mouth, is clear when one imagines what the Janie of the opening and closing frames, a woman who minces no words and who is utterly indifferent to public reaction, might say. For a black woman to say she had to kill a black man because, as Lucy had advised Isis, she loved herself more, because he had become a mortal threat to her, or because he had begun to act like a white man are words that would alienate some segments of her audience and be used by others. To circumvent those problems, Hurston uses her own "fish-net" in narrating the conflict between Janie and Tea Cake, intentionally telling a story with "holes" in it, strategic gaps and silences—how Janie responded to Tea Cake's beating, what exactly she says in court, what she did and thought on the Muck during the weeks after Tea Cake's death— that mask the conflict in their relationship.

The narrative handling of Tea Cake is equally masterful. Again, what would have been lost in a first-person narration by Janie is critical. She would not be able to provide, for instance, either Tea Cake's radically changed thoughts about Janie or his conversation (208) with Sop and his friends, both of which are important and unbiased signals of the changes that have taken place within him. The narrative approach Hurston takes allows her to convey "the understanding" of what has happened to him; but to avoid having this critique become a weapon in the hands of her own jurors, Hurston is careful to veil his violence toward Janie, to treat his "mad dog" qualities, which could so easily evoke the vengence directed at Mrs. Robbins and feed the kind of stereotypes John Pearson fears, symbolically. As careful in picking her words to describe Tea Cake's illness as Pheoby is in picking her way to Janie's door, Hurston exploits ambiguity in her description of him, using careful phrasings that seem to exonerate Tea Cake by making him a noble victim at the same time that they pinpoint the reality of what is destroying him.

Perhaps the best example of this strategy is found in Hurston's sole reference to Janie's assessment of Tea Cake's illness and death. In narrating Janie's testimony at her trial before the divided audience that mirrors Hurston's own, the narrator conveys only a summary (and even then in indirect address) that is fraught with ambiguity: "She tried to make them see how terrible it was that things were fixed so that Tea Cake couldn't come back to himself until he had got rid of that mad dog that was in him and he couldn't get rid of the dog and live. He had to die to get rid of the dog. But she hadn't wanted to kill him. A man is up against a hard game when he must die to beat it. She made them see how she couldn't ever want to be rid of him" (278). An excellent example of how Hurston works to convey "the understanding" but mask the intragroup conflict, this passage is accurate in its implied reference to the death of Tea Cake the "bee-man" and Janie's love for "him," the

malignity of the "mad dog" and the reason Janie had to kill "it," but it
is also ambiguous enough to mesh with the scenario described by Dr.
Simmons and the sheriff. By exploiting gaps, ambiguities, and silences
in this way, Hurston intentionally tells a tale that can be read as "mink
skin" or "coon hide," a story of a black woman's resistance to male oppression that sometimes looks surprisingly similar to the jury's version
of Janie's relationship with Tea Cake. To protect the story of a black
woman killing her husband from misuse by black men or white people,
Hurston uses elements of traditional romance ultimately to subvert
the genre. Buried beneath the romantic surface is the story of a woman
tempted to succumb to the passive female role assigned her in the pro-
totypical white woman's story but who does not, a woman who does
finally love herself more, who neither dies at her lover's hands nor with-
ers away after his death.

Hurston's need to camouflage female resistance is perhaps strongest
in the scene in which Janie actually shoots Tea Cake. Just as she had used
elements of the supernatural to mask female resistance of "Black Death"
and *Jonah's Gourd Vine,* Hurston camouflages female aggression against
sexual oppression in this scene through the use of romantic elements,
carefully describing Janie's shooting of Tea Cake both to imply the import of her act and to veil its volatile implications. To do so, she depicts the internal struggle in Janie's mind between one woman tempted
to protect her lover whatever the cost and another who protects herself from aggressive threat even in the person of her beloved. The entire
passage battles between two different selves and two different narrative voices. When Janie first notices the gun under Tea Cake's pillow
she responds with surprisingly rational thought, sizing up the situation,
weighing alternatives, and taking action. Rushing to see if it is loaded,
she checks the ammunition, starts to load the gun, but thinks with fore-
sight, "he might break it and find out she knew. That might urge his
disordered mind to action" (270). Neither immobilized by devotion nor
content to be sacrificed, she whirls the cylinder to make sure his first
three shots will be blanks. Her actions methodical, knowledgeable, and
deliberate, she then finds the rifle and strategically moves it to the
kitchen "almost behind the stove where it was hard to see" (270). Similarly, immediately before shooting Tea Cake, Janie is in control of her
actions, moving "deftly" (272) as she raises her gun, assessing Tea Cake's
aim with enough calm to recognize its accuracy. No actions of an ac-
quiescent woman like Arvay, who is paralyzed by her husband's vio-

lence, they are, in fact, those of a traditional male hero who skillfully and calmly slays the monster.

Attempting to protect her story from white appropriation and "the killing tools" of black men, Hurston is careful to temper this portion of the narrative with elements of traditional romance. As the narrative reveals Janie unhesitatingly moving to save herself, a different voice (articulating the battle within Janie) utters reassuring words in sharp contrast to her actions: "Tea Cake wouldn't hurt *her*. He was jealous and wanted to scare her. She'd just be in the kitchen as usual and never let on. They would laugh over it when he got well" (270). This passage and others in this section—"Of course she was too fussy, but it did no harm to play safe. She ought not to let sick Tea Cake do something that would drive him crazy when he found out what he had done" (270–71)—both convey the inner conflict in Janie and camouflage the self-possession and undeniable violence of her action. With the real dramatic tension in this scene arising from uncertainty not about what Tea Cake will do so much as about what Janie will, Hurston's narrrative vacillation mirrors Janie's struggle: will she play this scene as the lovestruck and passive "tender woman" described by Sop or as one of his "ol rusty black women" (218–19) who defends herself.

Although the narrative excuses Janie's actions and the momentous answer to this question that her behavior finally bespeaks as the mere instinct (272) of a scared human being fighting for her life, Hurston shows Janie exhibiting the power imaged in the storm, in Big Sweet, and in her own earlier defiance of Joe when she shoots Tea Cake, acting (as other strong black women in her fiction sometimes must) to purge from her life the racial, spiritual, and sexual threat that Tea Cake has come to represent.[25] At that moment, the woman whom nearly everyone in her life—Nanny, Joe, Sop, and finally even Tea Cake—has tried to make live as a white woman, rejects that role. Only because she resists her greatest temptation to play it and breaks out of the narrow margins of traditional romance is she able to emerge as the autonomous black woman we see in the opening and closing frames of the novel.

This moment, a critical one for Janie in her quest, is also the most volatile one for Hurston in her narration. Hurston thus rounds out the scene with a picture of Janie coddling a dead Tea Cake in her arms:

> It was the meanest moment of eternity. A minute before she was just a
> scared human being fighting for its life. Now she was her sacrificing self

with Tea Cake's head in her lap. She had wanted him to live so much
and he was dead. No hour is ever eternity, but it has its right to weep.
Janie held his head tightly to her breast and wept and thanked him
wordlessly for giving her the chance for loving service. She had to hug
him tight for soon he would be gone, and she had to tell him for the
last time. (273–74)

Whereas Hurston here uses the tableau that so affects the white jurors
and underpins their interpretation of Janie's experience, it is important
to recall how tangential it is to Pheoby's. As the fact that she does not
respond to Janie's story with vows to take her "sacrificing self" home to
give Sam some "loving service" suggests (in fact, "sacrifice" and "service" are hardly the words any of Hurston's readers would use to epito-
mize Janie and Tea Cake's relationship), Hurston works here to allow a
story of female resistance to "pass" as romance, to create an ending that
would make possible Janie's "acquittal" with Hurston's own divided
audience. That this was Hurston's struggle in the passage is supported by
a look at earlier versions of it. Defining "loving service" in the manuscript as "cooking and washing his clothes and such intimacies as patch-
ing overalls" (103, JWJ), Hurston deletes that phrase (almost as if she
realized it strained credulity, however well it masked the import of
Janie's actions) and substitutes the second and third sentences to create
a more plausible but still traditional romantic ending for an explosive,
conflict-ridden narrative sequence.

The narrator of *Their Eyes Were Watching God* thus tells a Janus-faced
story, a tale not only of a woman torn between two identities but
one that exploits the resulting ambiguities in relating it to a heterogenous audience. As in the John tales, which succeed because the divided audience finally hears two very different stories in them, Hurston
uses elements of romance in narrating Janie's temptation to succumb to
it ultimately to mask her treatment of contentious "family matters."
Just as white people could hear John tales but miss the import, hear
"some scraps" but "not understand because they had nothing to hear
things like that with. They were not looking for any hope in those days"
("High John," 70), Hurston counts on and even exploits misunderstand-
ing by some segments of her audience. But the story of a black woman's
struggle to define herself as neither mule nor white woman is also there
for the Pheobys in Hurston's audience who are looking for hope and
models of female resistance. Drawing on traditions of black expressivity

in this way, Hurston—even though writing in Nanny's world and, like her, unable to "preach a great sermon about colored women sittin' on high" (32)—is able to "save the text" (32), to tell for those listeners a story not of traditional romance but of quest, not of selfless female devotion but of survival and self-affirming autonomy.

4 The Ways of White Folks in *Seraph on the Suwanee*

HAVING USED WHITE CULTURAL models of male and female identity as the thematic backdrop for *Their Eyes Were Watching God,* Hurston focused directly on that world in *Seraph on the Suwanee.* Although Hurston's last published novel is often read as evidence of her growing conservatism or ambivalence about race and gender, careful reading of its metaphors against those of *Their Eyes Were Watching God* lays bare Hurston's most thorough critique of the dominant culture, one that details the emptiness of its models of identity and relationships for black women and men. Describing the world in which Nanny suffered and Starks apprenticed, Jim Meserve is, in fact, the "big light" and "boss-man" Starks emulates and Arvay, the white woman "settin' on the porch" Nanny romanticized and naively wanted Janie to be. By wrapping this critique in the cloak of romance, a version of the "poor girl marries rich boy" story she claimed was the favorite white theme, and by seeming to validate the traditional American values of hard work, tough men, and loyal women, Hurston hoped to write a popular novel, one that would be financially successful, marketed by book clubs, and made into a Hollywood film.[1] The "crooked stick" method she developed to achieve popularity for this deeply dystopic novel about white people developed through her relationship with Marjorie Kinnan Rawlings, whose depictions of Southern whites had already garnered critical and popular acclaim.[2]

Hurston became friends with Rawlings, to whom she would eventually dedicate *Seraph on the Suwanee,* during the early 1940s. Hurston had written Rawlings, who had become extremely successful and popular with the publication of *The Yearling* in 1938 and *Cross Creek* in 1942, praising her writing and was invited to visit Rawlings at Cross Creek.

Rawling's account of that visit provides the quintessential portrait of Hurston successfully presenting herself to a potential white patron as a colorful, amusing, even brash—but unthreatening—black woman who "has no use for the Left Wingers who consider her a traitor" and who "puts full responsibility for negro advancement on the negroes themselves" (Bigelow and Monti, 223). Rawlings was charmed by the "marvelous" folktales and personality of the woman she described as "a lush, fine-looking café au lait woman with a most ingratiating personality, a brilliant mind, and a fundamental wisdom that shames most whites" (Bigelow and Monti, 223).[3]

Whereas Hurston's relationship with Rawlings—her own obsequiousness and Rawlings's condescension—is a discomfitting one, it is important to remember that (like Isis in "Drenched in Light"), Hurston had much to gain from it.[4] Although it is unclear whether Rawlings actually helped promote *Seraph on the Suwanee* with her publisher, Scribner's, it is a fact that they published the novel at a time when Hurston was not having much luck with other publishers. Letters do indicate that Rawlings not only lent Hurston money while she was writing the novel but also congratulated her editor for publishing the novel and praised Hurston's writing to him.[5] From Rawlings, a Pulitzer Prize winner whose novels were sold to the film industry, translated into numerous languages, and marketed as Book-of-the-Month selections, Hurston also had a model of a novel that might sell.

On the surface Hurston seems to have paid careful attention to Rawlings's work. In fact, the basic situation and characters of *Seraph on the Suwanee* strikingly parallel one of Rawlings's sketches in *Cross Creek,* that of Tom Glisson, a poor Southern white who rises above his poverty.[6] Like Jim Meserve, Tom Glisson has no education, but "he talks with a flair for the picturesque and the dramatic" (14). Undeterred by his lack of inherited wealth, he vows that "'[his] young uns would get a better chance than their daddy'" (14). Even the family he works to support resembles the Meserve one: a son, like Kenny, who has been to the University of Florida and another, "a tragic cripple" (14). The lesson Rawlings draws from this sketch is validation of the Horatio Alger myth of the rise to prosperity, a moral that could as easily apply to the story of Jim Meserve: "it is hard to feel sympathy for what seem off hand less fortunate people, knowing what can be done with courage and hard work and thrift" (15).

The similarities to *The Yearling* are more broadly thematic. Like

Seraph on the Suwanee, it focuses on and glorifies the community of Southern white males, detailing the male-bonding ritual of the hunt, for instance, in much the same way Hurston treats shrimping. Both novels bitterly criticize a female figure, who lurks on the boundaries of this world as an impediment to male desires.[7] Just as Arvay never seems to "do her part" or even understand the significance of Jim's until the end of the novel, Jody's mother is a humorless shrew who fails to appreciate "frolicsome people" (67) and who "don't hold" with important male activities like "ramblin'" (10). Part of Jody's growing up in *The Yearling* involves coming to the kind of male wisdom about women expressed by Jim Meserve. Jody learns that women are basically "onaccountable" [unpredictable] (167): "[They] were all right when they cooked good things to eat. The rest of the time they did nothing but make trouble" (324).

The public response in reviews of *Seraph on the Suwanee* indicates how well Hurston could gauge her audience. Invariably, reviewers read the book as a positive picture of Southern white culture—in the words of one reviewer, "as earthy as a vegetable garden planted in rich soil, and as wholesome" (Rugg, 11). Jim was always seen as the novel's admirable hero, a "real man" who selflessly overcomes adversity, "motivated by his determination to enhance Arvay's life rather than by personal ambition" (Hedden 2) and Arvay as the major stumbling block to his success, "a textbook picture of a hysterical neurotic" (Slaughter 24) who overcomes her weakness with his help. The theme perceived was "that of a woman saved, brought finally out of her feeling of insecurity that has crippled her life, by the wholesome affection of a real man" (Brickell, "A Woman Saved").[8]

That Hurston works with the values of her model in a manner much more complicated than mere imitation is suggested by a comparison of the opening of *Cross Creek* and *Seraph on the Suwanee.* The title of the first chapter in *Cross Creek,* "For this is an enchanted land" (7), accurately forecasts Rawlings's view of rural Florida's landscape and white society. Hurston's opening two paragraphs promise a very different evaluation:

> Sawley, the town, is in west Florida, on the famous Suwanee River.
> It is flanked on the south by the curving course of the river which
> Stephen Foster made famous without ever having looked upon its wa-
> ters, running swift and reddened by the chemicals leeched out of drink-

ing roots. On the north, the town is flanked by cultivated fields planted
to corn, cane potatoes, tobacco and small patches of cotton.

However, few of these fields were intensely cultivated. For the most
part they were scratchy plantings, the people being mostly occupied in
the production of turpentine and lumber. The life of Sawley streamed
out from the sawmill and the "teppentime 'still." Then too, there was ignorance and poverty and the ever-present hookworm. The farms and
the scanty flowers in the front yards and in tin cans and buckets looked
like the people. Trees and plants always look like the people they live
with, somehow. (1)

As the setting forecasts, Hurston depicts Southern white society as dis-
eased and degenerate, a stark contrast to the Muck of *Their Eyes Were
Watching God.*[9] Entering the Florida world depicted in *Seraph on the
Suwanee,* we leave behind the rich and wild fecundity of the Everglades
for the pale insipidity of Sawley and the domesticated prettiness of
Citrabelle with its "picnicky, pleasury look" (73). In place of Janie and
Tea Cake's spiritual communion and sexual vigor, we are shown Jim and
Arvay's neurotic failure to communicate. Unlike the pear tree in *Their
Eyes Were Watching God,* emblem of an ideal, balanced relationship between women and men, the pear trees of *Seraph on the Suwanee* are pale
and sickly ones with pears "that were only fit for preserving" (8). The
wild imbalance between male and female in this novel is, in fact, imaged
in the central metaphor that replaces the pear tree, that of the mulberry
tree. Whereas in the marriage imaged in the pear tree of *Their Eyes Were
Watching God* blossom and bee, female and male exist in cooperation and
mutual service, Hurston's first description of the mulberry tree, its "new
green leaves, punctuated by tiny fuzzy things that looked like green
stubby worms" (37), prefigures the pervasive rape imagery and the female violation at the novel's core. Even the title of Hurston's novel about
whites echoes a passage from *Their Eyes Were Watching God* that highlights cultural lethargy and spiritual desolation: it is Mrs. Turner, infirm
and colorless worshiper of white features, who dreams of "a heaven of
straight-haired, thin-lipped, high-nose blond white seraphs" (216), and
it is her "gods" that Hurston unmasks in this novel.[10] Thus, while *Seraph
on the Suwanee* seems to recapitulate the values of Rawlings's work,
Hurston actually writes a book that is perhaps her most subversive attack on the values of what she called "Anglo-Saxon" civilization. In
Seraph on the Suwanee, she exposes the foundation of that culture as one

resting on oppression of white women, exploitation of people of color, and domination of Nature. To make this critique (and still get the book published), she presents it from behind the trickster's mask of praise, subtly developing her themes through a complex set of symbols developed in other works.

A major strand in her critique involves relationships between white men and women. Although for postwar white America, Arvay may have seemed a Cinderella figure, rescued from poverty and sexual frustration by Prince Charming, Hurston gives us a quite critical view of life on a pedestal, revealing the specific ways in which love is "de prong" even well-to-do white women get hung on. Despite her wealth and seemingly ideal life, Arvay's existence as a "seraph"—ironically, exactly what Nanny wanted for Janie—is one of the emptiest Hurston has portrayed. Just as being Jim's "pet Negro" (61) does not fundamentally alter Joe's servitude, Arvay's status as pampered "pet angel" only thinly masks her degradation. In contrast to the vigor and equality of Janie and Tea Cake's love, marriage in this world involves male repression and control of female sexuality as well as female emotional service to men. It takes the whole novel for Jim to "help" Arvay adjust to this view of marriage, but by the end she embraces her role as sexless seraph and nurturing mother.

The sexual politics of Jim and Arvay's relationship is overlain with a seemingly positive portrait of Jim Meserve. Dashingly handsome in good Hollywood fashion, Jim, despite his poverty, retains the "flavor" of his plantation-owning ancestors: "He was like a hamstring. He was not meat any longer, but he smelled of what he had once been associated with" (7). Inherently "quality white folks," blessed with "the gift of gab" (8) and "the nerve of a brass monkey" (8), Jim pulls himself up from poverty, becoming a major social and economic power in Citrabelle. He also seems to be the ideal husband in the community, fulfilling his role as devoted provider for his family, working for a wife he claims to cherish. As he tells Arvay when, after years of marriage, he has finally decided to leave her, "'I saw you like a king's daughter out of a storybook with your long, soft golden hair. You were deserving, and noble, and all I ever wanted to do was to have the chance to do for you and protect you.'" (263).

Jim's view of himself as Arvay's knight in shining armor and the magnanimity of his "big protection" are, of course, only his side of the story. Hurston undercuts this version of their relationship in Jim's lengthy speech to Arvay about why her inadequacy has driven him to leave. In this monologue, in which Jim reviews the history of their marriage and details Arvay's failure to appreciate his devotion to her, Hurston subtly undercuts Jim's premise, demonstrating that his primary motive has consistently been a self-centered rather than an altruistic one. Chastising Arvay for her lack of appreciation for the still operation that had launched his economic rise, for instance, he stresses the danger involved in that venture: "I went in with Joe stilling likker, and run a heavy risk of going on the chain-gang to get hold of enough money to put you up closer to where I felt that *my* woman ought to be" (264). Arvay, who "crumple[s] and flutter[s] one hand against her chest" (264), is silent in response to Jim's harangue, but the text in describing the actual event is not: "No law was going to touch that still. The law was present at the [first] run" (96) and at the last (129). With similar hauteur he reminds Arvay that he had had the swamp cleaned off "as a honor and a comfort to you" (265), but the text stresses his deafness to Arvay's pleas years earlier for Jim not to buy it and build their house on its edge (79–81). Even the death of Earl in Jim's biased rendition of their relationship is Arvay's sole responsibility, a mistake he tried to prevent (264). His role in Earl's fate is clear, however, in his response to Arvay's pleas, after Earl's first unsuccessful attack on the Corregio family, to send them away (126); planning to use Alfredo in his shrimping endeavor, Jim had refused Arvay's request, characteristically placing his own personal and economic interests first.

Jim's lengthy tirade, complex (as is the entire novel) because the narrator provides no intrusive evaluation and because Arvay herself is no verbal match for him, is a telling revelation of Jim's values. In addition to the ways his claims conflict with the actual narration of events, he inadvertently reveals his views of marriage and his real reason for leaving Arvay. He rightly points out that there exists no spiritual communion in their relationship: "But come right down to the fact of the matter, you and me have never been really married. Our bonds have never been consecrated. Two people ain't married until they come to the same point of view" (266). What these words mean to Jim, however, is clear in another of his self-righteous comments: "I'm sick and tired of hauling and dragging you along. I'm tired of excusing you because you don't understand. I'm tired of waiting for you to meet me on some high place and locking arms with me and going my way" (266). Their marriage is not consecrated, in Jim's view, because Arvay has failed to "go his way." He claims to want a vigorous love from Arvay, but the action he really desires is devoted reverence: "'I don't want [your] stand-still, hap-hazard kind of love. I'm just as hungry as a dog for a knowing and a doing love. You love like a coward. Don't take no steps at all. Just stand around and hope for things to happen out right. Unthankful and unknowing like a hog under a acorn tree. Eating and grunting with your ears hanging over your eyes, and never looking up to see where the acorns are coming from'" (262). The "knowing and doing love" Jim fails to find in Arvay is, finally, not the kind of mutual support shared by Janie and Tea Cake, but one in which a dehumanized Arvay "look[s] up" in gratitude to her husband; the understanding he yearns for is a relationship in which Arvay knows her place, "standing under" her husband. Like Starks in his marriage to Janie, Jim places Arvay economically above other women in the novel but decidedly beneath him, in the position of seraph who decorates and worships at the altar of her god.

Significantly, the attitudes toward women Jim expresses throughout the novel echo almost verbatim those of Jody Stark. Just as Jody tells Janie, "'When Ah see one thing Ah understand ten. You see ten things and don't understand one'" (111), Jim berates Arvay for her lack of insight: "'I see one thing and can understand ten. You see ten things and can't even understand one'" (261). Beneath Jim's professed adoration for women lies a chauvinistic view of them as helpless and mindless creatures protected and guided by men.[11] Like Starks, who is willing "'to think for women and chillun and chickens and cows [since] they sho don't think none theirselves'" (110), Jim magnanimously takes on this role, convinced that "women folks were not given to thinking nohow. It was not in their make-up to do much thinking. That was what men were made for. Women were made to hover and to feel" [105]). Even in their courting, Jim's "great solicitude" (21) barely masks his condescension and the threat to Arvay's self that marriage to Jim represents; she is, for him, a "precious play-pretty" (20), pleasant to look at but fundamentally frivolous. His loving nickname, "Little Bit" (64), and his references to her "sweet little self" (16) forecast the self-diminution she will experience just as his names, "baby-child" (74) and "baby wife" (112), augur her infantile role as wife. Although Arvay, even before marriage, accepts the subordinate role assigned her in Jim's definition of marriage, it is one that makes impossible the kind of spiritual and physical communion, the reciprocity and equality, enjoyed by Janie and Tea Cake. Arvay thinks,

> In so many words he had said, "Love and marry me and sleep with me.
> That is all I need you for. Your brains are not sufficient to help me with
> my work; you can't think with me. Let's get this straight in the begin-
> ning. Putting your head on the same pillow with mine is not the same
> thing as mingling your brains with mine anymore than crying when I
> cry is giving you power to feel my sorrow. You can feel my sympathy
> but not my sorrow." (35)

As she rightly intuits, relationships between women and men in Jim's
world are not those in which husband and wife "partake with everything" but ones characterized by rigid, unequal gender divisions. Unlike
Tea Cake, Jim never does domestic chores; and unlike Janie, Arvay never
works or plays alongside her husband. Significantly, when she is finally
invited onto the shrimp boat at the end of the novel, her participation
is limited to sex and cooking.

The images Hurston uses to describe their love and the ones they
themselves use to express it—ones of power, possession, hunger, and
domination—are stark indicators of their warped relationship. Ominously, both see love not as mutual support but as a form of slavery. Jim
tells Arvay at one point, "Love ain't nothing else BUT compellment"
(154) and (echoing Joe Starks) straightforwardly tells Brock Henson
what form this "compellment" will take in his marriage to Arvay: "'A
woman knows who her master is all right, and she answers to his commands'" (33). As Arvay later recognizes, her marriage is a master/slave
relationship: for much of the novel, she vaguely resents her "enslavement" (134, 137) but is throughout unable effectively to resist it. Love
for Jim is also "hunger" (22, 262, 267), a thinly veiled desire to devour
Arvay, to absorb her self within his own. Arvay yearns to play the role
of the dominated; love to her is not the active engagement in life it is for
Janie, but a "refuge" (24, 154) from it, a chance not to gain an autonomous identity but to lose hers in Jim's, "To be forever warm and included in the atmosphere that he stirred up around him" (24).

As these images suggest, the relationship between Jim and Arvay in
the book is never a real spiritual union between equals. Although Arvay
hopes to gain power over Jim through her sexual attractiveness to
him, Jim is the real victor who controls her energy, reducing her to a
"baby-wife" (112) and "pet angel" (103) whom he sexually "handles . . .
like she was a little child" (240). To tame the wildness in Arvay is Jim's
motive from the beginning of their relationship as his jokes that he

"know[s] how to handle" (17) her and finds her "worth the trouble of breaking in" (18) suggest. Whereas Jim only intends such words to indicate his affection for Arvay and determination to marry her, the metaphors used to describe their relationship underscore his domination of her: as early as their courting, Arvay, standing before Jim with "her eyes stretched in fear like a colt that has been saddled for the first time" (14), is clearly no match for him.

Part of the "saddling" that white women experience in *Seraph on the Suwanee,* as the frequent horse and rider metaphors in the novel suggest, is a sexual one. The young Arvay, with no healthy channel for the thoughts that "made her body plague her in miserable strange ways" (11), retreats into thinly veiled dreams, a repressive religiosity, and hysterical fits just as her mother had in her youth (6). Although Jim feels he liberates Arvay and "fill[s] the bill" (263) sexually for her, Hurston symbolically suggests that he actually harnesses Arvay's sexual energy. His success in doing so is evident in Hurston's description of Arvay's early fits. The sexual innuendoes implicit in the description of Arvay "sprawled out on the horse-hair sofa clenching hands and teeth and bobbling around and up and down" (6) are even more pronounced in the manuscript version of this scene:

> Arvay was on her back, but she was not limp and passive. She was bowed up as if from strychnine poisoning with only her heels and shoulders in contact with the sofa. Her hair was falling in a soft golden mass behind her head. Her hands were clinched tight, and her eyes, though open, were rolled back in her head so far that only a slit of the white showed. The skin of her face was suffused with blood, and her mouth stretched back in a grimace with her teeth clenched tight. (41–42, HC)

This scene, suggesting powerful (albeit frustrated) female sexuality, reveals the intense and spirited sexual potential Arvay possesses before she becomes Jim's passive seraph. In a less repressive environment and with a less oppressive mate, planted in the more fertile soil of *Their Eyes Were Watching God* with a bee-man like Tea Cake, even Arvay, Hurston suggests, might have blossomed.

The men in this book, who flee in horror at Arvay's fits, are clearly not ready for such robust female sexuality. Significantly, only Jim is undeterred; in fact, by dropping turpentine in her eye, he is literally responsible for putting an end to such experiences. Even more broadly, Hurston suggests, in the social milieu of the novel, marriage as an institution means the repressing of a woman's sexual powers, the taming of her passion. With unwitting insight, the townspeople think that "fits were things that happened to some young girls, but they grew out of them sooner or later. It was usually taken as a sign of a girl being 'high-strung.' Marriage would straighten her out" (6).

And, unfortunately, for Arvay, it does.

The scene of Jim and Arvay's first sexual encounter under the mulberry tree perfectly foreshadows the dynamics of their future relationship. Ominously, for neither participant is love or even physical passion the motive: for Arvay, this "surrender" represents an opportunity for her to expiate her guilt over her lust for her brother-in-law, Carl; for Jim, it is a premeditated act of rape, designed to show Arvay who is boss and to achieve the domination of her he feels he lacks.[12] This motive is clear from his conversation with Joe immediately before this rendezvous. When he tells Joe his worries about his relationship with Arvay, Joe responds with this advice: "'Most women folks will love you plenty if you take and see to it that they do. Make 'em knuckle under. From the very first jump, get the bridle in they mouth and ride 'em hard and stop 'em short. They's all alike, Boss. Take 'em and break 'em'" (46). Following Joe's direction, Jim undertakes the rape with the motive of taming Arvay, of subduing the elusive wildness within her.

Thinking that the mulberry tree is sacred to Arvay and forcing her to reenact her childhood play (50) before he rapes her, Jim stages this scene as Arvay's rite of passage into womanhood. In an ominous foreshadowing of the spiritual violence and domination she will endure in their marriage, she experiences not the encouragement of voice that Janie enjoys with Tea Cake but an enforced silence (51), her role as helpless victim and passive prey further suggested in the description of Jim carrying her away "growling like a tiger which had just made a kill and was being challenged" (54). Ultimately reduced to a sexual object in her relationship with Jim, Arvay leaves the mulberry tree to begin a life of passive sexual availability, her underwear left hanging on its branches. In this drastic inversion of the sexual relations imaged in the pear tree, there are no images of female vigor, no "arching sister-calyxes" or even "the strychnine poisoning" of Arvay's early fits, but only suggestions of self-annihilation and passivity:

> She pressed her body tightly against his, fitting herself into him as
> closely as possible. A terrible fear came over her that he might somehow
> vanish away from her arms, and she sought to hold him by the tightness

of her embrace and her flood of kisses. It seemed a great act of mercy
when she found herself stretched on the ground again with Jim's body
weighing down upon her. Even then she was not satisfied. Somehow, she
seemed not to be able to get close enough to him. Never, never, close
enough. (53)

In his self-satisfied brag that Arvay will "keep on getting raped"
(57) every day of her life, Jim unwittingly speaks the truth about what
their marriage will mean—both physically and spiritually—for her.[13]
Arvay is right to see the degrading image of her "drawers swinging ever
so gently in the breeze" (54) as "a kind of sign and symbol" (54) of her
new life. She is wrong later, however, to see the mulberry tree as her
"tree of life" (308) and a symbol of her triumph, for it is in fact the place
of her first defeat and the beginning of her spiritual death at Jim's
hands.[14] By carefully detailing this sexual encounter and so richly contrasting it with the pear tree of *Their Eyes Were Watching God,* Hurston
underscores the fact that, although Arvay may seem a Cinderella figure,
she in fact becomes a glorified "spit cup" in her marriage.

As the images associated with Arvay's first sexual experience suggest, objectification and submission characterize her physical relationship with Jim. The vigor of her early sexual feelings thus dissolves into
passivity in Hurston's descriptions of Arvay's sexual response after their
marriage: "Her body got warm and she seemed to be sinking, sinking,
down through the mattress, through the floor and through the world
on some soft cloudy material, and drifting off through the rimbones of
space. Passive, passive, receptive and dreamlike, until she felt Jim's first
kiss on her lips. It came as a great mercy and a blessing, and Arvay de-
parted from herself and knew nothing until she came to earth again and
found herself in the familiar bed" (158). The kind of female sexuality
depicted here, one characterized by passivity, receptivity, and loss of self,
contrasts sharply with that imaged in the pear blossom. In fact, none of
the sexual relations for women in this novel are robust expressions of
their passion; rather, sex often operates as a soporific, draining female energy. The situation for Angeline, who has already been made a "seraph"
in her father's naming of her, promises to be similar. That her physical relationship with Hatton will echo Arvay's "drows[y]" (157) sexual experience is evident when Arvay, interrupting their lovemaking in
her living room, sees Angeline "drooping" as if "under a heavy dose of
laudanum" (181).

Hurston's critique of the white world's model of male sexuality is also suggested imagistically in her treatment of Earl, the child conceived under the mulberry tree and the appropriate symbolic offspring of such a twisted relationship. The sexual violence from which he springs mirrored in his own aggressive behavior, Earl seems hardly human from birth, so deformed that only through Arvay's constant attention is she able to shape his body into human form (69). Although Arvay feels responsible for Earl's condition and Jim assumes he comes from her side of the family (125), Hurston's images associate him with Jim's predatory sexuality and that of several black male characters in other works who draw their models of masculinity from a white world.[15] The sexual "hunger" that Jim brags about but that the novel exposes as destructive is undeniable in Earl's voracious appetite. His first word was either "eat" or "meat" (76), and even as an infant, he "attacked [so] ferociously when put to the breast" (68) that Jim worries he will "eat [Arvay] clear up" (69). Later, echoing Tea Cake's attack on Janie, Earl actually does bite Arvay's hand, evidence (in addition to his "inhuman screams" and "snarly howls" [100]) of his dehumanized and predatory masculinity.

Hurston also uses the symbol of the dog here as in "Muttsy" and *Their Eyes Were Watching God* to depict Earl as the embodiment of an aggressive and destructive male sexuality. Just as Jim courts Arvay "like a well-trained dog tackling a bob-cat" (8) and later tells her that he is just as "hungry as a dog" (262) for love, Earl's attack on Lucy Ann is described as that of a "mad dog" who hunts and finally devours his prey.[16] Arvay hears in Earl's room "A whimpering, whining that broke into a kind of yelp now and then as it grew more insistent. Something like a dog penned up in a strange place, or when a hunting dog sees its master take down the gun and is impatient to be off on the chase" (112). Escaping from his cage, running to the grove "like a hound dog hunting for the scent" (123), Earl assaults Lucy Ann in a scene that imagistically echoes his father's rape of his mother under the mulberry tree. The perversion of male sexual impulse is unequivocal here. There has been no sexual contact between Earl and the girl; rather, after watching her "hungrily" (124), he finally bites her on the neck, hand, and leg, in a symbolic attempt to devour her.[17]

Although Hurston exploits popular tastes in heroes and love stories in shaping Jim and Arvay's relationship, she also subtly reveals in the novel's "love scenes" that Jim's sexual behavior is similarly driven by a desire for power. They all echo the dynamics of initial rape under the mulberry tree (Jim often physically overpowers Arvay and invariably manipulates her sexual feelings for his own purposes), and they further suggest that domination rather than sex is his primary motive. In the novel's second "love scene," for instance, which occurs after the death of Earl, Jim's reason for approaching Arvay is to regain the emotional power over her he feels he has lost in Arvay's obsessive grief over Earl's death and to reinstate himself as the sole object of her attention. Urging her to forget Earl as he arouses her, Jim (deaf to Arvay's protests) is able to attain physically the goal that has eluded him verbally. Made more "Passive, passive, [and] receptive" (158) through their liaison, Arvay, convinced that "she could part with anything, even principles, before she could give up this man" (158), immediately afterward abandons her mourning for Earl and transfers her affection back to Jim.

Significantly, this is the last scene in which Jim and Arvay actually have sexual relations, and the later scenes that promise some torrid encounter lead to no sexual consummation. The next one, which occurs after Jim and Arvay have been in Gainesville to see Kenny perform, arises directly out of Jim's rage at Arvay's threats to leave without him. The power dynamics of the bedroom scene after they return home, one in which male violence and female objectification again masquerade as passion, echo those of the rape under the mulberry tree. Just as he had earlier ripped off her bloomers, Jim here rips off her dress and orders her, "'Up with that petticoat and down with them pants before you make me hurt you'" (216). Summarily silenced when she starts to protest (215) and as easily overpowered as "a mouse under the paw of a cat" (215), she is, as Jim announces, his "'damn property'" (217), once again humiliated, dehumanized, and objectified under the guise of romantic passion. Despite its ominous parallels with the mulberry scene, however, this scene does not end in sexual consummation but in the suggestion that Jim's real motive is to verify his power over Arvay and her acquiescence to it. Because in this case she professes her "bondage" to Jim (218) and even threatens to kill herself (218), their encounter is strangely and totally asexual: Jim "stretched himself full length upon her, but in the same way that he might have laid himself down upon a couch" (218). With sex merely a maneuver by Jim for control, the scene ends with Jim's "happy arrogance" and Arvay's "hovering" devotion (219).

In the "reconciliation" scene between Jim and Arvay on the shrimp boat at the very end of the novel, Hurston develops a similarly complex portrait of the sexual relationship between Jim and Arvay. The implicit violence of Jim's sexuality is evident when Jim bounds into her cabin "like he was stalking a prey" (347) and reinforced in his "growling" (347, 349) words:

> "Don't you holler!" Jim growled. "Putting me on the line like you did! I ought to take my belt to you and run your backside crazy!" All of a sudden, Jim stood over Arvay on the bunk and offed with his jacket and flung it from him without looking to see which way it went. He tore at the buttons of his shirt frantically and threw it as if it had done something to him. "Holler if you dare! You had better not even cheep!" (347–48)

Silencing and dehumanizing Arvay in this scene, Jim's advances again sap her sexual energy so completely that "her eyelids flutter[ing] and droop[ing]" (347), her arms "in a languorous curve" (349), she "almost los[es] consciousness" (349). With Jim even more quickly able to reaffirm her passivity and subjugation, this scene ends with a disconcerting depiction of mother and child:

> Jim was gripping her shoulders so hard until it hurt her, and trembling over his body like a child trying to keep from crying. Like a little boy who has fled in out of the dark to the comfort of his mother. After a while, Jim sighed deeply, and his head slid down and snuggled on her breast. From long habit, Arvay's fingers began to play through his hair in a gentle way. Almost immediately, Jim sighed and went off into a deep and peaceful sleep. (349)

As these scenes suggest, Hurston presents a more complex psychological portrait of Jim's sexuality than is suggested by his own expressions of lusty virility. His love for Arvay is ultimately not sexual but infantile, an attempt to recreate a relationship with his mother, who is the most important woman in his life. Attracted to Arvay because "All of the agony of his lost mother was gone when he could rest his head on Arvay's bosom of nights" (105), Jim is no "bee" in search of a "blossom" but a child seeking uncritical and undivided maternal devotion. As Arvay realizes later in the novel, Jim is not finally "the over-powering general that she had took him for . . . but a little boy to take care of, and he hungered for her hovering" (351). This need for "hovering" rather than a vigorous sexual partner requires that he harness Arvay's sexual energy, making her his sexless seraph and nurturing mother.

The insecurity that ultimately motivates Jim's domination of Arvay is clear in another of Hurston's symbolic snake scenes, one replete with phallic imagery reminiscent of *Jonah's Gourd Vine* and "Sweat." Jim plans this snake-handling scene as an expression of his masculinity and expects Arvay to see his actions as "big and brave and full of manhood" (261). The domination inherent in his notion of manliness is suggested in his motive for staging this scene, a patently oppressive desire to terrorize Arvay and to gain psychological control over her. Even in this scene, however, which so starkly images Jim's sense of himself, he is revealed not as the "real man" he repeatedly claims to be but as a child who requires female confirmation of his fragile identity. Performing "Just like a little boy turning cartwheels" (254) for a doting mother as he handles the snake, Jim needs Arvay's acknowledgment of his power in order to feel "big and brave and full of manhood" and must repeatedly in the novel diminish her sense of selfhood to extract it.

His masculinity a compensation for dependency and weakness (just as Earl is both the most aggressive and the most fearful male in the novel [70, 80]), Jim is depicted in this central scene as fundamentally ineffectual when his theatrical plans backfire. In the conclusion of the scene, reminiscent of "Sweat," Jim successfully terrifies Arvay, but in Hurston's suggestion that his conception of masculinity is ultimately as destructive for him as for Arvay, he is nearly killed by the snake. With this unexpected turn of events, Jim again reveals his dependency and impotence, for he must be rescued by Jeff while Arvay stands frozen. In an embarrassing scene for both men, Jeff takes over the role of ministering mother, saving Jim from the snake, "hover[ing] and guard[ing]" Jim as if he were "an infant child" (256). While Jim berates Arvay that she has "crapped out" on her "biggest chance in the world to make a great woman out of [her]self" (260), he is really distressed that, in her failure to save him, she has refused to play a maternal role. Her refusal to "serve" and to "hover" as a decent mother should is reason enough for him to leave her.

Arvay's behavior in this scene is equally complex. A part of her yearns to play this role for Jim: "In her consciousness Arvay flew to Jim and slew that snake and held Jim in her arms like a baby. Actually, Arvay never moved. She could neither run to the rescue nor flee away from the sight of what she feared would happen" (223). Although Arvay accepts Jim's interpretation of cowardice as the reason for her inaction (255), we can see a more complicated set of conflicting desires at work. A part of Arvay recognizes the threat that the snake, as a symbol of Jim's manhood, represents for her and can "feel in her own body the fiery pang from the long, curving fangs" (254). Arvay's subconscious, always a more accurate sensor than her divided conscious mind, is quite willing to see Jim's oppressive masculinity destroy him. Her inaction is as real (if more tepid) a sign of female self-defense as Delia's impassive behavior at the end of "Sweat" or Janie's shooting of Tea Cake.

By the end of the book, however, Arvay abandons even such feeble attempts at defiance. Returning home from her mother's funeral, she begins to act "just like Mister Jim" (314), as Janie and Jeff notice, and to "prefer [his] ways of handling things" (314). No longer fighting him, she finally "goes his way" and accepts total responsibility for the problems of their marriage (341). The path is now smooth for Arvay and Jim's relationship: she has become his "seraph" and accorded Jim the paradoxical status he has demanded, that of God to be worshiped and child to be hovered.

Arvay's final defeat is symbolically and powerfully foreshadowed in the crossing of the bar scene at the end of the novel, perhaps Hurston's starkest symbolic treatment of the male/female conflict central to the novel.[18] Echoing her description of the hurricane in *Their Eyes Were Watching God,* Hurston casts the foaming, boiling sea as a godlike force counter to male domestication and control, a potentially liberatory power that Jim must harness and control to maintain his dominance. The language used to describe Jim's steering of the boat through the churning waters, with its sexually explicit overtones, underscores his ultimate victory. In a thinly veiled recapitulation of their relationship, driving the *Arvay Henson* as the boat "throb[s] out towards the bar" (326) in the same way that he sexually manipulates and dominates Arvay, Jim finally subdues this "storm" just as he had tamed Arvay's earlier "hurricane" (32).

Arvay's self-annihilation is evident in her changed response to Jim in this scene. Unlike Hurston's strong black women who resist their oppression, Hurston's seraphs and "pet angels" repeatedly not only accept but even abet theirs. Just as Angeline taunts Hatton, "So rape me, I'll help you" (179), Arvay serves Jim here at the end of the novel in his project of symbolically defeating her. When (in a scene imagistically reminiscent of the earlier snake episode) the mate wraps his arms around Jim's leg in an attempt to keep him from making the unnecessarily dangerous attempt to cross the bar before the tide is up, Arvay is no longer torn about her position. Ironically, she now displays a "doing love," but it is to be the agent of her own destruction. Violently attack-

ing the shipmate, she becomes a "she-bear in her rage" (329); her passion, however, is not that of Hurston's strong black women, "tigers" who
defy their oppressors, but of an utterly vanquished female who adores
and protects hers.

The role left for the domesticated Arvay is clear after the boat crosses
the bar into calm waters. Just as the sea, whose "calm surface rose and
fell like the breast of a sleeping woman" (343), is now harmless and unthreatening, Arvay slips into the maternal role Jim assigns her, ministering to the crew, delighted to serve men who act "like boys" (341).
Defining her spiritual defeat as the ultimate happiness, she foregoes a
sexual relationship with Jim and embraces her role as his mother. In bed
with Jim at the novel's end, "She shifted her body sufficiently to lie on
her right side, and her arms still about the sleeping Jim, snuggled him
more comfortably in the narrow bunk and held and hovered him as if
he had been her little boy" (349). Her passion domesticated, she thinks
of Jim with adoration explicitly equated with feelings for her children:
"Inside he was nothing but a little boy to take care of, and he hungered
for her hovering. Look at him now! Snuggled down and clutching onto
her like Kenny when he wore diapers. Arvay felt such a swelling to
protect and comfort Jim that tears came up in her eyes. So helpless sleeping there in her arms and trusting himself to her" (351). For Arvay, who
sees it as "her privilege to serve [Jim]" and to give him "the hovering
that he needed" (351), the boat rocking gently on the calm sea is an
image of peace and belonging; for Hurston, it is one of submission and
harnessed female energy: "The *Arvay Henson* rode gently on the bosom
of the Atlantic. It lifted and bowed in harmony with the wind and the
sea. It was acting in submission to the infinite, and Arvay felt its peace.
For the first time in her life, she acknowledged that it was the only way"
(349).[19]

Although Arvay feels elevated by the end of the novel, like the princess Jim has told her repeatedly that she is, Hurston paints a very different picture of white women's place in a society that defines eroticism as
rape, romance as domination, and marriage as female emotional service to men. To highlight Arvay's degradation, despite her social status,
Hurston stresses her affinities with many of the black women to whom
she feels decidedly superior. Women whose lives appear to be extremely
different—Kenny's black friend, Belinda, the black prostitute, Fast Mary,
and Arvay—find themselves in similarly degrading positions in their relationships with white men, their objectified status starkly symbolized

by their lack of underwear. Arvay fails to realize the bitter truth in her comment that her bloomers left swinging on the branches of the mulberry tree are "a kind of sign and symbol" (48). They are evidence that, no matter how comfortable her life and no matter how much she feels like a Cinderella, her relation to white men often betrays surprising parallels to those of black women she distrusts and resents.

The relationships all three women have with white men are built on the elevation of the male and the dehumanization of the female. "Bossy like his father," Kenny chooses Belinda as his favorite playmate, for instance, "because Belinda was persuaded that he was very smart and showered admiration in various ways upon him" (108). His part in the seemingly lighthearted incident at the railroad station—ordering Belinda to stand on her head and parade her bare bottom before the amused passengers—provides further evidence, as the townspeople note, that "He t[akes] after his Pappy all right" (112). Even though he had not planned the consequences, it is certainly significant that Kenny profits from Belinda's humiliation and that Belinda sees no degradation in her situation. Although they are too young for their relationship to be sexual, it is—like the adult ones in the novel—built on female debasement and service to men.

Surprising affinities between Arvay and Fast Mary surface when she arrives at the Meserve house to protest Kenny's humiliating jokes about her lack of underwear. Arvay's jealous worry that "Jim had been fooling around [with] that Mary" (164) and his casual sexual banter with her before he realizes Arvay is eavesdropping further emphasize the ease with which Jim can move sexually between the two women. Whereas Arvay clings to the class and race differences that assure her superiority over Mary, Hurston emphasizes some commonalities in their sexual relationships. Even though Fast Mary can be had "for a fish sandwich and a drink of gin" (162), the scene with Arvay and Mary arguing in front of the house (163–66) over who is more virtuous is bitterly ironic, for in their relations with white men, they are both prostituted "spit cups."

The imbalanced and ultimately lifeless models of manhood and womanhood found in Jim Meserve's world are only one strand in the rich critique of it that Hurston weaves in *Seraph on the Suwanee.* Just as the pear tree becomes a symbol not merely of sexual but of broader social relations in *Their Eyes Were Watching God,* the dynamics of the mulberry tree in *Seraph on the Suwanee* reverberate throughout Jim Meserve's world, echoed in his relationships with Nature and with people of color. Just as his marriage with Arvay is, on many levels, built on rape, his relationships to Nature and black people are also insidiously oppressive and destructive demands—as his name indicates—that they serve him.

Hurston suggests the underlying unity in Jim's actions by associating Arvay imagistically with Nature—the trees, the swamp, and the sea that are so important in his rise to power. Just as Jim professes to worship Arvay, he also loves the woods because he finds there the same mothering protection and solace he seeks from Arvay. His behavior, nevertheless, is equally destructive, for Jim either mutilates the trees in his turpentining venture or domesticates them in his groves; in both cases, the trees become symbolic perversions of Janie's pear tree and stark contrasts to Tea Cake's woods.

This demand that Nature serve him is also played out in the development of the swamp, Jim's most grandiose and profitable financial scheme. Reminding the reader of the parallels between this swamp (the "finest stretch of muck outside the Everglades" [79]) and the Muck in *Their Eyes Were Watching God,* Hurston stresses Jim's blindness to the spiritual power embodied in it; for him, it "'ain't nothing but a lot of big trees and stuff growing together'" (80) that he desires to possess (80). Seeing its "richness" only in material terms, he repeatedly responds to this rather obvious symbol of dark, mysterious female space by focusing on the potential monetary gain it embodies: "There's a big fortune hid in that dark swamp. All it needs is the brains and the nerve to get it out" (192). With the Howland Development that he dreams of throughout the novel, Jim achieves his goal, extracting his profits, buttressing his social position, and destroying the swamp. Hurston subtly suggests the spiritual violence tied to this "progress" as Arvay looks at the "Raw, dark gashes made by the bulldozers" (196) that transform the wild and fertile swamp into a new domesticated space of expensive homes, golf links, and a club house (196). Creating a world grounded in class and racial hierarchies in addition to male/female inequalities, the Howland Development Company "came along and stratified the town. The original line of the swamp gave accent like a railroad track. Those who belonged moved west" (197).

Hurston stresses the consistency of Jim's actions by drawing parallels between Arvay's fate at the hands of Jim and the swamp's. Just as Arvay empathizes with trees, she is also identified with the swamp (despite her initial fear of the place) and senses her affinities with it when it is being destroyed: "Arvay was surprised at finding herself feeling in sympathy with the swamp . . . it seemed a pity and a shame for those trees to be destroyed" (195). The destruction of the swamp is understandably "very personal to her though she never said so to anyone" (171), for it recapitulates the spiritual annihilation and domestication she has experienced in her marriage to Jim. Arvay pinpoints the real danger in her life as the swamp is being destroyed. As the sun shines through (195), a symbol of Jim's victory, she vaguely senses that "This Howland Development seemed infinitely more threatening to her than the dark gloom of the swamp had been" (197), but she fails to recognize fully the implications of her feeling.[20]

Jim's love for shrimping stems from equally complex motives. As always, he professes to love the sea:

> The colors charmed and pleased Jim. There was the delicate green close
> at hand and flipping inward toward the faint outline of the Florida coast.
> To starboard and infinity, it took on a blue-green, and where the sun
> rested on it, it seemed to be overlaid by a silvery veil. . . . There was an-
> other thing that fascinated Jim about the sea, the seemingly infinity of
> form. No matter how much you saw, the sea had still other marvels of
> shape and color. (223–24)

Significantly, Arvay is also associated with the sea through parallels frequently drawn between her "Gulf-blue eyes" (4) and her sexual feelings. Just as Jim is fascinated with the varied colors of the sea, he is mesmerized by the change in the color of Arvay's eyes when she is sexually aroused. At one point, for instance,

> He seized Arvay midway in a passage from the table to the stove and
> held her tight and kissed her and murmured sweet soothing things until
> that mysterious green light appeared in Arvay's blue eyes. Arvay's eyes
> had some strange power to change like that when she was stirred for
> him. Each time that she succumbed to his love making, Arvay's eyes
> gradually changed from that placid blue to a misty greenish-blue like
> the waters of the sea at times and at places. It warmed him, it burned
> him and bound him. (106)[21]

Attracted to the mystery in Arvay and the sea, he nevertheless must symbolically rape both in an effort to control them.

In her descriptions of shrimping, Hurston suggests the underlying unity between that activity and the predatory model of male sexuality depicted in the novel. The process, which involves dropping a red flag as "a marker over the shrimp, and drag[ging] back and forth through them" (225), takes on explicit sexual overtones in the barroom banter of the shipmates (221, 228). The power Jim enjoys in his sexual relationship with Arvay is echoed in his love of shrimping. While he struggles to make Arvay see him as a king and revere him appropriately, shrimping gives him a less conflict-ridden "chance to stick his head in a crown" (227). As captain of a shrimping fleet, he is undisputed god, "some kind of king, only bigger and better" (203), with the power of death in his hands and all of creation floundering at his feet.

In her description of shrimping, Hurston develops the symbolic violation of the sea it entails. The "strange unimaginable-shaped things" (335) that inhabit the depths and are victims of gratuitously vicious carnage when the men pull up their nets are symbolically feminine creatures (one kind is even called a "damn whore's-egg" [336]) with whom Arvay, subconsciously aware of her fate at the hands of men, identifies. Seeing her own life symbolically reenacted, she "watche[s] the slaughter with pity" (336) and once "involuntarily let[s] out a scream" (338). Her lament that "Turtles and hard shelled things had a chance. Few soft-bodied things had a chance" (336) is an unrecognized statement about the fate of the feminine in Jim's world. Without the mask that protects blacks from white intrusion or the emotional wall that black women such as Janie and Lucy erect to protect themselves from oppressive men, Arvay is also one of those "soft-bodied things." As she watches the carnage, she "shrink[s] like a Portugues man o' war on the beach" (337), a spineless victim who (unlike Hurston's strong black women) has mustered little defense against male domination.[22]

Whereas Arvay is momentarily moved to pity at this sight, Hurston at the end of the novel emphasizes not only Arvay's victimization by Jim but also her internalization of his values. Determined to show a "doing love" and to battle other women who might want Jim, she promises, "She was going to deal with things. Oh, yes she was! And she was not going to fool around with the try-net. She was going over board with the drag and sweep the very bottom" (303). Arvay's language here, much more than mere borrowing of metaphor, bespeaks her ultimate acceptance of Jim's worldview.[23] Given the values associated with the sea-depths and with shrimping, Arvay here expresses her acceptance of the aggressive, rapacious behavior that has characterized white males in the novel and her willingness now to support their subjugation of "soft-bodied things."

Jim's effect on the black characters in the novel is equally pernicious and insidious. Although they move only on the margins of *Seraph on the Suwanee,* Hurston carefully shows that their world does not escape unscathed by the values that dominate the novel. Like Arvay, in fact, the black characters are domesticated and diminished, stunted in the soil of white culture, as the name of one shipmate—Stumpy—graphically suggests. The strength and independence of Janie in *Their Eyes Were Watching God* is parodied in the mindless fawning of Janie in *Seraph on the Suwanee* who "turns large soft eyes on Arvay with deep emotions" (313) when given a ham and a bag of pecans. Janie's mate is not the Tea Cake of *Their Eyes Were Watching God* but a pale and sickly reflection, the "faithful" retainer, Jeff, who invariably carries out Jim's orders. Tea Cake also resurfaces in miniature in the faceless shipmate, Cup-Cake, a stereotypical black figure who constantly "beam[s]" and grins (332). Further, just as Arvay is, in many ways, a slave in her relationship to Jim, black men are consistently feminized in their relationship with him. Titty-Nipple's name starkly reveals the maternal role black men play for white men in the absence of white women: Jeff "hovers" Jim when Arvay fails to do so, and Cup-Cake cooks for him when she is gone.

Just as Jim saps Janie's energy and uses her to elevate his own social position, Jim's relationship to black characters in the novel is (despite his good humor and apparent generosity) equally exploitative. Every one of his financial ventures—from his still operation to his turpentining, citrus groves, development projects, and shrimping fleet—depends on the expertise and the efforts of black workers. Whereas Jim takes personal credit for clearing the swamp for the housing development, Hurston points to the black men who provide the labor, the "gangs of husky black roustabouts" (195) who make his dreams real but do not participate in them: when the completed Howland Development they build "stratifie[s] the town . . . like a railroad track" (197), they find themselves living on the wrong side of town.

Jim also similarly usurps the rich verbal art of black culture for his own profit. Blessed with the "gift of gab," he is able to insinuate himself into the black community, not so much to participate in its rich traditions but to extract gain for himself. Knowing nothing himself about citrus production but aware that black men "were the ones who actually knew how things were done" (74), Jim entertains them with his treats and his stories (74). His participation in the banter of the jook and the tale-swapping on the porch front—the intimacy he seems to enjoy in contrast to Arvay's racist reserve—is a self-serving investment from which Jim knows he will profit. Such appropriation and exploitation of black culture are also echoed in Kenny's seemingly harmless appreciation and popularization of Joe's music. As Jim tells Arvay,

> white bands up North and in different places like New Orleans are taking over darky music and making more money at it than the darkies used to. Singers and musicians and all. You do hear it over the radio at times, Arvay. Kenny claims it is just a matter of time when white artists will take it all over. Getting [so] it's not considered just darky music and dancing nowadays. It's American, and belongs to everybody. Just like that swamp. (202)[24]

Like the swamp, Joe's music becomes domesticated, "owned," and used for white profit in Kenny's hands. A rich black musical tradition, thus, becomes "Kenny's piece" (238); and Kenny, not Joe, reaps the financial rewards from it (238). Following Kenny on his musical tour and awarded not a share of the profits but a set of "changing-clothes" (251) in exchange for his talent, Joe travels not as a respected black musician but as a nursemaid. Accepting the surrogate mother role as eagerly as Jeff or Cup-Cake, ministering to white men in the absence of white women, he reassures Arvay, "'I'll sure hold his feet to the fire and keep him straight. Without a doubt, Miss Arvay. You know that Kenny ever would mind me. It'll be just like you was there'" (252).

The damaging effects on black people living in a Jim's world are also outlined in the changes that occur in Joe and Dessie's relationship. Even though Jim sees his role as one of benevolent protector of his pet (a role Joe never disputes), the money Joe receives from Jim cuts him off from his roots and finally culturally impoverishes him. In what looks like a move upward, bowing to Jim's "pressure . . . [to] put some of his likker money into two lots in Colored Town" (117), Joe moves his family to town where he starts to build a fine home, an "unfinished structure" (117) that symbolizes his hollow life. Working for white folks all his life finally takes the same toll on Joe that it does on his namesake from *Their Eyes Were Watching God:* imitating his "boss-man," Joe sets himself above his community and brags about "Doing things on a high-toned scale" (117), but his "success" destroys his egalitarian relationship with Dessie. When he spiritually deserts that relationship for the superficial life of philanderer and self-proclaimed "Heavy-set Daddy" (117), Dessie's life becomes as miserable as Lucy's, and her relative economic prosperity as empty as Janie's. As the fate of every black character in

Seraph on the Suwanee suggests, living in Jim Meserve's world adulterates black culture and destroys a healthy black identity, both male and female. Just as the young Janie in *Their Eyes Were Watching God,* unsure of who she is when she lives in white people's backyard, adopts whatever name they give her, black characters who live in the shadow of Jim Meserve— Belinda who claims Arvay as her mother (114), Joe and Jim who refer to themselves as "Meserves" (252, 313)—draw their identity from and in fact revere the figures of their own oppression.

As the adoration universally showered on Jim suggests, the world where "the white man is de ruler" depicted in *Seraph on the Suwanee* is one with the hierarchies but not the racial or sexual tensions of the social worlds described in *Mules and Men, Jonah's Gourd Vine,* or *Their Eyes Were Watching God.* Virtually devoid of resistance, stabilized by acquiescence and complicity, it is peopled not by "fractious" mules who slip their halters but by victims who accept their saddling and whose energy is expended only in jockeying with one another for favor with their rider. Detailing the diminishment of black people and white women in this way, Hurston thus paints a picture of racial and sexual domination in ironic contrast to the idealized relationships Stephen Foster immortalized and she alluded to her in title. Unlike Foster, who (as Hurston reminds us at the beginning of the novel) wrote "without ever having looked upon [the Suwanee River]" (1), she takes an intimate look at a white world whose exploitative hierarchies deny full humanity to all people—male and female, black and white.

5 "Crossing Over" and "Heading Back": Black Cultural Freedom in *Moses, Man of the Mountain*

PROVIDING A BACKDROP AGAINST which she wants her audience to read *Moses, Man of the Mountain,* Hurston depicts Moses in her introduction as a figure rooted in African traditions and religion, related to gods in Haiti and Africa.[1] For blacks throughout the world, she suggests, Moses is admired not as a servant of God who accepted the Ten Commandments but as "the fountain of mystic powers" (xxii), a god whose power rivals that of the Judeo-Christian deity. Thus, Moses (like the heroes in the African American tales of black superhuman power narrated in *Mules and Men*) represents an important image of blackness, one of awesome power rather than subervient bondage: the worship of Moses by people of African descent focuses on "his rod of power, the terror he showed before all Israel and to Pharaoh, and THAT MIGHTY HAND" (xxii).[2]

Hurston's introduction thus sets up the novel as one of black cultural affirmation. Depicting Moses as a black hoodoo man and drawing on a rich tradition in African American folklore to develop him as a liberator of black people, Hurston seems to forecast an extremely positive portrait of Moses.[3] Finally, however, this introduction, like many comments she made about her other works, is a diversionary tactic, for the story of Moses she tells is a much richer one, significantly more complicated in its evaluation of him, his leadership, and the nation he creates. Having exposed the dangers she saw in black people's uncritical assimilation into and emulation of Jim Meserve's world, Hurston, through Moses and his epic religious and political struggle, examines on a broader scale than she had before the cultural choices facing black people: sexual, social, and economic relations grounded in black traditions and the world of the Muck or the recreation of Jim Meserve's oppressive hierarchies.

Another side of Moses, one quite different from the heroic image sketched in Hurston's introduction, is found in some of her unpublished manuscript materials. Her description of him in "The Elusive Goal: Brotherhood of Man" as "the Dictator" who "arranged to force acceptance of his 'Ten Sayings' on the people" (3, HC) jars with the traditional African American conception of Moses. More developed and even more critical is the character sketch contained in a typescript in the Scribner's archives at Princeton University. Titled "Just Like Us: An Analysis of the Hebrews and the Modern Jews as They Were as Against Our Traditional Conceptions," the manuscript consists of a five-page foreword and a fourteen-page outline of a projected work, which (Hurston asserts) would present a fairer, more accurate picture of the Jews than has been passed on in the Christian tradition. In contrast to the view of Jews as "a stiff-necked people who were ungrateful to the God who brought them out of the land of Egypt, etc., that they were forever turning from God and being unruly" (2, SC), Hurston proposes, instead, one of a group so "individualistic . . . that they made extremely poor subject-people" (1, SC). Their biggest "sin" (a virtue, certainly, for Hurston) was simply "insisting on doing some thinking on their own" (2, SC).

In this manuscript, Hurston's portrait of Moses and the role he played in the history of the Jews is hardly that of liberator. After conceiving of his new religion and choosing the Hebrews as the group to "bend to his way of thinking" (1, SC), he soon establishes "a dictatorship" (2, SC), instituting extensive laws to transform this individualistic, free people into a mentally enslaved and socially restricted group (2, SC). Hurston further emphasizes the oppressive cruelty characterizing Moses' iron rule. Echoing Joe Starks's form of "leadership" in Eatonville, setting himself above the community, Moses "holds himself coldly aloof from the people" (3, SC) and demands absolute subservience: "The price of escape from Egypt was eternal and unquestioning submission" (3, SC), and the price for defiance, death (4, SC).

Although this version of Moses' character and actions seems in sharp conflict with the one Hurston expresses in her introduction to *Moses, Man of the Mountain,* there are, in fact, two Moses in the novel. The first, under the tutelage of Mentu, represents one of Hurston's ideal male characters. Like Tea Cake, this early Moses is also a "bee-man," emotionally expressive, attuned to Nature, and supportive of women. Moses in the second half of the novel, however, becomes a very different char-

acter, one more like Joe Starks—disdainful of women, alienated from
the common people and from his own feelings. With striking parallels
between his personal and political behavior, Moses, who starts out committed to freedom for the common people, becomes a dictator as ruthless as the Pharaoh he sought to overthrow. Rejecting his African gods
and the values they represent to worship the god of Jim Meserve's world,
Moses ultimately creates an oppressive, hierarchical, patriarchal state.
Whereas Hurston's novel seems revolutionary in depicting Moses as
black, the work is, in fact, much more broadly iconoclastic. Hurston's
purpose is not merely to debunk a mythic conception of Moses but to
confront contentious issues of black cultural identification and freedom.
Hurston's message for her contemporaries is conveyed not simply in a
tale of liberation but in one about the hazards to be encountered on the
journey toward it.

     That Moses would seem a hero for leading the Jews out of Egypt is
partly a reflection of the despotism evident there. The Egyptian state
created by the Pharaoh, with its obvious similarities to American slavery,
reflects many of the values Hurston repeatedly decried. The Pharaoh
with his phallic "rod of state" (52) epitomizes a politically repressive
and sexist state, one rooted in force and unnatural law (one of his first
acts is to make "The birthing beds of Hebrews . . . matters of state"
[11]). Like Joe Starks, he is a "big voice," a demogogue who uses words
to elevate himself above the common people (31). Hurston satirically
deflates his tyrannical pretensions through the grumblings of his subjects: "Why, he's got a law about everything under the sun! Next thing
you know he'll be saying cats can't have kittens. He figures that it makes
a big man out of him to be passing and passing laws and rules. He thinks
that makes him look more like a king" (15).

     The effects of this system on the oppressed Hebrews echo those
Hurston had seen in the lives of African Americans. Divisions within
the community spring up as "Hebrew began to suspect Hebrew" (26),
and husband and wife argue about whether to kill their children mer-
cifully or to hide them. The deleterious effects on the gender identities
of men and women are also familiar. Men feel emasculated, mules with
no "say-so" over their lives (18) rather than men (17, 19). When "the
Hebrew womb [is crushed] under the heel of Pharaoh" (11), Hebrew
women suffer as deeply as African American ones, silenced like Janie
and Lucy and forced to stifle even their cries of childbirth (11). Under
such slavery, motherhood also becomes so twisted that women can no

longer care for their children; just as Nanny is forced to hide her child in the swamp, Jochebed must abandon her infant to the river to save its life. Women's oppression is pervasive in this society, extending beyond the slave class into that of the elite—even the daughter of the Pharaoh "must lend her support to the female robes of state. She must lend her ears to the sound of mighty words boiling out of futile men. She must bear something in male form, for after all that is what she was born for—a passageway for boy children" (53).

Destined for a leadership role in this state, possessed with enough charisma and natural talent for warfare perhaps to have become pharaoh, Moses (largely as a result of his relationship with Mentu) rejects this state and the values it represents. Significantly, Hurston suggests Mentu's affinities with the values of black folk culture in the characteristics she gives him. As a mentor, Mentu is no big "Muck-de-muck" but an illiterate stableman who responds to young Moses' questions with "answers in the form of stories" (54), including one about Tara the Monkey, a "smart aleck" (56) figure who resembles the monkey of African American folklore. Unlike the Pharaoh who needs his pyramids as tangible proof of historical continuity (35), Mentu's faith rests with an oral folk tradition of story and proverb: "These, his images and happenings of the mind, scrambled from his lips and entertained the listeners for a day, then went to join the thousands of other dreams where they dwelt. Where did they hide? He did not know. But he believed that they did not die. They were stronger and more enduring than men" (54–55). In the relationship between Moses and Mentu, which echoes in many important details that between Janie and Pheoby in *Their Eyes Were Watching God,* the older Mentu plays a nurturing, guiding role similar to that of the more experienced Janie at the end of the novel. Instead of preaching or lecturing, he tells stories that broaden Moses' experience and deepen his thinking. Just as Pheoby " 'grow[s] ten feet higher from jus' listenin' " (284) to Janie's tale, Mentu's tales foster Moses' spiritual growth. Moses' encounter with Mentu is thus an important emotional experience for him, for it represents his first relationship that is not based on hierarchy, control, or self-aggrandizement.

The philosophy Mentu passes on to Moses should also be quite familiar to readers of *Their Eyes Were Watching God* and other of Hurston's works. Echoing the egalitarian gender dynamics of the voodoo pantheon Hurston had described in *Tell My Horse* (137–54), Mentu repeatedly stresses the importance of both the male and female principles of life. For Mentu, this "bi-sexual" concept of creation results in equal emphasis on male and female to describe reality. As he teaches Moses, "'Most things are born in the mothering darkness and most things die. Darkness is the womb of creation, my boy. But the sun with his seven horns of flame is the father of life'" (55). Espousing a philosophy of human connection with Nature rather than control over it, Mentu teaches Moses the secret ways of her creatures. With affirmation of life as the key note of his teachings, he subtly argues against the egotistical desire to transcend the human and to defy the natural that characterizes the Pharaoh's endeavors. When he sees Moses building a playhouse that imitates the Pharaoh's monuments, he responds (with satiric deflation of Moses' budding pretensions) in the role of one of his animal characters. The lizard, he tells Moses, "'thinks all structures are made for nesting. He thinks you have been building a nest for your mate to lay eggs in. He says you take too long about so that your mate must be ready to bust from holding her eggs so long. He asks why do men build such high nests for their mates? Are they afraid their eggs will be stolen?'" (58). With this humorous dig at the Egyptian Pharaoh who sees his palace not as "a residence" but as "the seat of authority" (65), Mentu shows Moses the unnatural folly of the value system the Pharaoh represents and the danger of human endeavor cut off from everyday life.

The differences between Mentu's philosophy and that of the Egyptian state is also suggested in the snake imagery Hurston associates with him. In contrast to the oppressive phallic symbol of the Pharaoh, Mentu's snake is a symbol of wisdom rather than domination (72). Directing Moses to the Book of Thoth (73) for understanding rather than controlling Nature, the hoodoo Mentu teaches him is a power to "enchant" (73) that involves not strong-arming Nature into submission but uniting in a oneness with and deep appreciation of its mystery. Significantly, the Pharaoh's priests do not know this book (74); they know some "tricks" by which to control Nature (61–62, 72, 74) but possess no "real knowledge" (81). What Mentu wants for Moses, echoing what Janie desires for Pheoby (*Their Eyes Were Watching God,* 19), is quite different. Just as Janie tells Pheoby that "' 'tain't no use in me telling you somethin' unless Ah give you de understanding to go 'long wid it'" (19), Mentu tells Moses that the theatrical magic of the priests "'is learning but not wisdom. Learning without wisdom is a load of books on a donkey's back. I want *you* to understand'" (74).

These views, based on a reverence for Nature and appreciation of the experiences of ordinary women and men, constitute the philosophical foundation for Moses' development early in the novel. While raised in a culture of artificial hierarchies and brutal domination, Moses encounters through Mentu the values Hurston frequently attached to black folk culture: human relationships based on equality and mutual support, human endeavor tied to natural human needs. The power of this philosophy is evident in its effect on Moses, for under Mentu's influence, he abandons the way of life symbolized by the pharaohs. While as a warrior, he had denied his own feelings, he learns to value the bi-sexual character—reason/emotion, day/night—within himself that Mentu had taught him to recognize; he sees that "he was two beings. In short, he was everybody boiled down to a drop. Everybody is two beings; one lives and flourishes in the daylight and stands guard. The other being walks and howls at night" (82). Cultivating his spiritual and emotional powers, Moses becomes "a man of thought" (93) who spends his days thinking and feeling (96, 99, 100). This spiritual transformation leads Moses to a changed notion of power. Like Janie who grows toward exercising a "'power tuh free things'" (*Their Eyes Were Watching God,* 92), Moses, after killing an overseer, feels "a new sympathy for the oppressed of all mankind" (92) and a new sense of social responsibility; now when he looks at the Hebrews, "what he s[ees] touche[s] him so that he resolve[s] in his heart to do whatever was in his power to better their condition" (84). Significantly for Hurston, Moses' original urge to help the Hebrews arises in her version of history as a feeling of love rather than as a response to divine order.

When warfare loses its glamor, Moses also abandons the ideal of force on which the Pharaoh's political power rests. Vowing to fight only in self-defense (109), he comes to see man-made law as an important tool of oppression in the Pharaoh's regime: "'I feel the cursing thought of the law and power. I had always felt the beneficence of law and power and never stopped to consider that it had any other side. It was a sword with two edges. Never mind whether it is directed against me honestly or not. That has nothing to do with its power to injure me" (99). Wholly rejecting the Egyptian social system and the values on which it rests, Moses, like Jochebed and Janie and other of Hurston's women for whom "the dream is the truth" (*Their Eyes Were Watching God,* 9), embraces a vision of an ideal society that guides his actions: "He found his unformed wishes taking shape. He was wishing for a country he had never seen. He was seeing visions of a nation he had never heard of where

there would be more equality of opportunity and less difference between top and bottom" (100). What he here imagines is also Hurston's
ideal—the world of the Muck in *Their Eyes Were Watching God,* in
Nanny's words, a "'place way off in de ocean where de black man is in
power'" (29). Unsure of where to find such a place, Moses nevertheless
rejects his past, spiritually "crossing over" into a realm not infused with
these values:

> Moses had crossed over. He was not in Egypt. He had crossed over and
> now he was not an Egyptian. He had crossed over. The short sword at
> his thigh had a jewelled hilt but he had crossed over and so it was no
> longer the sign of high birth and power. He had crossed over, so he sat
> down on a rock near the seashore to rest himself. He had crossed over
> so he was not of the house of Pharaoh. He did not own a palace be-
> cause he had crossed over. He did not have an Ethiopian Princess for a
> wife. He had crossed over. He did not have friends to sustain him. He
> had crossed over. He did not have enemies to strain against his strength
> and power. He had crossed over. He was subject to no law except the
> laws of tooth and talon. He had crossed over. The sun who was his
> friend and ancestor in Egypt was arrogant and bitter in Asia. He had
> crossed over. He felt empty as a post hole for he was none of the things
> he once had been. He was a man sitting on a rock. He had crossed over.
> (103–4)

"Crossing over" involves much more, of course, than merely traversing
borders. Hurston uses a rich symbol of freedom from slavery in African
American folklore to symbolize a broader form of spiritual freedom, not
merely Moses' movement beyond the reach of Egyptian law but his escape from spiritual enslavement to a set of cultural values.

What Moses has rejected in the Pharaoh's state and what he has
embraced in Mentu's philosophy have specific historical, religious, and
symbolic significance for Hurston. Although Hurston develops her
analysis of race and gender in Egyptian and Jewish religion quite cryptically, numerous historical references in the novel reflect wide reading
in Egyptian and Jewish history and religion.[4] That she saw a chance to
"plough up some literary" in this subject matter is suggested in a letter
she wrote while a student to Fannie Hurst in which she comments on
one of her classes: "I wish some of these spring days that you can come
up to Anthropology 110. It is about the religions of primitive people
and is full of things a writer could use as a dog is of fleas" (quoted in
Wilentz, 30). None of Hurston's novels is more indebted to her "spyglass
of anthropology" for its richness and complexity than *Moses, Man of the*

Mountain. In fact, the philosophical conflict between the Pharaoh and Mentu that is primary in the first part of the book reflects the major conflict within the history of Egyptian religion, commented on in all of the major histories of Egypt—that between the worship of the sun and that of Osiris and Isis. Mentioned frequently were their different origins: Osiris and Isis were considered indigenous African figures while the sun-gods were usually thought to have been brought in from the East (Budge, *The Gods,* I. xiv; Budge, *Osiris,* I. vi). As every major historian noted, these two strains in Egyptian religion also exhibited class differences: the worship of a remote, untouchable sun was associated with royalty throughout the history of Egypt whereas the cult of Isis and Osiris, intimately connected with a tangible Nature and desirable afterlife, enjoyed broad popularity among the common people.[5] The common people in *Moses, Man of the Mountain,* likewise, show little enthusiasm for the worship of the sun, repeatedly associated with the Pharaoh and other royalty in the book (52, 66). The Egyptian foreman may gaze at the sun with "awe" and "reverence" (13), but the workers recognize that " 'Horus may be all those good things to the Egyptians, brother, but that sun-god is just something to fry our backs' " (13). Significantly, Moses' "crossing-over" involves a rejection of the god associated with his Egyptian nobility: "The sun who was his friend and ancestor in Egypt [becomes] arrogant and bitter" when he forfeits his social rank.

Especially attractive for Hurston was a feature commented on by nearly every Egyptologist she might have read, namely the bi-sexual character of popular Egyptian religion. As in voodoo and African religions she described in *Tell My Horse,* Egyptian gods were nearly always (with the exception of the sun-god who lacked a female counterpart) thought of in the popular imagination in male and female pairs. The equality between male and female such balance symbolized is especially clear in the case of the central figures in the Osirian faith, Isis and Osiris. Other features of this relationship, in addition to this male and female balance, strongly echo elements in the early relationship between Janie and Tea Cake in *Their Eyes Were Watching God* and help explain Hurston's consistent attraction to these figures.[6] Like Janie and Tea Cake on the Muck, Isis and Osiris are closely connected with Nature in Egyptian mythology. A process as central to human civilization and survival as the inundation of the Nile was seen as a reflection of the relationship between the two deities. Osiris, associated (like Verigible Woods) with trees, functioned as the personification of the yearly death and rebirth of the vegetative world. As the central "verdure-god" (Breasted, *Dawn,* 24), Osiris was seen as a god of fertility; the natural birth and rebirth brought about through his relationship with Isis, paralleling the richness flowing from the relationship between Janie and Tea Cake, imaged for Hurston the creativity inherent in a balanced relationship between male and female.

Like Tea Cake, the Osiris popular with the Egyptians was also a god devoted to human pleasures, one who was "given to mirth and jollity and took great pleasure in music and dancing" (Budge, *Osiris,* I. 231). The everlasting life he promised souls was not that of a disembodied, transcendent world of spiritual contemplation but the paradise of the Muck, a "Field of Peace, where wheat and barley grew in abundance, and where a man would possess a vine, and fig trees, and date palms, and be waited upon by his father and his mother, and where he would enjoy an existence more comfortable than that which he led upon this earth" (Budge, *The Gods of the Egyptians,* I. 334).

Whereas Osiris represented the feminized "bee-man" Hurston valued, one associated with natural fecundity, female equality, and human pleasure, Isis, associated with the preservation of life, reviving Osiris, her son (after he was stung by scorpions), and even Nature, personified the kind of active and nurturing female Hurston created in the characters of Janie and Big Sweet. Isis received these powers from the god Thoth, the "arch-magician," and became known as "the lady of enchantments," a great magician "with mighty words of power" (Budge, *Egyptian Religion,* 55): "At her bidding the powers of nature ceased or modified their operations, and she could make everything, both animate and inanimate, to perform her will" (Budge, *Osiris,* II. 279–80). Her powers to revivify the dead were considered so significant that many of the formulae set out in *The Book of the Dead,* a set of rituals to assist dead souls in their journey toward everlasting life, were specifically designed to secure her protection (Budge, *Book of the Dead,* clxxxvi). Isis, thus, becomes a most powerful figure in the Egyptian pantheon, hailed as "the mighty lady, the mistress of the gods" (Budge, *Gods,* I. 363).[7]

Although Hurston never explicitly states so in *Moses, Man of the Mountain,* she inserts cryptic details to associate Moses with this Osirian worldview early in the novel. Offering sacrifices to Isis and referring prayerfully to the the Judgment scene over which Osiris and Isis reign, Moses (as many Egyptologists had pointed out) also possesses many of Osiris's characteristics. Mysteriously related to Apis, the sacred bull with special markings that was universally identified with Osiris (Budge, *Osiris,* I. 397–404, *Moses,* 128, 321), Moses becomes an Osirian character under Mentu's tutelage, a figure (like Tea Cake) devoted to Nature, female equality, and celebration of life.[8]

The Osirian faith Moses learns from his lowly mentor is also implicitly referred to in Mentu's own association with other key elements of the Osirian faith, especially Thoth, the god of wisdom. Just as Thoth was nearly always depicted with a dog-headed ape at the Judgment of dead souls in Egyptian symbolism, Mentu is repeatedly associated with monkeys in *Moses, Man of the Mountain* (56, 57, 71, 72, 80). Like Mentu's understanding, Thoth's wisdom was grounded in communication with Nature. Thoth was worshiped as the "arch-magician" (Budge, *Book of the Dead,* ciii) who gave magical words to Isis and who was author of *The Book of the Dead.* It is the power and knowledge from this African tradition that Mentu introduces to Moses.

Hurston's most cryptic indicator that Moses' wisdom and power are not Hebraic but Osirian is her extensive quotation from a traditional Egyptian tale, "Setna and the Magic Book," in her description of Moses' trip to Koptos in search of the Book of Thoth. In the following parallel passages, I have quoted from a standard version of this tale, that given by Petrie in *Egyptian Tales,* one often referred to by other commentators. My purpose in detailing Hurston's borrowing is not so much to identify her source (although her extensive quotation makes that clear) but to suggest how emphatically she places Moses in an Egyptian and pagan rather than Hebraic and monotheistic tradition. For years Moses is haunted by the memory of Mentu's story about a mysterious book

in the middle of the river at Koptos in an iron box; in the iron box is a bronze box; in the bronze box is a sycamore box; in the sycamore box is an ivory and ebony box and in the ebony box is a silver box; in the silver box is a golden box and in that is the book. And there is a deathless snake by the box to guard it. (*Moses,* 74)	in the middle of the river at Koptos, in an iron box; in the iron box is a bronze box; in the bronze box is a sycamore box; in the sycamore box is an ivory and ebony box; in the ivory and ebony box is a silver box; in the silver box is a golden box, and in that is the book. It is twisted all round with snakes and scorpions and all the other crawling things around the box in which the book is; and there is a deathless snake by the box. (*Tales,* II. 95)

As Mentu tells Moses, reading this book and learning the spells in it, confers power on the reader. It is a book

"which Thoth himself wrote with his own hand which, if you read it, will bring you to the gods. When you read only two pages in this book you will enchant the heavens, the earth, the abyss, the mountain, and the sea. You will know what the birds of the air and the creeping things are saying. You will know the secrets of the deep, because the power is there to bring them to you. And when you read the second page, you can go into the world of ghosts and come back to the shape you were on earth. You will see the sun shining in the sky, with all the gods, and the full moon." (*Moses,* 73)

"which Thoth himself wrote with his own hand, and which will bring you to the gods. When you read but two pages in this you will enchant the heaven, the earth, the abyss, the mountains, and the sea; you shall know what the birds of the sky and the crawling things are saying; you shall see the fishes of the deep, for a divine power is there to bring them up out of the depth. And when you read the second page, if you are in the world of ghosts, you will become again in the shape you were in on earth. You will see the sun shining in the sky, with all the gods, and the full moon." (*Tales,* II. 93–94)

Years later Moses, of course, actually goes to Koptos. He tells Jethro about his trip in words that again echo verbatim the traditional tale. After offering sacrifices for four days,

On the morning of the fifth day he had called a priest to him and with his powers had commanded the priest to make a magic cabin that was full of men and diving tackle. Moses himself put the spell on it and put life in it and gave the men breath and said to them, "Workmen, go to the place in the river where the book is, and work for me." Then he had sunk the cabin in the water. In three days they had come to the place in the river where the box was and made a shoal out of sand to make the water shallow. They worked night and day.

Then he found the box all wrapped around with scorpions and snakes and different other kinds of reptiles. But he knew what to do for them so

"And the morning of the fifth day came; and Naneferkaptah called a priest to him, and made a magic cabin that was full of men and tackle. He put the spell upon it, and put life in it, and gave them breath, and sank it in the water. He filled the royal boat with sand, and took leave of me, and sailed from the haven; and I sat by the river at Koptos that I might see what would become of him. And he said, 'Workmen, work for me, even at the place where the book is.' And they toiled by night and by day; and when they had reached it in three days, he threw the sand out, and made a shoal in the river. And then he found on it entwined serpents and scorpions and all kinds of crawling that they all laid sleeping as if they were dead. Then he met the deathless snake. So the snake got ready for a hard fight and Moses fought him all the next day. Moses did not win over the deathless snake but then the snake did not beat him, so they met and fought again the next day. At sundown Moses felt that he had the advantage of the snake to a certain degree, so he called up all of his power of mind as well as his body, for if he won he would have more power than any man on earth and also the deathless snake would come under his command. And he wanted the obedience of the snake. So late in the third day, he beat the snake and commanded the snake to meet him anywhere in the world that he might call. So the snake did not appear to resist him anymore. (*Moses*, 153)

things around the box in which the book was; and by it he found a deathless snake around the box. And he laid the spell upon the entwined serpents and scorpions and all kinds of crawling things which were around the box, that they should not come out. And he went to the deathless snake, and fought with him, and killed him; but he came to life again, and took a new form. He then fought again with him a second time; but he came to life again, and took a third form. He then cut him in two parts, and put sand between the parts, that he would not appear again." (*Tales*, II. 98–99)

Like the protagonist of "Setna and the Magic Book," Moses acquires phenomenal power from reading the book:

So Moses read the book and then he was able to command the heavens and the earth, the abyss and the mountain, and the sea. He knew the language of the birds of the air, the creatures that people the deep and what the beasts of the wild all said. He saw the sun and the moon and the stars of the sky as no man had ever seen them before, for a divine power was with him. (*Moses*, 154)

"He took the book from the golden box, and read a page of spells from it. He enchanted the heaven and the earth, the abyss, the mountains, and the sea; he knew what the birds of the sky, the fish of the deep, and the beasts of the hills all said. He read another page of the spells, and saw the sun shining in the sky, with all the gods, the full moon, and the stars in their shapes; he saw the fishes of the deep, for a divine power was present that brought them up from the water." (*Tales*, 100)[9]

It is this power that Moses uses throughout the rest of the novel. In thus suggesting an Egyptian origin for Moses' magic (and for Hurston, as for many of her contemporaries, that meant black), Hurston was not out of line with historians and anthropologists of her day. Nearly all quoted the Bible description of Moses as "learned in all the wisdom of the Egyptians" and "mighty in words and in deeds" (Acts 7:22) as evidence that he knew Egyptian magic.[10] Moses' first demonstration of Yahweh's power, for instance, his turning a rod into a snake before Pharaoh, was recognized by Egyptologists as a staple Egyptian magic trick.[11] Egyptologists found evidence of Moses' familiarity with Egyptian magic in other of his actions. Budge actually suggests that the plagues—including turning water into blood (6) and commanding the waters of the sea (7)—that Moses visited as signs of his God's power were also no different in kind from the tricks in the repertoire of an Egyptian magician (*Egyptian Magic*, 6).

Even more specifically, Hurston also suggests, in calling attention so dramatically to this tale, that Moses' power derives from that of Isis. Koptos, the goal of Moses' pilgrimage, was famous for its temple to Isis, as Petrie points out in his remarks on "Setna and the Magic Book" (122). Again echoing the actions of that tale's protagonist (*Tales,* II. 97), Moses actually admits to Jethro that he worships in her temple (153). Such a connection between Moses' miraculous powers and those of Isis was seen by many commentators Hurston would certainly have read. Mercatante, for instance, points out that many people have historically seen the biblical passage as evidence that Moses possessed words of power like those of Isis (90). Budge also interprets the biblical phrase, "mighty in words," as meaning that "like the goddess Isis, [Moses] was 'strong of tongue' and uttered the words of power which he knew with correct pronunciation" (Budge, *Egyptian Magic,* 5).

In carefully tracing the source of Moses' power back to an Egyptian rather than a Hebrew source, Hurston thus suggests the indebtedness of Judaism to Egyptian religious beliefs and practices.[12] Instead of depicting Judaism as a sweeping away of an African religion, Hurston shows how the religion that was to become the foundation of modern European culture usurped the power of an earlier African one. In at least as radical a fashion, she also shows the foundation of Judaism, seen by numerous writers such as Freud and Briffault as a fundamentally patriarchal one, to rest ultimately on a more egalitarian gender symbolism. Thus, while Moses associates almost exclusively with father figures in the second half of the novel, early in the story he demonstrates an unashamed attachment to female figures, including Isis, his wife, and his mother. Even Mount Sinai, ultimately identified as the abode of the "father" is earlier distinctly feminine in Moses' mind, a nurturing, "sheltering mountain" (142) with "heavy hips" (288) and "big pregnant-looking clouds around the top" (345), a symbolic "mother" (120–21) he yearns to embrace.

How Moses comes to forget the African wisdom he had acquired from Mentu and to reject the "gods" of his egalitarian worldview is the basis for the rest of the novel. The second half of *Moses, Man of the Mountain* chronicles the transformation of this "natural man," one like Tea Cake in touch with the male and female within himself, into a stern, oppressive patriarch. On a broader social level, the novel explores how an African religion built on nature worship and respect for the feminine is usurped by a patriarchal religion, one grounded not on equality and natural law but rather on hierarchy, repression, and coercive power.[13] Hurston makes the conflict in Moses' life between these two radically different worldviews explicit by introducing another mentor for him in the second part of the book. While Moses loves Jethro as much as he had Mentu, he is a very different personality who espouses an opposing belief system, one (ironically) that Hurston had earlier sketched in her portrait of the Pharaoh. In contrast to Mentu's gentle strength, Jethro is explicitly depicted as a very different kind of man, a "patriarch" (115) who values and displays "ferocity" and "sternness" (264).

Jethro's attitudes toward women also echo those of the Pharaoh and other of Hurston's oppressive men. Clearly a misogynist, Jethro immediately expresses his sexist beliefs when he and Moses meet by bemoaning his "shameful" situation in having only daughters (117). When Moses suggests that Zipporah help them fight the thieves (just as Tea Cake had invited Janie into "male" activities like playing checkers and shooting a gun), Jethro responds with an opinion conflicting with later events: "'But Moses, she is nothing but a woman. She wouldn't be a bit of service in a fight'" (123). Even when Moses prevails and the women perform admirably in the battle, Jethro reacts consistently. Unlike Tea Cake who fixes dinner with Janie after they have both labored in the fields, Jethro denies the equality their joint campaign reflects and orders the women to "'get to doing around'" (126) and fix breakfast. Like other oppressive male characters Hurston has created, Jethro also silences women. His wife never asks where he has been, knowing "she would get no answer" (138); when Zipporah, accustomed to a more egalitarian relationship with Moses, does ask, Jethro tells her "to work harder on the weaving of the new tent of camel's hair and not to be so talkative" (138). Viewing women as impediments to more important male endeavors, such as building empires, Jethro repeatedly chastises Moses for his attachment to Zipporah. Love and desire are unmanly, "feminine" concerns for Jethro (135), in conflict with social action and political leadership. As he tells Moses, "'You have more greatness about you than any man I ever heard of, Moses. Don't over-pull your belly on this love business and destroy it'" (135). Jethro's affinities with Joe Starks resurface several times when Jethro (in a comment inserted later than the manuscript) tells Moses he "hate[s] to see [him] wasted on a woman" (135–36); he concludes, "'Women pull men aside'" from the "'work [they] got to do'" (272).

Like Mentu's, Jethro's eyes too have "power in them" (115–16). In him, however, Moses encounters a definition of power very different from Mentu's. Whereas Moses at this point conceives of power as wisdom, understanding, and the ability to free things, Jethro consistently pushes Moses to exercise power as control and coercion. Jethro immediately and ominously echoes the Pharaoh's system when he meets Moses. Distressed that "'Law and order is in a terrible state in Midian'" (117), he reveals a number of familiar values in his explanation of what that means:

> "Well, I tell you, Moses, my house has always been powerful. From generation to generation it was that way. Right and justice prevailed in all Midian. But for the last few years a weak King has been on the throne and the robbers and things are just about to take us. Nobody is afraid of the King so people do not respect their chiefs and the country is gone to the dogs. Nobody can have any more than he has the might to protect. It all started with the downfall of the Hyksos in Egypt many years ago. Bands of them retreating before the Egyptians' army overran this country and got things so upset we just haven't been able to get straight since. No real unity any more. If a chief hasn't got an army of his own, he's in a mighty poor fix." (118)

For Jethro, justice is no broader than protection of private property, respect no deeper than fear, and peace inconceivable without military might. Jethro's wish is not for social equality but for wealth and sufficient "might" to protect it. That material profit is part of his scheme is clear when Moses attacks the robbers and retrieves Jethro's cattle. When Jethro's wife comments that it "'looks like we've got a few cows here that we didn't have before'" (126), Jethro is not moved to return them out of concern for justice like that which inspired Moses to help him; instead, he responds "with a cheerful tone of voice," "'Well, I am not going to tote a casket in my pocket about it. . . . I don't expect to take to bed sick over it for even one day'" (126).

Jethro's imperialistic leanings are cultural as well as material. He is not content merely to practice his own religion; rather, like Constantine and other cultural imperialists masquerading as religious enthusiasts Hurston criticizes in *Dust Tracks on a Road,* he "feel[s] the command to bring other people beside the Kenites to know this god and worship him" (137). His concern for the Hebrews stems not from his empathy with their suffering as Moses' earlier had but from his view of them as potential converts and subjects, people likely to accept a new religion because they, in his words, have "'no god of their own and no more protection than a bareheaded mule'" (156). Like Jim Meserve, Jethro views people in terms of their potential role in this endeavor and treats them as dehumanized instruments to be used for his purposes. Although language for Mentu is important for the deep and meaningful communication it fosters, it is for Jethro merely an instrument of control. The folk idiom his people speak is not a sign of group identity and poetic creativity but a tool that can be used to mold popular opinion. As he tells Moses, "'It's always a great advantage when you're managing people to be able to speak their kind of language. Stiff words frighten poor folks'" (122). Moses, at this point, however, sees language as Mentu and Hurston do: he "'want[s] to talk the dialect of [Jethro's] people'" because "'Its [*sic*] no use of talking unless people understand what you say'" (121).

Jethro's relationship with Moses is also finally an instrumental one sustained by Jethro's desire for power and awareness of the role Moses can play in helping him "become the wealthiest man in Midian" (145). As Mentu had suggested, all love is tempered with something; in Jethro's case, it is not lizard-talk and open communication but plenty and power that underlie his attachment to Moses: "'We all love you. . . . look what you have done for us. You came and found us in a pretty low state. Me a chief that had next to no power and you have built me up around here. You found our cattle gone and got us more than we had. Why, we are eating high on the hog now, and all because you are here with us'" (140). Jethro is also attracted to Moses because he is the best "'piece of ruling material'" (159) Jethro has ever seen. Although he is delighted that Moses is "'Just full of that old monarch stuff'" (125), such qualities, suggesting a propensity to lord over the common people, are not ideals of Hurston's.

Moses may possess these "talents," but in the early part of his relationship with Jethro, he is not interested in developing them. For quite a time, Moses is adamant about his beliefs, insisting on "asking Nature her secrets" (158) and listening to her answers. Taking on the task of persuading Moses to change his plans, Jethro reveals himself to be a "teacher" (128) very different from Mentu, one who directs Moses to Nature for the purposes not of communing with it but of extracting the information needed to control it. With this technological wizardry, Jethro plans for Moses to gain, not wisdom or understanding, but power and control, the status of "King over all the local chiefs" (145), who " 'looks like God' " (275) to the common people.

As a mentor, Jethro uses methods that are also quite different from Mentu's. Instead of the selfless affection and respect that Mentu showed Moses, Jethro, seeing Moses' desire to study as "a serious failing" (145), repeatedly expresses scorn for Moses' interest in Nature and thought. When Moses leaves in search of the magic book, Jethro again reveals his insensitivity to the kind of power and understanding Mentu valued; for Jethro, power is mere strategic advantage: " 'You go down and come back with the power, if it is to be had. It might come in handy some time' " (149).

That Jethro is a consummate despot, one who knows how "to handle" people (274), is also evident in the ways he engages his student. Instead of the narratives fostering spiritual growth that Mentu tells, Jethro "teaches" through lecture, argument, and directive. In their conversations, far from two-way, non-hierarchical interchanges, Jethro is a symbolic attacker and Moses the victim. Even though delicate in his approach at first, Jethro "never let up on the subject [of freeing the Hebrews]. Moses kept on refusing but it got harder and harder to do so. Jethro had a feather touch but he crowded Moses farther and farther into a corner until Moses went around with a harried look" (158). When persuasive argument and gentle persuasion fail, Jethro resorts to more devious methods. Keenly aware of Moses' devotion to the mountain, he dangles it like a carrot before Moses, forbidding him to go up to the mountain without permission (128) and promising to take him when he is " 'ready' " (136). In one of the novel's most iconoclastic revisions of biblical history, Hurston strongly suggests that Jethro single-handedly orchestrates the Burning Bush episode to ensure that Moses will go into

Egypt and return with Hebrew followers. Worried that Moses will change camps after reading the magic book in Egypt, he plans a dramatic use of his own hoodoo powers, announcing in a telling aside: "'Well, he might think I'm through with the thing, but first and last he's going to find out different. I ain't been to Koptos, it is true, and had no fight with no never-dying snake, but maybe there is still something about snakes that he can learn. The backside of that mountain may be too hot to hold him yet'" (159).

Describing the bush with a convenient rock under it (160) to hide Jethro while he creates the illusion of fire, Hurston strongly suggests that Jethro, still Moses' "master in magic" (144), orchestrates this scene to further his control over him. Jethro, in fact, creates Yahweh in this section, becoming the voice of the God who directs Moses' actions. In striking but predictable ways since for Hurston "Gods always behave like the people who make them" (*Tell My Horse*, 232), Jethro fashions a god like himself, a stern patriarch, a "great voice" (160) who "command[s]" (161) Moses to pick up a snake (161) and "order[s]" (161) him to go into Egypt. Inspiring "fear" (161) like Joe Starks and other of Hurston's "big voices," Yahweh squelches the voices of his followers, telling Moses (when he expresses concern about his ability to communicate with the Hebrews), "'I'll speak for you'" (162).[14] In addition to demanding silence, this god also degrades and humiliates his worshipers so that even someone as courageous as Moses is reduced to an abject wretch, "shrivel[ling] and shr[i]nk[ing]" (161) in his presence. From this point forward in the novel, "god" is no longer a bi-sexual concept such as that expressed by Mentu or embodied in the Egyptian myth of Isis and Osiris but another oppressive patriarch, the "god" worshiped by Joe Starks and Jim Meserve. Usurping the mother's abode on the mountain, this father demands gratitude and uses murder to enforce it; when people return to their African gods, the Voice cavalierly tells Moses, "'Go stop them before I get too tired of their ingratitude and kill them'" (288). For Hurston, this God, who epitomizes the Western world he will eventually rule over, is an unnatural father, who instead of supporting life, denies it.

In the Burning Bush episode, Hurston further reveals the philosophical significance of this new God in her description of the snake transformed into a walking stick. In addition to reducing this awesome and miraculous evidence of Jehovah's power to the status of staple trick of Egyptian magicians, Hurston makes this episode a quite symbolic turning point in Moses' life and in human history. The "serpent" (162), so richly associated with Mentu and Isis, understanding of Nature and wisdom, becomes from Jethro's and Jehovah's influence, a "lifeless thing" (162), in fact, a phallic "rod" (162) of oppressive power in Moses' hands. With such a radical philosophical shift, once the "serpent . . . become[s] a rod" (163), everything changes, so much so that both for Moses and for the Hebrews who accept this new religion, "Life could never be again what it once was" (163).

When Moses vows to take Jethro for his father (124), to adopt his gods and his ways, and to give Jethro his life to use as he sees fit (143), he betrays Mentu and his own earlier beliefs. Forsaking the mother and rejecting the feminine, following the voice only of the father, Moses comes more and more to resemble the Pharaoh he despises so that it is more than a mirage that the Presence of Moses' God descending on Mount Sinai resembles "a Pharaoh assuming his throne" (278). Using his own rod of power in equally oppressive ways, he lets himself be led by values that recreate a system as racist, sexist, and oppressive as that governed by the Pharaoh. Like the god he worships, Moses finally rules by command, becoming such an "absolute rule and law-giver" (345) and overbearing "bossman" (224) that the people soon recognize they have "just swapped one Pharaoh for another one" (296).

Because Moses is as adept as John Pearson at "washing himself with his tongue like a cat," this portrait jars with comments Moses himself makes about his mission. Rather than his coercion and cruelty, he stresses his selflessness and consistent refusal to crown himself king. The significance of this refusal is qualified, however, by Moses' own earlier astute observation about titles. When Jethro advises him to seize power but to forego the title of king, Moses—who, at this point, still remembers Mentu—responds, " 'Jethro, it's not the title I am afraid of, it's the thing itself. It makes no difference what he calls himself, king or ruler, who sends the young men out to be killed and takes the people's cattle away from them. Titles ain't nothing but nicknames' " (158). Although Moses may never wear a crown or bear the title of king, he becomes "the thing" he describes. Taking more than cattle from people he conquers, spending a "whole day counting up and dividing the spoils taken from the Amalekites. Horses, cows, mules, camels, women, wine and jewelry" (261), he becomes more ruthless than the rogues he had defeated for Jethro years earlier.

In becoming such a stern patriarch, Moses increasingly cuts himself off from the female side of his soul and his everyday, domestic life. While he had early felt (much to Jethro's distress) that "'a whole life-time would be too short to search out all [Zipporah's] wonders'" (134), under Jethro's tutelage, he gradually forsakes his wife and family. His public mission wars with his private life (302) until finally, as Moses admits, Zipporah "'los[es] the husband [she] used to have'" (267). Losing contact with and respect for a set of values Hurston associates symboli-cally with the feminine, Moses gradually becomes as sexist as Jethro. Instead of embracing Miriam as an equal, he consistently treats her in a condescending manner, showing no respect for her role in the liberation of the Hebrews by "gather[ing] folks together by twos and threes and chang[ing] weakness into resolution" (323). Despite the fact that she is "'a two-headed woman with power'" (171) and "a big prophet" (268), Moses lets her participate in his mission only because "'she would be useful in handling the women'" (171). In his response to Miriam, Moses shows how far he has come from his early days. In contrast to his former egalitarian belief that women should participate in both the public and private spheres—including even battle—he has by this time come to see women's "natural" place as the home. When Miriam criticizes him, Moses responds in the voice of Jethro, Joe Starks, or Jim Meserve; he denigrates Miriam (described in "Just Like Us" as "the first Women's rights champion" [2, SC]) as a frustrated spinster who only meddles in worldly affairs because she has no man: "'Miss Miriam, your case is piti-ful. The trouble with you is that nobody ever married you. And when a woman ain't got no man to look after, she takes on the world in place of the man she missed'" (300). One of Hurston's many feisty women, Miriam refuses to play the role of worshiper that Joshua so eagerly as-sumes. Like Big Sweet, she "specifies," speaking out against the injustices and class inequalities characterizing Moses' rule (269). When she persists in defying Moses' authority, he heartlessly curses her with leprosy and banishes her for seven days, a spiritual defeat from which she never re-covers.[15]

As this episode suggests, compassion is another spiritual loss for Moses once he becomes obsessed with political power. To stress this change, Hurston embellishes her biblical source to include brief but graphic descriptions of the suffering Moses decrees. For instance, after the death of the Pharaoh and the Egyptians at the Red Sea, Moses gazes on a sight of human carnage, "the dead bodies of the Egyptian soldiers . . . flung up along the shore in scores, flung helter-skelter like dolls"

(243). Moses is "torn by the pitiful sight of all the sudden death" (243) but immediately rationalizes that defeat would have been worse for his victims. Cutting himself off from his feelings, focusing only on his goal of creating a Hebrew state, seeing people as more or less effective "instruments" in his cause, Moses repeatedly commands harsh and gratuitous cruelty. As early as the plagues, he focuses not on the suffering his actions cause but on their strategic efficacy to show the power of his new god and to recruit followers. Moses never seems to notice that the people who must suffer include many more than the Pharaoh himself, but Hurston includes details that remind the reader of this human reality. During the plague of darkness, for instance, the ones who perish are not the Pharaoh or even his family, but "Old ones, sick and poor; children, women trampled to death during the darkness when the nation was stampeded by fear" (218). Although Moses never notices the parallels, his curse of death on Egyptian firstborn children punishes the innocent as cruelly as the Pharaoh's own earlier decree that Hebrew male infants die.[16]

The change in Moses' ethics is graphically reflected in his final conversation with Aaron on Mount Hor. He reveals, for instance, how thoroughly his mission is grounded in duplicity, admitting his lie in telling Aaron that he had been called by God. Knowing Aaron will not live to tell this fact, Moses now admits that "'I thought I needed you for the big job I had to do because you were of the Hebrews" (333). Moses also uses God as an excuse for his own ruthlessness; whereas he tells Aaron he must die because the Lord said "all the old folks who came out of Egypt had to die in the wilderness" (331), the text had earlier made it clear that this was Moses' own decision after the Golden Calf episode (316–17). As this last act suggests, human beings no longer matter to Moses. Whatever is required to make a great nation is legitimate regardless of its toll on individual women and men. Admitting that "'nothing and nobody has been spared to make this nation great'" (335), Moses repeatedly (and often inadvertently) acknowledges in this final conversation with Aaron the brutality of his leadership. When Aaron complains, for instance, that Moses killed his sons after the Golden Calf episode "'Just for dancing and making a little ceremony before a god of Egypt that we had always known'" (335), Moses, twisting the meaning of words beyond recognition, claims that he did not kill Aaron's sons but rather an idea: "'What they signified had to die if Israel was to be great'" (335). Moses here further reveals the kind of inhumanity that can result when political expediency is the ultimate value: "'Aaron, the future of Israel is higher than pity and mercy'" (335). It is higher also than human happiness; for as Aaron points out Moses has failed to make his people happy (332). In his response ("'I never said I'd make them happy people. I promised to make them great'" [332]), Moses unintentionally highlights how divorced from human needs his mission ultimately is. This project takes its toll on Moses as well as his followers. Forsaking feelings and relationships, he has (as he tells Aaron) been forced to "'quit being a person . . . [and] to become a thing, a tool, and instrument for a cause'" (334).[17] Thus, it is no surprise that when Aaron has served his purpose of propping up Moses' leadership and begins to question it, Moses murders him in premeditated (311) cold blood so that he can install (as Hurston had suggested in her outline [4, SC]) his more subservient son as high priest.

The values Yahweh and Moses stand for are as clearly evident in the state he creates as in his relationships with people. Again, Moses' words and actions rarely mesh. Despite his claim that possessions in the Pharaoh's world only "stir up ambition and create unhappiness" (244) and that "'Leaders have to be people who give up things [rather than] people who grab things'" (263), the society Moses molds is as crassly materialistic as the Pharaoh's Egypt. Willing to pay any price for his warped concept of freedom, Moses, instead of teaching the people the meaning of spiritual freedom, reinstitutes the state finery he had earlier rejected, giving Aaron and Miriam "'rich regalia to dress in to keep [them] from feeling like slaves again'" (263). Although Moses may personally forego flashy wealth, he self-consciously (and hypocritically) makes his wife "'as elegant as Pharaoh'" (267), decking her out with some "'jewelry out of Egypt and a few Amalekite pieces [he] saved for her from the stuff after the battle'" (266). He forgets his earlier insight about material wealth, but the Hebrews' jealousy of Zipporah's ornaments proves how much "ambition" and "suspicion" the Pharaoh's kind of wealth breeds. Moses, again forgetting Mentu's teaching about the folly of grandiose monuments, even creates burial tombs "greater than Pharaoh" (336) for Miriam (323), Aaron (336), and himself (349).

As Moses' new state demonstrates, a religion based on intimidation and coercion quite logically leads to a society based on laws and commandments. When power loses its rich associations with understanding and degenerates into force, orders rather than conversations become central. Working with a notion of power as control, Moses takes "the ten words of power and he made ten commandments out of them" (281). As always, his stated motive for developing rules sounds quite lofty (and self-congratulatory): "Now men could be free because they could govern themselves. They had something of the essence of divinity expressed in order. They had the chart and compass of behavior. They need not stumble into blind ways and injure themselves. This was bigger than Israel itself. It comprehended the world. Israel could be a heaven for all men forever, by these sacred stones" (285). The exalted rhetoric notwithstanding, Moses' attitudes about human behavior jar with many values Hurston held dear. "Order," a "chart and compass" in human behavior, may seem desirable for Moses, but for Hurston such words connote "pigeonholes," restriction, and oppression. Further, Moses' desire to "save" people from injuring themselves is a trap into which Mentu and the mature Janie (who knows that experience is the only real teacher since "'you have tuh go there tuh *know* there'" [*Their Eyes Were Watching God*, 285]) would never have fallen. He even forgets his own earlier awareness, learned from Mentu, that "'You have to go to life to know life'" (105). Moses' aspirations to be the law-giver not just for the Hebrews but for the whole world would also have troubled Hurston, bothered as she was by economic and cultural imperialism in her own day. Even within its own borders, the state Moses creates is no "heaven"; despite Moses' confidence that "Israel is going to know peace and justice" (285), events immediately suggest that "rules" cannot create such a utopia.

Hurston's critique of Moses and the ethic underlying the Western world also stems from the nature of his laws. Striking first of all is their sheer number. Just as the Pharaoh had rules for every aspect of human life to the point (as the Hebrews note) of absurdity, Moses writes laws to govern almost every aspect of human life. Like the Pharaoh, Moses develops rules that conflict with nature and ultimately deny life. How unnecessary many of these are—except to curb happiness and "squinch the spirit"—is clear when Jethro chastises Moses (as he does frequently) for sleeping with his wife. Moses rejects such silly prudery in a voice as exuberant and as light-hearted as Tea Cake's: "'I believe I'm guilty [of hurrying to Zipporah's tent]. It's your daughter's fault. It's a shame the way this woman keeps me running after her, but it looks like there ain't no help for it. I reckon I'll have to keep it up until I die'" (272). In another hypocritical repression of his followers, however, Moses almost immediately orders the Hebrews not to sleep with their husbands and wives (278), promulgating a rule as fundamentally unnatural as the

Pharaoh's control of "the Hebrew womb." Instead of affirming life, as Mentu had urged and as Isis and Osiris had symbolized, Moses forgets Mother Nature and becomes himself the unnatural, life-denying father of the Hebrews.[18]

For Hurston, these developments constitute not a gain but a loss for humankind. As she reveals in the Golden Calf episode, this intense battle is one between two very different but powerful worldviews. Even a man as imposing as Moses cannot easily destroy the religious and cultural legacy of Egypt. When he destroys the altar built in his absence, the battle is still not over: "The law from Sinai had broken the idol of Egypt, but the sacred tablets had themselves been destroyed in the clash. Egypt against Sinai. It was going to be a hard struggle" (289). Hurston revises biblical history here to present Egypt, the historical loser in this battle, as the cultural better. The "sinners" have, after all, merely sacrificed to gods who nurture and care for them, Isis who "'will sure help you if you pray to her and pray right'" (282–83) and Apis who "'[n]ever [did] go back on us'" (283). Their life-affirming pagan worship offers a stark contrast to the repression and denial Moses enforces. Hurston's rendition of this ceremony echoes many other celebrations that she has joyfully described in her other works. After worshiping, "Then they finished the altar part of it and got up to play. They cast off clothes and they cast off care. Drums and cymbals and harps and voices singing loud and happy. Shining bodies moved and turned and collided joyfully. Maidens danced in ecstasy with closed eyes and nobody looked too closely at faces. Joy was the feeling, joy!" (284). The "wild and savage shout of voices and drum" (285) that so sickens Moses is for Hurston an example of Africa's rich cultural expression. Whereas he (like Mrs. Turner or Joe Starks) sees filth (288) when he descends to the sight of revelry, Hurston sees in this celebration the life-affirming exuberance characterizing African song and dance from West Africa, to the Caribbean, to the Jook of the rural South. What is lost when this African culture is crushed by a repressive, rule-bound one is significant for her: "Before Apis and Aaron [the people] were clothed in joy, and license. Before Moses and Sinai they were naked to their souls" (289).

Moses' response to such spontaneity is that of a stern father who punishes ruthlessly for disobedience. Standing ominously before the people "like a crucifix" (292), he once more orders mass murder, this time of his own people and for the "sin" of joyful self-expression, telling his followers: "'You all know what a foul thing has happened in Israel today. You know better than I do who the leaders and agitators were. If this is to be a great nation, it must be purged of such evil-doers, or all Israel must perish. You have you eager weapons, men. Spare not a soul who is guilty'" (292). Nowhere does Hurston show more graphically "the terror" of Moses and the deadliness of his god than in this scene.[19]

Near the end of the novel, Moses looks out on the nation of Israel, proud of this "sight such as the world had never seen before" (344), a nation "set apart from other nations" (344). While he (and history) judge this "a splendid and orderly sight—a magnificent spectacle" (344), a step forward for human civilization, Hurston strongly hints that it is culture no different in fundamental values than the one the Pharaoh created, one claiming the same exclusivity of its god (16) and intensified nationalism. Superficially different in appearance—Tabernacle and the Tent of the Testimony instead of pyramids and graven images—it is quite similar inside with its "gold and silver vessels, and candlesticks and basins. The rich and jewelled vestments of the priests and attendants and the instruments of worship" (344). Just as the Presence descends like the Pharaoh assuming his throne, the Tabernacle sits "brooding in the plain and hovering its mysteries like the sphinx" (344). Even Moses seems aware that something valuable has been lost in what he has created. As he tells Joshua rather mournfully, "'I have made a nation, but at a price'" (336). And at a high one for Hurston, for he has sacrificed equality, communion with Nature, openness to other people and to experience, and finally happiness to create such a spectacle. Also significant for Hurston is the loss of individuality and personal freedom that results from exclusive focus on "the nation." As Moses admits to Joshua, he has had to squelch both to achieve his abstract political goal: "'You can't have a state of individuals. Everybody just cannot be allowed to do as they please. I love liberty and I love freedom, so I started off giving everybody a loose rein. But I soon found out that it wouldn't do'" (340).

In another blasphemous revision of her biblical source, Hurston shows Moses recognizing the error in his ways late in life. He seems to realize, for instance, that his goal of "giving" the Hebrews freedom has been fundamentally misguided:

> He had meant to make a perfect people, free and just, noble and strong, that should be a light for all the world and for time and eternity. And he wasn't sure he had succeeded. He had found out that no man may make another free. Freedom was something internal. The outside signs were just signs and symbols of the man inside. All you could do was to give

the opportunity for freedom and the man must make his own emancipation. (344)

His aim to make freedom "eternal," he now realizes, was also impossible, for no genuinely human experience is everlasting: " 'This freedom is a funny thing. . . . It ain't something permanent like rocks and hills. It's like manna; you just got to keep on gathering it fresh every day. If you don't, one day you're going to find you aint' got no more' " (327). Recognizing the impossibility of permanence given the temporality of human experience, Moses here echoes the kind of understanding Janie arrives at by the end of *Their Eyes Were Watching God*. Love, like freedom, is not a material commodity but a fluid experience, different for each human being: " 'love ain't somethin' lak uh grindstone *dat's* de same thing everywhere and do de same thing tuh everything it touch. Love is lak de sea. It's uh movin' thing, but still and all, it takes its shape from de shore it meets, and it's different with every shore' " (*Eyes*, 284). Moses' own understanding of human individuality leads him to a more modest assessment of his project than he has yet uttered: "They might not be absolutely free inside, but anyway he had taken from them the sorrow of serving without will, and had given them the strife of freedom. He had called to their memories the forgotten words of love and family. They had the blessing of being responsible for their own" (346). Most important in any society, he now realizes, is not "order," "power," or "the state," but humbler domestic matters—the freedom to love strenuously, to bear and raise children as one chooses, and, in the words of Amy in *Jonah's Gourd Vine*, to "treasure" them.

By the end of the novel, Moses longs once more for human happiness. Drawn once more to the sphere of "female" domesticity and suddenly yearning to be with his family, he looks forward to conversing with Zipporah about "simple things . . . like asking about who was still living and who was dead and things like that" (348). Hoping that "the Voice wouldn't trouble him again" (348), he seeks a similar kind of communion with Nature and yearns again to contemplate her mysteries (348). As these passages suggest, Moses here misses the life Mentu had earlier taught him to value. Even more radically, Hurston suggests that Moses returns at the end of his life to the social values and religious sentiments he has spent much of his life trying to destroy.[20] She makes this important point by reintroducing powerful allusions to Mentu in her seemingly whimsical conclusion to the novel. While Moses builds the tomb that will shroud his escape in mystery, he encounters a talking lizard who speaks to him of a "'glorious time'" when "'[his] ancestors ruled the world'" (349). When Moses expresses interest in such stories, the lizard directs Moses to another lizard, the "'keeper of memories'" (350): "'Listen,'" he says, "'you must go east to a great mountain called Sinai and climb to the very top. There is a great flat stone on the very top and on that stone is another stone that is the very peak. And under that peak stone, and resting on the flat stone, is a bearded lizard who knows all the things that used to be'" (350–51).

This lizard echoes Mentu in important ways. Just as the bearded lizard will tell Moses "'how the world was made, and the heavens'" (351), Mentu used to tell Moses "tales of creation": "Those first days of the world, which he called the 'Kingdom Age,' when people lived as long as trees" (61). Furthermore, Mentu often used the lizard as a voice through which to speak his wisdom to the youthful Moses. It was through the lizard, for instance, that Mentu had gently chided Moses for his attraction to grandiose monuments. Mentu had also playfully drawn parallels between himself and the lizard who "'is old like me and a little hungry like me'" (58) to get food from Moses. Hurston echoes this scene in the novel's conclusion; just as the youthful Moses had produced a swarm of flies for the lizard (59) and some food from the Pharaoh's table for Mentu, Moses (almost as if he senses Mentu's presence) at the end of the novel "produce[s] a small swarm of flies" (350) for his lizard friend to eat.

In making such extensive allusions to Mentu here at the end of the novel, Hurston drastically revises her biblical source, underscoring how completely Moses reevalutes his life and his beliefs. At the end of the novel, he returns not to the Decalogue for the answers he needs but to an older, African folklore. To obtain these answers Moses must journey back to Sinai, to listen not to Yahweh's voice but to "lizard-talk," the African foundation buried under Judeo-Christian tradition. Spiritually seeking Mentu and his own personal and cultural roots at this point, Moses actually abandons the religion with which he is associated in European culture. "Turn[ing] away from his memories of fire-spitting mountains and night-vigils with God" (351) and turning his back on Israel, Moses finally "crosses over" by "head[ing] back" (351)—like Hurston herself—to his African traditions and the alternatives to Jim Meserve's world they offer.

6 "With a Harp and a Sword in My Hand": Black Female Identity in *Dust Tracks on a Road*

WHEN HURSTON CAME TO treat a black woman's search for identity in describing her own life, she emphasized that (like so many of her characters) she too grew up in a racial and gendered world of "mules and men," facing many of the obstacles experienced by black women in her earlier works and struggling against the dominant cultural definitions of blackness and womanhood. Striving to avoid the "diminished" fate of white women and black people who in Jim Meserve's world merely accept powerlessness and acquiesce to domination, Hurston, in her autobiography as in her other works, finds images of wholeness, strength, and power for black women not in the gods and seraphs of Jim Meserve's world but in mythic black traditions. While images of titanic power guide her own sense of identity and often shape her treatment of issues in her autobiography, Hurston ultimately emphasizes the necessity of flexibility in a world of "mules and men." Carefully assessing power relations in her own life and charting her varied responses to them, Hurston underscores the importance of black women learning when to fight and when to negotiate or dissemble, when to specify and when to signify, when to be a "tiger" and when to be a trickster.

Not only about the difficulties of self-affirmation in a world of mules and men, Hurston's autobiography was written by a woman immersed in the same milieu. No work more graphically demonstrates the problems Hurston encountered in trying to negotiate her heterogenous audience or more deeply challenges the early blithe optimism about doing so expressed in "Drenched in Light." As a black woman of several major works, two Guggenheim awards, and considerable fame (as she reminds the readers of her autobiography [212]), she originally planned to specify in Big Sweet fashion in her autobiography, to speak out against values of the dominant world when embraced by whites or blacks.[1] Although her experience with editors suggests that Hurston had perhaps misgauged that audience and the power of her own arsenal to confront it directly, she had at her disposal another discursive strategy learned from High John and black women with their keys. Without sufficient power "to stand off a panzer division," she finally took the trickster's approach, veiling her critique of Jim Meserve's world instead of "giving a reading on it." This discursive flexibility, Hurston's judgments even as she wrote about when she could play the titan with her sword and when she needed to be the trickster with a harp, results in a profoundly ambiguous autobiography that reveals more about her position as a black woman writer than about the paradoxes of her personality or the contradictions in her views.

The fundamental ambiguity of Hurston's autobiography is reflected in the extremely divergent response to the work at the time of its publication. As with so many of her works, white reviewers, applauding its "gusto" (Rose) and "robust" "exuberan[ce]" (*Booklist*), focused on the richness of Hurston's colloquial language, "her graphic metaphors and similes" (Sherman) and her stylistic "seasoning—not overdone—of the marvelous locutions of the imaginative field nigger" (Stong, 6). They also praised the lusty humor of the book, one (in the words of one reviewer) "as vivid as a poinsettia, as beautiful as Cape Jasmine—and as vulgar as a well-liquored fish-fry" (Chamberlain). Many responded quite positively to Hurston's seemingly noncombative treatment of race, approving specifically of her arguments against race consciousness. Stong, for instance, expressed relief that "The race-consciousness that spoils so much Negro literature is completely absent here" (7) and praised as "sensible" (7) her belief "that if the stuff is in you it is likely to come out and that if it isn't it doesn't make any difference whether you are white, black, green, or cerise" (7). Chamberlain also singles out this aspect of *Dust Tracks* for praise, announcing that "one fully understands her contempt for people who generalize about 'the Negro problem,' or 'the race issue.'" His reasons for recommending the book involved exactly the issues that would trouble others: "If you want to feel warm inside about a concrete individual at one end of the scale, and the whole of the American democracy at the other, 'Dust Tracks on a Road' is a book among a hundred for you to read."

Sensing how "heart-warming" (and how reassuring) *Dust Tracks* would be for many readers, other reviewers criticized Hurston for pandering to white readers in her treatment of race. In "From Eatonville, Florida to Harlem," Arna Bontemps sarcastically points to Hurston's personal relationships with whites, the "line of substantial friends who saw in the exuberant unspoiled colored girl the kind of Negro they wanted to encourage," and sees her desire to ingratiate herself with them as the central shaping force behind her approach to race: "Miss Hurston deals very simply with the more serious aspects of Negro life in America—she ignores them. She has done right well by herself in the kind of world she found." Harold Preece, reviewing the book in *Tomorrow,* even more bitterly called the book "the tragedy of a gifted, sensitive mind, eaten up by an egocentrism fed on the patronizing admiration of the dominant white world."[2]

Even with Hemenway's publication of chapters deleted before publication that show how Hurston originally planned a much more critical and confrontational ending to her book, *Dust Tracks on a Road* seems fundamentally contradictory, alternately an affirmation of racist stereotypes and a testament to black pride. Hurston's repeated references to ambiguous experiences and the difficulty of interpreting them suggest, however, her awareness of the tensions and contradictions her book, in its final form, would display. The very phrase itself—"My People! My People!"—can, she points out, have two radically different meanings. Uttered by upper-class blacks, it expresses the distance they wish to feel from the behavior of blacks they see as beneath them (215–17). The very same words can, however, express the opposite feeling:

> Maybe at the other end of the coach another couple are saying the same
> thing but with a different emotion. They say it with a chuckle. They
> have enjoyed the show, and they are saying in the same tone of voice
> that a proud father uses when he boasts to others about that bad little
> boy of his at home. "Mischievous, into everything, beats up all the kids
> in the neighborhood. Don't know what I'm going to do with the little
> rascal." That's the way some folks say the thing. (293)

Dust Tracks on a Road displays a similar kind of paradoxical complexity. Far from providing the straightforward proof of her false consciousness some have seen there, it is rather deeply ambiguous, a form of "double talk" (62) like that Hurston heard on Eatonville's porch-front or in the dressing rooms of actors with the drama troupe (137). As Hurston herself learned as she became skillful at deciphering this language, the "outside meaning" of words is often not the intended message. What Hurston says about the expression, "My People! My People!" is equally true of her autobiography: "It is the interpretation that is difficult" (291).[3]

Hinting at the complexity of her own experience at the very beginning of *Dust Tracks on a Road,* Hurston stresses the importance of her roots for understanding who she is:

> Like the dead-seeming, cold rocks, I have memories within that came out of the material that went to make me. Time and place have had their say.
> So you will have to know something about the time and place where I came from, in order that you may interpret the incidents and directions of my life. (3)

The rest of the chapter, which details the history of Eatonville, provides a key for deciphering Hurston's personal history. If one looks at Eatonville in the present, one sees an all-black town, but behind this appearance lies a very complicated history. Hurston's unusual hometown was not born as a black town; rather, she suggests, "Eatonville is what you might call hitting a straight lick with a crooked stick. The town was not in the original plan. It is a by-product of something else" (3). Oddly enough, as she describes its history, Eatonville was the "by-product" of white actions, from the three white "adventurers" who originally settled there to the white property owners who donated the land.

In telling the story of Eatonville Hurston stresses the benevolent good will of whites. When black people came to work in white Maitland, they found "The best of relations . . . between employer and employee" (8) and an Edenic-sounding place to live: "No more backbending over rows of cotton; no more fear of the fury of the Reconstruction. Good pay, sympathetic white folks and cheap land" (8). This paradise of racial harmony, Hurston suggests, continues into the present: "White Maitland and Negro Eatonville have lived side by side for fifty-six years without a single instance of enmity. The spirit of the founders has reached beyond the grave" (10–11).

This strand in Eatonville's history (which seems to suggest that race is socially unproblematic and even inconsequential) is not, however, the whole story Hurston tells in this first chapter, for she describes another set of "founders," in addition to Captains Lawrence and Eaton, in Eatonville's past. As she points out, the place was not always a racial

Eden but once a "dark and bloody country" (4) in which Indians and black slaves joined forces in war against whites. Indian chiefs such as Miccanopy, Billy Bow-legs, and Osceola who led these insurrections are thus an equally important part of the "material that went to make" (3) Hurston. Had Osceola not been captured, Hurston points out, history would have been quite different from the harmonious situation she describes; in fact, "the struggle would have lasted much longer than it did" (5). This duality in Eatonville's past parallels that in Hurston's autobiography, for both histories are only superficially expressions of idealized race relations. Beneath the placid exterior of her hometown, buried in "the dead-seeming, cold rocks" of Hurston's past, lies war, a defiance of oppression very much a part of both "the material that went to make [her]" (3) and of her autobiography.

The published version of *Dust Tracks on a Road* is a discomfiting book because Hurston rarely expresses her defiance directly. Often "hitting a straight lick with a crooked stick" instead, she repeatedly emphasizes the necessity of this skill for a black woman to survive in a world that conspires to "squinch [her] spirit" and silence her voice. Documenting numerous instances in which her own iconoclastic voice had been silenced during her childhood, Hurston indicates that this problem was no less serious in her adult writing career. Although the "psychic bond" (175) between Hurston and Mrs. Charlotte Osgood Mason may have been real, Hurston must have felt equally real the psychic violence in her "lacerat[ing]" rebuke, " 'Keep silent. Does a child in the womb speak?' " (176), and her control (including legal ownership) of Hurston's words. At times the silencing is more subtle but no less real in effect. When Hurston describes the writing of *Jonah's Gourd Vine,* she emphasizes the difficulty of writing a story that "was not what was expected" (206) by publishers and readers. Because her story "seemed off-key" (206), "I was afraid to tell a story the way I wanted, or rather the way the story told itself to me" (206).

One of the few black women in *Dust Tracks on a Road* who seems immune to such pressures is Big Sweet. If a black woman can "back [her] crap"—and Big Sweet certainly can—then she may engage in straightforward verbal assault; in *Dust Tracks on a Road* (as in *Mules and Men*), Big Sweet is constantly "specifying," "giving readings," and otherwise taking on all opponents. As Hurston suggests, however, this behavior is reserved for very few:

If you are sufficiently armed—enough to stand off a panzer division—
and know what to do with your weapons after you get 'em, it is all
right to go to the house of your enemy, put one foot up on his steps,
rest one elbow on your knee and play in the family. That is another way
of saying play the dozens, which also is a way of saying low-rate your
enemy's ancestors and him, down to the present moment for reference,
and then go into his future as far as your imagination leads you. But if
you have no faith in your personal courage and confidence in your arsenal, don't try it. It is a risky pleasure. (187)

Rather than risk this pleasure, Hurston shows herself throughout the
published version of *Dust Tracks on a Road* taking the indirect verbal
route to survival, often quite unabashedly lying to authority figures
when necessary.[4] The response by her father and his colleagues to her
"analysis" of religion ("It seemed to me that somebody had been fooled"
[268]) taught her the price of thoughtless honesty: "When they got
through with me, I knew better than to say that out loud again" (268).
Her questions remain, but "When I was asked if I loved God, I always
said yes because I knew that that was the thing I was supposed to say"
(268). In addition to lying to one of the editors of Lippincott's about the
book she was supposedly working on ("Mind you, not the first word
was on paper when I wrote him that letter" [209]), Hurston includes
another revealing anecdote about her early literary experience. Significantly, her "first publication" (153), tacked to the blackboard at Morgan,
was an "allegory" (153) poking fun at the administrators of the school.
This training in the trickster's more covert method of attack, which was
to serve Hurston throughout her literary career, is evident in the published version of *Dust Tracks on a Road*. Although (as the chapters restored by Hemenway suggest) Hurston planned her most open and confrontational treatment of race in her autobiography, her experience with
editors in writing this autobiography merely reconfirmed her understanding of how black women had often best dealt with powerful
whites. Instead of being silenced or abandoning her message, she finds
an indirect way to express herself.

One of the ways Hurston camouflages racial conflict and critical
commentary in her autobiography (and one of the reasons some have
found the book politically naive and hopelessly ahistorical) is by casting
her story in the form of timeless myth, one shaped as a quest, grounded
in visions, and filled with allusions to European myths.[5] Its language and
tone evoke the placidity and universality of fairytale, a world seemingly

unsullied by mundane social problems. As Hurston uses this mythic material, however, it is just as rooted in the sociopolitical realities of race and gender as the folktales in *Mules and Men* are. Myths function as both mask and vehicle for her racial analysis and for her treatment of specific whites in her life.

The complex way in which Hurston deals with race is foreshadowed in her discussion of her first encounter with whites from outside her hometown. Cast as a mythic initiation ritual, Hurston's anecdote is, on the surface, bothersome because of the idealized conception of race relations it seems to depict. The story is especially discomfiting, occurring as it does in the chapter, "The Inside Search," one filled with examples of black people's repression and rejection of her as a child. Like "Drenched in Light," however, with which it is closely related, this story has two quite distinct and opposing levels of meaning. Superficially, the story details the beneficence of the two white fairy godmothers, mysterious supernatural figures with strange "baby pink" fingertips (48) who rescue the extraordinary child hidden in poverty. Faced with the trial of reading a passage from the myth of Persephone and Ceres, the young Zora passes the test and is invited to the royal palace (in this case, the Park Hotel) where she feasts on what must have seemed the equivalent of ambrosia for a Southern black girl—"strange things, like stuffed dates and preserved ginger" (51). Passing her final reading test, she is then given an appropriately mysterious and mythical-sounding present, "a heavy cylinder done up in fancy paper, tied with a ribbon" (51).

Another carefully crafted "allegory," this story presents a more complicated view of the dynamics of relationships between blacks and whites than initially seems the case. Beneath apparent racial harmony, white benevolence, and Hurston's own seeming enthusiasm for being elevated above and set apart from her fellow black children lies an extended, astute analysis of white patronage. Hurston, first of all, subtly suggests a motive more complicated than simple benevolence behind white patronage. Just as the woman in "Drenched in Light" ultimately embraces Isis for a selfish reason (her need for warmth and light), the Northern whites Hurston describes have their own personal reasons for visiting black schools. Not so very different from many white enthusiasts during the Harlem Renaissance, these women approach a black world with a certain degree of voyeuristic "curiosity" (46) about the "strange" (46) exoticism of another culture. As white supporters and patrons later in Hurston's life would, these people too "came and went, came and went" (46). Hurston's "fairytale" thus highlights a harsh racial truth: white interest in black folks' talents (as history after the Harlem Renaissance and as Hurston's own personal experience proved) is transitory, waxing and waning in whimsical and, for black artists, uncontrollable fashion.

Further, Hurston's gifts come with strings attached, for she is not simply given fine things; she must perform for them. The white women, who define what she must do to win her prize, not surprisingly construct her test within their own cultural terms: she must read a Greco-Roman myth and *Scribner's Magazine.* The artifice of this performance is also suggested by the formulaic, prescribed role Zora must play in the presence of these women. She must, in fact, lie in this first relationship with white patrons:

> They asked me if I loved school, and I lied that I did. There was *some* truth in it, because I liked geography and reading, and I liked to play at recess time. Whoever it was invented writing and arithmetic got no thanks from me. Neither did I like the arrangement where the teacher could sit up there with a palmetto stem and lick me whenever he saw fit. I hated things I couldn't do anything about. But I knew better than to bring that up right there, so I said yes, I *loved* school. (50)

The threats to the black self and the divisive effect on black community posed by white patronage are also evident in the gifts of money and fine clothes Zora receives. The "red coat with a wide circular collar and red tam" (53), though not exactly the dashing gypsy costume of Isis in "Drenched in Light," is certainly glamorous attire for the young Zora, but Hurston underscores how these gifts, evidence of initiation into a white world, alienate her from other black people. Just as Janie was ostracized when dressed in the Washburn's cast-offs, Zora here admits: "My chums pretended not to like anything that I had, but even then I knew that they were jealous" (53).[6]

This anecdote, neither evidence of Hurston's adoration of whites nor a tragic story of cooptation, details a relationship between black girl and white adults as complicated as that in "Drenched in Light." Whereas the white people's power is undeniable—they define the tests and choose the rewards, Zora demonstrates the power tricksters always possess in Hurston's work. Even though the whites choose (often inappropriate) gifts and have their own (often culturally insensitive and chauvanistic) understanding of what they are rewarding, Zora maintains her freedom to assign very different cultural meanings to their gifts. Regardless of the meaning the white women see in the money they pay for her performance, Hurston responds to it with unsullied aesthetic sensibility: "Perhaps, I shall never experience such joy again. The nearest thing to that moment was the telegram accepting my first book. One hundred goldy-new pennies rolled out of the cylinder. Their gleam lit up the world. It was not avarice that moved me. It was the beauty of the thing" (52). Hurston's ability to sift through white culture for what meshes with her cultural values (and serves her own purposes) is also expressed in her response to the white women's gift of an Episcopal hymnbook. Instead of rejecting it as a symbol of cultural imperialism or ridiculing it for the white ignorance of black culture that it bespeaks (what *would* John Hurston's daughter need with such a hymnal?), Zora picks and chooses according to her own "inside juices" and cultural tastes. She memorizes the few songs she finds "the most beautiful" (52) and jettisons the rest: "Some of them seemed dull and without life, and I pretended they were not there. If white people like trashy singing like that, there must be something funny about them that I had not noticed before. I stuck to the pretty ones where the words marched to a throb I could feel" (52).[7]

Hurston thus reveals the complexities of white patronage and initiation into a white world. Instead of fleeing from the potential psychic damage such relationships could inflict, she depicts herself enjoying the gifts and avoiding the price, like High John de Conquer, "winning in a permanent way . . . with the soul of the black [wo]man whole and free" ("High John de Conquer," 70–71). The history of her hometown—an all-black town that "was not in the original plan" (3) of the white "explorers" but "a by-product" (3) of a white town—reinforced this lesson and demonstrated that black cultural independence can begin in the most unlikely places. That the white benefactors might have given the land simply to regain political control of their town did not (luckily) keep Hurston's cultural forebears from accepting the gift. Although Hurston's defiance of white standards and her own cultural independence was probably not part of her patrons' plan in supporting her, Hurston was never ruled by their intentions or interpretations. Very much a product of Eatonville, "the material that went to make [her]" (3), Hurston shows herself early in life, like her hometown, becoming adept at "hitting a straight lick with a crooked stick" (3).

Professions of appreciation notwithstanding, Hurston displays the same savvy understanding of other rich white patrons. The story of her

relationship with the wealthy white man who happened by at the moment she was born and assisted in the childbirth seems at first a disconcerting story of white salvation. Described as a mythic superhero, "a
centaur" (43), who "was supposed to be so tough, it was said that once
he was struck by lightning and was not even knocked off his feet, but
that lightning went off through the woods limping" (43–44), he becomes Zora's mentor, about whom she seems to express only the most
positive of feelings. Nevertheless, many quite subtle ironies lurk just beneath the surface of this story. Embedded in her breezy description of
this relationship, for instance, is a coldly realistic assessment of the white
man's feelings. Certainly not as enthusiastically as he would have acted
toward a white godchild, motivated primarily by "pride in his own
handiwork" (30), this man maintains only a "pinch of interest in [Zora's]
welfare" (30) that keeps him (irregularly) returning to see how she
is doing.[8] Although Hurston treats details with seeming good humor, it
is highly significant that the white man gives her another name,
"Snidlits," "explaining that Zora was a hell of a name to give a child"
(41). In addition to ridiculing the white man's taste in names ("Snidlits"
is, by anyone's standard, "a hell of a name to give a child"), this man's
renaming reflects the same appropriation of black identity seen in the
white people's renaming of Janie as Alphabet in *Their Eyes Were Watching God*.

The advice this man repeatedly offers—" 'Snidlits, don't be a nigger.
. . . Niggers lie and lie' " (41)—is likewise ambiguous and complex.
Without Hurston's explanatory footnote on the meaning of this expression, it would evidence a set of racist beliefs no doubt held by this
stereotypical white Southern man. A stark denigration of who she is, it
also reflects white pressure on black people to reject their own cultural
identity. Hurston's footnote, "The word Nigger used in this sense does
not mean race. It means a weak, contemptible person of any race" (41),
is more complicated than the naive attempt to save face for her patron
that it seems to be. In fact, despite the footnote that explicitly seems to
wipe out race as an issue, the story highlights the man's racism: his use
of "nigger" as a universal derogatory term is, unquestionably, rooted in
his equation of "weak," "contemptible," and black. Even more significant is Hurston's youthful response to this comment. Just as she
tossed out those Episcopal hymns that failed to nurture her dreams, she
here disregards the racist component of his advice, salvaging and internalizing only those remarks and proverbs that nurture her own spunky

sense of herself as a black female. Allowing the racism in the expression, "nigger," to roll off her back and following her own experience that (contrary to his injunction) *proves* lying definitely has its place, Zora is silent in response to this advice, embracing instead aphorisms like "getting hurt is part of fighting" (43) and "kill dead and go to jail" (42) that capture the intensity of her own feelings. Finding it corroborated in her everyday experience, she also remembers in great detail his advice about survival: "if you can't back your crap with nothing but talk, you'll catch hell" (42). When "doubleteened," he warns, she had better "'Use [her] head'" (42): "'Don't you try to fight three kids at one time unlessen you just can't get around it. Do the best you can, if you have to. But learn right now, not to let your head start more than your behind can stand. Measure out the amount of fighting you can do, and then do it. When you take on too much and get licked, folks will pity you first and scorn you after a while, and that's bad!'" (41–42). Hearing echoes of the wisdom she has learned from the High John stories of her own culture, Zora responds enthusiastically to this advice, "assuring" the white man that she will "'Do de best [she] can'" (42). Not shackled by the white man's intended meanings, Hurston thus transforms what could have been a debilitating lesson in racial self-hatred into one that nurtures her dreams of self-determination.

Mrs. Charlotte Osgood Mason is also presented as a more complex mythical white person than might initially seem the case. Although she may have seen herself as the fairy Godmother in the lives of the black people for whom she served as patron, much of Hurston's description makes her sound more like Cinderella's wicked stepmother. Her oppressive behavior is depicted as extreme, for she often "lay [Hurston] by the heels" not only for her actions but also "for what [she] was *thinking*" (176). A stern law-giver like Moses, she punishes any infraction of her "law" (176, 177), paternalistically forcing her "children" to be silent when *she* feels they speak inappropriately (176). Like the other patrons, she too imposes her own definitions on black people, deciding for black artists how they should express themselves and chiding them for what she sees as "'dissipating [their] powers in things that have no real meaning'" (176). The irony of an old wealthy white woman telling Hurston or Langston Hughes that their work had "'no soul in it'" (177) could not have escaped either of them. A mother figure who (more like Hurston's father) demands obedience, only being "as tender as mother-love when she felt you have done right spiritually" (177), Mrs. Mason provides a stark contrast to Hurston's biological mother, who supported Zora's rebellious childhood acts of self-definition and helped her avoid becoming a "mealy-mouthed rag doll" (21).

Violence and death also figure prominently in Hurston's description of her relationship with Mason. A predator/prey metaphor lurks, for instance, beneath Hurston's folksy expression that she often felt like a "rabbit at a dog convention" (176) in Mason's company and an echo of Ned's oppressive whip in the description of her tongue as "a knout" (177). Death also lurks in Hurston's childhood vision of the "old faceless woman . . . beside a tall plant with [an] off-shape white flower" (58), a much starker prefigurement of Hurston's later relationship with Mason than the seemingly idealized parallels with Persephone might suggest. Although she acknowledges the importance of some modicum of financial stability in her life in her admission that Mrs. Mason represented an "end of [her] pilgrimage, but not of [her] life" (58), those "queer-shaped flowers" (58) are (as the manuscript version of this chapter [309, JWJ] makes explicit) lillies, symbols of Mrs. Mason's deadly threat to Hurston's artistic, cultural, and personal autonomy. Hurston camouflages the paradoxical nature of relationships with whites—their attractive and deadly qualities—in her interpretation of this vision. As Hurston admits, she profited from her relationship with Mason and other powerful whites, experiencing "peace and love and what goes with those things" (58) as a result of their financial support; but to win that love—"what [went] with those things"—was often ugly, no matter how cleverly Hurston's fairytale language masks it. Hurston ultimately stresses, however, her ability to make the most positive use of this double-edged patronage, at once so seductive and so potentially deadly. She is not a totally helpless "rabbit at a dog convention," as she suggests immediately after expressing this feeling: "[Mrs. Mason] would invite me to dinner at her apartment, 399 Park Avenue, and then she, Cornelia Chapin, and Miss Chapin's sister, Miss Katherine Garrison Biddle would all hem me up and give me what for. When they had given me a proper straightening, and they felt I saw the light, all the sternness would vanish, and I would be wrapped in love. A present of money from Godmother, a coat from Miss Chapin, a dress from Mrs. Biddle" (176). The white people may have left this evening, confident of their superiority, self-satisfied from having given Hurston a "straightening," but Hurston's interpretation of the same experience is quite different. Far from feeling like a defenseless, "hemmed-in" rabbit, she exits instead as the trickster Brer

Rabbit, who, having survived against more powerful enemies, emerges with the spoils.[9]

Although Hurston repeatedly shows herself receiving material support from whites that aided her search for identity, her autobiography makes it clear that she did not get her model of womanhood from the same source. In fact, in *Dust Tracks on a Road,* she soundly rejects white definitions of the ideal female and posits a detailed alternative myth of black female identity. Rejecting traditional myths of female identity from within the white world as inadequate as models for a young girl who wants to "stretch [her] limbs in some mighty struggle" (56), she lampoons the stories she was given about girls—always white girls—because they only reinforced the passive and helpless role assigned her. These heroines disgust the young Zora because they are both physically and spiritually pale in comparison with her fantasies:

> There were other thin books about this and that sweet and gentle little girl who gave up her heart to Christ and good works. Almost always they died from it, preaching as they passed. I was utterly indifferent to their deaths. In the first place I could not conceive of death, and in the next place they never had any funerals that amounted to a hill of beans, so I didn't care how soon they rolled up their big, soulful, blue eyes and kicked the bucket. They had no meat on their bones. (54)

Hurston highlights distinctions between this kind of female self and the much more vigorous one she envisages in her chapter, "Friendship," which details her relationships with Ethel Waters and Fannie Hurst. An excellent example of the way Hurston deals with race in her autobiography, this chapter, in which Hurston depicts herself as a close friend to both black and white women, seems to evidence Hurston's racial even-handedness but actually accentuates contrasts. The affinities among Fannie Hurst, Miss M— (the member of the drama troupe Hurston worked for), Arvay Meserve in *Seraph on the Suwanee,* and the little girls in Hurston's childhood stories suggest an image of white womanhood very different from the model of the black female self Hurston embraces.[10] Whereas Hurston appears tolerantly amused at Fannie Hurst's vagaries, her portrait of Ethel Waters is a striking contrast, echoing many positive aspects of the black female self that she stresses in her own life and in those of her characters.[11] Someone who has also "been in Sorrow's kitchen and licked out all the pots," Waters, Hurston suggests, responds to hardship with the same vigorous engagement of life that Janie displays after Tea Cake's death. As assertive as Hurston's other verbal "lionesses," with eyes that flash fire (246) when she is angry, Waters is the woman with whom Hurston shares an intimate, mutually supportive friendship, as her echoes of the relationship between Pheoby and Janie suggest (244–45).

In contrast to the "great humanness and depth" (243) of Waters, Hurston describes Fannie Hurst as almost mindlessly shallow, "impish" (238, 239) and "so young for her years" (238). Consistently stressing her childishness, Hurston tells one story, for instance, about the time "I caught her playing at keeping house" (238), a tale bizarre in the immature picture of Hurst it paints: "What was my amazement to see Miss Hurst herself open the door and come in, greet herself graciously and invite herself to have some tea. Which she did. She went into that huge duplex studio and had toasted English muffins and played she had company with her for an hour or more. Then she came on back up to her office and went to work" (239).[12] Her lengthy anecdote about their unplanned trip through Canada, likewise, ends on this analytical note: "Here was Fannie Hurst, a great writer and globe famous, behaving like a little girl, teasing her nurse to take her to the zoo, and having a fine time at it. . . . She was like a child at a circus. She was a run-away, with no responsibilities" (242). Reflecting the early stories about white girls with "no meat on their bones," Hurston's portrait of Hurst reveals how undesirable it is for black women to emulate a white model of womanhood.

Despite her almost maternal tolerance for many white women in *Dust Tracks,* Hurston paints an ideal for black women that is more active and powerful. Big Sweet, respected even by white men—not docile white girls—is her ideal, one who explodes white definitions of femininity *and* blackness. As another woman in the camps tells her, " 'Dat Cracker Quarters Boss wears two pistols round his waist and goes for bad, but he won't break a breath with Big Sweet lessen he got his pistol in his hand. Cause if he start anything with her, he won't never get a chance to draw it. She ain't mean. She don't bother nobody. She just don't stand for no foolishness, dat's all' " (187–88).

To imagine such possibilities, Hurston suggests in narrating her childhood, was difficult because she was offered so few positive literary images of black women. Finding no models in the stories of white girls or in those about black women told by black men, Hurston suggests in "Figure and Fancy" that her youthful storytelling imagination was inspired to fill this void. In the stories she tells her mother, she creates a

child's mythology centered around a black female that rivals the proportions of the Bible. She revises the story of Christ walking on the water,
editing out the wrathful white male God who displays his power in
terrifying mortals. She told her mother "how the lake had talked with
me, and invited me to walk all over it. I told the lake I was afraid of
getting drowned, but the lake assured me it wouldn't think of doing *me*
like that. No, indeed! Come right on and have a walk. Well, I stepped
out on the lake and walked all over it. It didn't even wet my feet. I could
see all the fish and things swimming around under me, and they all said
hello, but none of them bothered me. Wasn't that nice?" (71). In place of
the patriarchal God she had critiqued in *Moses, Man of the Mountain* and
in the "Religion" chapter of her autobiography, Hurston here sees a maternal Nature that figures significantly in many of her works—a Nature that welcomes and protects Zora as her own child. As a young girl,
Hurston also reworks the creation myth in two significant ways: the
creator is herself a black woman and she creates woman first. In a direct
reversal of the biblical story, man only comes onto the scene to please
the woman. In her childish but already womanist imagination, she creates Miss Corn-Shuck, and "we had a lovely time together for a day
or two, and then Miss Corn-Shuck got lonesome for some company"
(73). She then fashions Mr. Sweet-Smell for her, a prefigurement of
the feminized, fun-loving Tea Cake. Even in this child's version of
Their Eyes Were Watching God, Hurston has created a real mate—not a
master—for woman, a partner who fosters rather than squelches female
growth.

As these stories and Hurston's disgust with those of passive blond
girls suggest, Hurston's search for stories of female equality and power
entails explicit rejection of white ideals. A central myth against which
she shapes her vision of female identity and her autobiography is that of
Cinderella. As she will show, it is not only a tale that fails to match black
women's experience but also a myth of female identity that is dangerous
for black women to emulate. In her one explicit reference to this fairytale, speaking of her poverty at Morgan College, she emphasizes the
difference between herself and Cinderella: "It would be dramatic in a
Cinderella way if I were to say that the well-dressed students at school
snubbed me and shoved me around" (149). The contrast is, however, one
of spirit rather than circumstances. Although Hurston rejects the notion of passive femininity underlying this myth, she describes the circumstances of her early life to parallel in striking degree those of

Cinderella.[13] Cursed with a wicked stepmother and a father who lav-
ishes gifts on Sarah while berating her, Zora is "put to scrubbing down
the stair steps" and "clean[ing] up the pantry" (106) at boarding school
and forced into "get[ting] up early in the morning and mak[ing] a fire
in the kitchen range" (129) at her brother's house. So "poorly dressed"
that to call it that would be "bragging" (130), she makes an early escape from this drudgery to the "enchanted" world of the theater (134).
She does not enter, however, as the Cinderella of the fairytale's end,
magically clothed in a ball gown and glass slippers; instead, dressed in a
"cheap" "little dress" (131), she "mount[s] up the golden stairs" (131)
not to attend the ball but to work as a maid. The blond white woman
she serves, on whom she puts the slippers and white dress (133), is the
real Cinderella who later marries Prince Charming and lives happily
ever after.

Hurston consistently refuses to cast herself in the role of abused
Cinderella even though the demeaning work she does would qualify
her for the role. Shaping a myth of a much more active female, consciously drawn in contrast to the white myth of the passive female rescued from her suffering by a man, she shows herself repeatedly treated
like Cinderella but stubbornly refusing to act like her. She does not
weep at the abuses of her stepmother, for instance, but rather beats her
to within an inch of her life. Unlike Cinderella, she is not humbled
by her poverty either as a homeless child (117) or penniless domestic
worker (118).

Whereas some white women like Miss M— and Fannie Hurst may
live a Cinderella existence, Hurston describes relationships between
black men and women to emphasize the folly of any black woman who
expects to travel that route to happiness and fulfillment. In spite of
Hurston's praise for the folklore on Joe Clark's porch and her attraction
for the place even as a child, her treatment of it in *Dust Tracks on a Road*
turns up no Prince Charmings ready to sweep black women away to
the palace.[14] Listening to the men talk, she hears expressed not adoration
but a hatred of black women that stems from the fact that they, unlike
Cinderella, fight to protect themselves. Light-skinned women are valued, on the other hand, because they conform to the white myth of
the passive female who submits to and serves men. Echoing Sop's comments to Tea Cake in *Their Eyes Were Watching God,* the story about black
women runs:

They brought bad luck for a week if they came to your house of a Monday morning. They were evil. They slept with their fists balled up ready to fight and squabble even while they were asleep. They even had evil dreams. White, yellow and brown girls dreamed about roses and perfume and kisses. Black gals dreamed about guns, razors, ice-picks, hatchets and hot lye. I heard men swear they had seen them dreaming and knew these things to be true. (225)[15]

As the banter of men suggests, black women are not objects of romantic idealization but scorned and dehumanized sex objects (62–63), reduced to the status of vessels for men's desires or food to be consumed in many of the men's derogatory metaphors. In the parlance of the porch-front, women are spit-cups, even in the imagery used to talk about them. As one man says disgustedly, " 'To save my soul, I can't see what you fooled with her for. I'd just as soon pick up an old tin can out of the trash pile' " (63).

The hilarity and camaraderie of the porch almost make us forget how frequently women are denigrated in these stories. Whereas it is also easy to overlook the absence of women, Hurston reminds us (as she had in *Mules and Men*) that they are, in fact, working while the men enjoy one another's company. When some wives call for help from the men, the men adeptly turn even that into a joke:

The wives of the story-tellers might yell from the backyards for them to come and tote some water, or chop some wood for the cookstove and never get a move out of the men. The usual rejoinder was, "Oh, she's got enough to go on. No matter how much wood you chop, a woman will burn it all up to get a meal. If she got a couple of pieces, she will make do. If you chop up a whole boxful, she will burn every stick of it. Pay her no mind." (64)

As the men reveal in their humor, they do not see their role as one of Prince Charming, rescuing the black woman from work. The story they tell, that of Sis Snail, who finally divorced her husband because he took seven years to get to the door when sent to get her a doctor (64–66), emerges as a more accurate story than Cinderella for capturing the male/female reality of Eatonville.

In writing about her own relationships with men, Hurston charts her life as a gradual and often painful process of rejecting this myth about romantic love. Finding ultimately that "Work [not love] is the nearest thing to happiness that [she] can find" (285), she nevertheless

shows herself earlier experiencing both the attraction and absurdity embodied in the tale of Cinderella and the popular mythology of Hollywood. This treatment of "love [as] de prong us black women git hung
on" begins with her first humorous story of falling in love, one that
shows not only the degree to which the myth of movie romance per-
vades even the life of a black girl from Eatonville but also the emotional
dangers of buying into this myth. Falling in love with an "older man,"
President Collier, Zora (in good melodramatic fashion) writes him love
letters and puts a brick in the bed of a "rival lover." Her fantasies straight
from Hollywood, she is mad with jealousy that he seems satisfied

> with some stale, old, decrepit woman of twenty-five or so. It used to
> drive me mad. I comforted myself with the thought that he would cry
> his eyes out when I would suddenly appear before him, tall and beauti-
> ful and disdainful and make him beg me for a whole week before I
> would give in and marry him, and of course fire all of those old half-
> dead teachers who were hanging around him. Maybe they would drown
> themselves in the St. John's River. Oh, I might stop them just before
> they jumped in. I never did decide what to do with all my disgruntled
> rivals after I dragged them away from the river. (106)

Her narration of this "torrid love affair" (107) is very amusing, but the
ending of the story should have taught the youthful Zora the danger
of romantic fantasy. When the teacher turns her in for putting the wet
brick in her bed, Zora is shocked at her lover's response: "Oh the perfidy,
the deceit of the man to whom I had given my love and all my lovely
letters in the hole behind the laundry! He listened to this unholy female
and took me into his office and closed the door. He did not fold me
lovingly in his arms and say, 'Darling! I understand. You did it all for me.'
No! The blind fool lifted up my skirt in the rear and spanked a prospec-
tive tall, beautiful lady's pants" (107–8).

In discussing the specifics of her adult love life, Hurston is not always
so amusing, but the same concern to debunk traditional stereotypes
drives her narration. Her marriage to her first husband, for instance, is
not the hazy, blissful day the romantic myth had led her to expect (250–
51). Her love of the "perfect man" is more complicated, for the tempta-
tions for Hurston are much graver in a relationship with a man who
seems the independent, vigorous, and passionate prefigurement of Tea
Cake. When Hurston tries to lend him a quarter until payday, his response is as romantic as Tea Cake's refusal to spend Janie's money:

> What did I do that for? He flew hot. In fact he was the hottest man in
> the five boroughs. Why did I insult him like that? The responsibility
> was all his. He had known that he did not have his return fare when he
> left home, but he wanted to come, and so he had come. Let him take
> the consequences for his own acts. What kind of coward did I take him
> for? How could he deserve my respect if he behaved like a cream puff?
> He was a *man!* No woman on earth could either lend him or give him
> a cent. If a man could not do for a woman, what good was he on earth?
> His great desire was to do for me. *Please* let him be a *man.* (253)

At this point, Zora is impressed, but as she notes, "That very manliness,
sweet as it was, made us both suffer" (253). The alliance between his
desire to do for her and his demand that she fulfill stifling traditional
female roles is evident in his first admission of love: " 'You know, Zora,
you've got a real man on your hands. You've got somebody to do for you.
I'm tired of seeing you work so hard. I wouldn't want *my* wife to do
anything but look after me. Be home looking like Skookums when I got
there' " (255). As the love-struck Zora only gradually realizes, this notion
of manliness—connected with protecting a woman from the world and
from work—also implies a conception of womanliness at odds with her
own. Whereas her lover talks like Prince Charming, eager to treat her
as Cinderella, he is exposed as a much more pernicious figure: "He was
the master kind. All, or nothing, for him" (257). Too often, Hurston's
own experience shows, "love" between a man and a woman can mask
a relationship of domination; the black woman enamored with white
fairytales risks finding herself reduced, as Hurston was, to a "slave"
(258).

Hurston's chapter on love explodes this romantic myth and posits
the possibility of a woman engaging men in a less passively stereotypical
way. Hurston works in many ways to show that male and female roles
can be reversed in love, with the black woman playing the role not of
Arvay but of Erzulie, powerful and sometimes haughty love goddess
of the voodoo pantheon, who is "not the passive queen of heaven and
mother of anybody . . . [but] the ideal of the love bed" (*Tell My Horse,*
144). As awesomely powerful as male gods traditionally are, she is "the
perfect female [who] must be loved and obeyed . . . whose love is so
strong and binding that it cannot tolerate a rival" (144). Playing Erzulie's
role in describing her relationships with men, Hurston often renders the
self-proclaimed Prince Charmings in her life as buffoons and reduces

their love poetry to ludicrously mixed metaphors: Men "pant in my ear on short acquaintance, 'You passionate thing! I can see you are just *burning* up! Most men would be disappointing to you. It takes a man like me for you. Ahhh! I know that you will just wreck me! Your eyes and your lips tell me a lot. You are a walking furnace!'" (262). Instead of responding in the expected manner, Hurston, as an adult at least, rejects the heroine's role in the traditional melodrama of love, commenting, "This amazes me sometimes. Often when this is whispered gustily in my ear, I am feeling no more amorous than a charter member of the Union League Club. I may be thinking of turnip greens with dumplings, or more royalty checks, and here is a man who visualizes me on a divan sending the world up in smoke" (262). Depicting herself as alternately preoccupied and indifferent, Hurston turns men's sexist metaphors back against them, reducing them to "dishes" less interesting than corn pone or turkey hash:

> Under the spell of moonlight, music, flowers, or the cut and smell of good tweeds, I sometimes feel the divine urge for an hour, a day or maybe a week. Then it is gone and my interest returns to corn pone and mustard greens, or rubbing a paragraph with a soft cloth. Then my ex-sharer of a mood calls up in a fevered voice and reminds me of every silly thing I said, and eggs me on to say them all over again. It is the third presentation of turkey hash over Christmas. (263–64)

When confronted by unwanted sexual advances, she responds not with "ladylike" concerns about virtue that doom Pinky but with imperious disdain: "I was lacking in curiosity. I was not worrying so much about virtue. The thing just did not call me. There was neither the beauty of love, nor material advantage in it for me. After all, what is the use in having swine without pearls?" (144–45).

Although Hurston, in her treatment of black women in love and poverty, soundly rejects Cinderella and Arvay as models for the black woman's identity, she seems consciously to draw on other white mythic models in her search for a dynamic vision of selfhood. Nevertheless, just as her seeming unctuousness in talking about white patrons and apparent even-handedness in speaking of white friends serve as a mask for more critical assessment, similarly, behind the appearance of dependence on figures such as Thor, David, and Persephone lie black female figures who are the real source of Hurston's ideal.

As Hurston searches for stories of heroic action to use in fashioning a black woman with some "meat on her bones," she discovers that the only ones that match her aspirations are about white males. Norse tales, particularly, capture Zora's imagination (a fact she herself recognizes as odd) because of the energy and strength they embody: "Why did the Norse tales strike so deeply into my soul? I do not know, but they did. I seemed to remember seeing Thor swing his mighty short-handled hammer as he sped across the sky in rumbling thunder, lightning flashing from the tread of his stead and the wheels of his chariot" (53). She is also impressed with "the great and good Odin, who went down to the well of knowledge to drink, and was told that the price of a drink from that fountain was an eye. Odin drank deeply, then plucked out an eye without a murmur, and handed it to the grizzly keeper, and walked away. That held majesty for me" (53). Heroic, too, is the self-denial of Hercules, who met Pleasure and Duty and "put his hand in that of Duty and followed her steep way to the blue hills of fame and glory, which she pointed out at the end" (53–54). As Hurston admits, this story "moved me profoundly. I resolved to be like him" (54).

Hurston's use of European mythology is more complicated than her expressions of enthusiam for these white male figures might suggest. Reclaiming action as a possibility for black women, she appropriates the heroic elements in those early stories she loved and applies them to herself. She emphasizes, for instance, that she did not just listen to the story of Hercules but swore herself "an oath to leave all pleasure and take the hard road of labor" (262). Like Odin who willingly sacrifices an eye for what he wants, Hurston is ready to pay a high price for her work rather than sacrifice it for love as the traditional myth would have her do. Hurston also reclaims for black women the symbols of male strength and energy, lightning and thunder, associated with Thor in those childhood stories. Symbolically wresting power from Anglo-Saxon males during her hoodoo initiation, when she dreams she "strode across the heavens with lightning flashing from under [her] feet, and grumbling thunder following in [her] wake" (191), she discovers a black source of this power defined in white culture as European and male. These symbols become more than a dream in the same ceremony when "the symbol of lightning was painted on my back . . . to be mine forever" (192). Even at the very end of the manuscript version of *Dust Tracks on a Road,* Hurston reaffirms a mythic image of black womanhood—as awesome as Thor—by depicting herself as the "cosmic" Zora who has "walked in storms with a crown of clouds about [her] head and the zigzag lightning playing through [her] fingers" (347).

Although Hurston seems here to depict herself as the spiritual heir of Thor, indebted to white culture for her identity, there is, in fact, another figure who parallels Hurston's self-description more fully. In *Mules and Men,* Hurston mentions several aspects of the character of Marie Leveau, the greatest conjure woman in American history, that she echoes in discussing her own experience both in *Mules and Men* and in *Dust Tracks on a Road.* Just as Leveau was associated with snakes (*Mules and Men,* 201) and the thunder and lightning of fierce storms (*Mules and Men,* 203), Hurston also emphasizes her own fascination with snakes (*Mules,* 164; *Dust,* 56, 192) and her symbolic association with storms. When she narrates one hoodoo initiation in *Mules and Men,* for instance, she quotes her teacher's vision of her "'conquering and accomplishing with the lightning and making her road with thunder'" (209) and his prophecy that she would receive wisdom from The Great One in storms (210). Repeating these symbolic identifications in *Dust Tracks,* Hurston also, in her childhood story about walking on the water (71), follows in the footsteps of Leveau, the "two-headed" woman, who every year during her feast walked upon the waters of Lake Ponchetrain (*Tell My Horse,* 202).[16]

With no black women authors available to her, David becomes her professed ideal of a writer, one who combines poetic sensitivity and vigorous action: "no matter where he went, he smote 'em hip and thigh. Then he sung songs to his harp awhile, and went and smote some more. Not one time did David stop and preach about sin and things" (54–55).[17] Usurping the ideals she had admired in David, the poet of the harp and the sword, she repeatedly depicts herself not merely as a melodious singer but as a fierce warrior who brandishes her own weapon. Hurston shows herself as such a fighter even as a child, willing to engage in pitched battle against oppressive and overbearing figures. Although Zora could have understandably resented her sister, she becomes "a tiger" (100) defending her against their stepmother just as Big Sweet becomes "a lioness" (190) fiercely protecting the weaker Zora against Lucy. Quite unlike Cinderella, who remains simply the weeping victim of her stepmother, Zora hates hers intensely and gleefully takes up her sword (in this scene literally a hatchet) to act on those feelings:

> The feelings of all those six years were pressing inside me like steam under a valve. I didn't have any thoughts to speak of. Just the fierce instinct of flesh on flesh—me kicking and beating on her budgy self—those

two ugly false teeth in front—her dead on the floor—grinning like a
dead dog in the sun. Consequences be damned! If I died, let me die
with my hands soaked in her blood. I wanted her blood, and plenty of
it. That is the way I went into the fight, and that is the way I fought it.
(101–2)

This willingness to fight to protect oneself and one's loved ones, a characteristic Hurston repeatedly attributes to black women, is a crucial aspect of the persona Hurston adopts in dealing with her own adversity.
Unlike the little white girls who sweetly pass into oblivion, women
"with some meat on their bones" value resistance rather than acquiescence. Prayer, thus, receives a sword-like stroke from Hurston because it
"seems to me a cry of weakness, and an attempt to avoid, by trickery,
the rules of the game as laid down. I do not choose to admit weakness.
I accept the challenge of responsibility" (278). Bitterness over racial oppression is even more forcefully rejected—not because it is unjustified—
but because of its psychic and emotional toll on the individual. As she
says, "I take no refuge from myself in bitterness. To me, bitterness is the
under-arm odor of wishful weakness. It is the graceless acknowledgment of defeat. I have no urge to make any concessions like that to the
world as yet" (280).[18] Far from being blind or insensitive to racial injustice, Hurston calls for battle as a way to correct it: "I am in the struggle
with the sword in my hands, and I don't intend to run until you run me"
(280). Assessing her career in the statement, "I have stood on the peaky
mountains wrapped in rainbows, with a harp and a sword in my hands"
(280), Hurston conveys the complexity of her discursive project in *Dust
Tracks,* her aim not only to espouse an ideal of racial harmony and sexual
equality but also to confront oppressive realities—to "smite 'em hip and
thigh."

David is not the only figure to brandish a weapon in Hurston's experience, and her sword is not simply borrowed from the Old Testament
figure she admires. In fact, numerous black women in Hurston's writings—Big Sweet, the young Isis in "Drenched in Light," the women in
men's nightmares, all with their knives and razors—can trace their line-
age back, not so much to David but more directly to the fierce Amazon
warriors with their swords that Hurston describes in *Dust Tracks* (201).
In her treatment of the black female self, Hurston takes a stereotype
of the black woman who (according to derogatory comments made by
black men) when threatened by a black man's fist in her face, dreams of

splitting his head open with an ax (226) and reinterprets it as an ideal. Hurston's black woman warrior, like Big Sweet, "'ain't mean, . . . don't bother nobody, . . . [but] just don't stand for no foolishness.'"

Proof that all the heroic warriors in Eatonville's history are not male is delightfully evident in Hurston's story (significantly narrated by herself rather than one of the men on the porch) about Aunt Caroline. Caroline's response to her philandering husband is not that of a passive victim but that of a lioness, one (like Big Sweet) strong and assertive enough to demand respect from men: "A knockdown didn't convince her that the fight was over at all. She would get up and come right on in, and she was nobody's weakling. It was generally conceded he might get the edge on her in physical combat if he took a hammer or a trace-chain to her, but in other ways she always won. She would watch his various philandering episodes just so long, and then she would go into action" (23). One day, ax slung over her shoulder, she follows her husband when he leaves, bearing shoes and sweets, to meet his girlfriend. Hurston's conclusion to the story is not only amusing but iconoclastic in its depiction of Jim as a ridiculous "furtive figure in white ["long drawers"] dodging from tree to tree" (24) and Aunt Caroline as heroic victor: "The axe was still over her shoulder, but now it was draped with Uncle Jim's pants, shirt and coat. A new pair of women's oxfords were dangling from the handle by their strings. Two stalks of sugarcane were over her other shoulder" (24). Women such as Caroline, whose strength rivals that of mythic white males, do not passively await a nonexistent Prince Charming or endure oppression in silence. Like Zora with her hatchet, Caroline with her ax, Big Sweet with her knife, and the women of men's nightmares with their razors, they brandish their weapons in a way that makes David and his sword seem mere bravura by comparison.

Awareness of Hurston's reliance on black traditions, despite her seeming indebtedness to white ones, her embrace ultimately of figures like Erzulie, Marie Leveau, and the Amazon warriors rather than Cinderella, Thor, or David, can be helpful in understanding what seems the European myth most central in *Dust Tracks on a Road,* that of Persphone.[19] Hurston foregrounds this myth by having herself read a full version of it for the Northern visitors to her school (48–49) and, as she does with other myths, by drawing parallels between the European myth and her own life. Imagistically echoing Persephone's wintry spiritual death and sojourn in a dreary underworld in telling her own story, Hurston suggests similarities between her fate and Persephone's: "The winters have been, and my soul-stuff has lain mute like a plain while the herds of happenings thundered across by breast. In these times there were deep chasms in me which had forgotten their memory of the sun" (322). Poverty—with its "dead dreams dropping off the heart like leaves" and "impulses smothered too long in the fetid air of under-ground caves" (116)—also contributed to spiritual desolation echoing that of Persephone.

This myth also seems to underlie the overall structural plan for *Dust Tracks*. As she makes explicit in the manuscript version, her final vision in her quest entails coming to the house of Mrs. Charlotte Osgood Mason (309), which she describes as "the end of [her] pilgrimage, but not of her life," a time when she would know "peace and love and what goes with those things" (58). This culminating vision seems to echo the end of the myth of Persephone, when "flying Mercury, the messenger of the Gods, brought Persephone back to the sunlit earth and restored her to the arms of Dame Ceres, her mother, that the world might have springtime and summer flowers, autumn and harvest" (49). Perhaps more than any other example, Hurston's use of this myth seems, with its emphasis on the importance of union with a white [god]mother figure, proof of Hurston's conflicted sense of identity. Nowhere does she seem more emphatically to affirm the centrality of whites in her life and her indebtedness to white traditions for grander visions of the self than the black world offered her. Although Hurston invites us to focus on her identification with the white woman Persephone, there is no Prince Charming (or Mercury) in her life who carries her to safety. As that significant omission and the double-edged way in which Hurston treats Mason suggest, Hurston's use of this myth is ambiguously complex. Just as she expresses enthusiasm for Thor and other white mythic characters but ultimately finds their "thunder and lightning" in an older black tradition, it is an African mythic female that inspires Hurston's autobiography. The white model of passive womanhood embodied in Persephone may be foisted upon her (it is, significantly, what her benefactors require her to read in order to be initiated into their world and to receive their gifts), but Hurston, as the names of her autobiographical characters in "Drenched in Light" and *Jonah's Gourd Vine* suggest, actually embraces as her ideal Persephone's precursor, the more dynamic and powerful African goddess, Isis.

The influence of this myth on *Dust Tracks on a Road,* although never explicitly pointed to, can be seen, first of all, in her shaping of the book as an anguished and painful journey. Whereas Persephone suffered as a prisoner in the underworld, Isis (as her famed Lamentations over the deaths in her family and her Wanderings to recover the body of Osiris suggest) was an active pilgrim. Similarly, Hurston's autobiography is structured not as a tale of imprisonment, but as one of pilgrimage (89, 115, 143, 146). Even more profoundly, Hurston embraces Isis and Osiris as an ideal male/female relationship for black people quite different from that of Prince Charming and Cinderella or Mercury and Persephone. As Hurston's entire chapter "Love" suggests, one of the biggest struggles of her life was her search for the kind of equality evident in the relationship of Isis and Osiris and imaged in her youthful fantasy of Miss Corn-Shuck and Mr. Sweet-Smell.

Admiring Isis's power rather than Persephone's passive victimization, Hurston suggests further parallels between herself and Isis by detailing the hoodoo initiation in which she gains similar magical powers. Like the Egyptian goddess, the famed "lady of enchantments" (Budge, *Egyptian Religion,* 55), she is also able to animate the dead. Transforming the mundane figure, Mr. Pendir, into a larger-than-life mythic alligator of "awful majesty" (80), she imaginatively brings this man back from death and oblivion as surely as Isis reanimates Osiris's corpse. Even though he "had no female relatives around to mourn loud" and "his name soon ceased to be called" (83) in the town, he lived in Zora's youthful imagination (83) and in her written story. Hurston also highlights the black woman's regenerative powers in her most explicit allusion to the myth of Isis, her discussion of writing *Their Eyes Were Watching God*. "Embalm[ing] all the tenderness of [her] passion" (260), she reanimates her ideal beloved in that book just as Isis had brought Osiris back to life. As these examples suggest, Hurston's mythic model is not built on Persephone's victimization and reunion with a white mother figure but rather on Isis's power and her creative use of it in a black world.[20] Like Isis, who collected and reunited the fragments of Osiris's body, Hurston uses her literary and anthropological power to fashion an "undiminished" version of black identity to counter the "mutilation" (204) she sees as the legacy of slavery.

Hurston also implicitly embraces a religion that echoes that associated with Egyptian worship of Isis. Aware of the dangers for black women who absorb the spiritual values of a culture that "squinches" their spirit, she rejects the white father religion of the Judeo-Christian tradition for many of the same reasons she had critiqued it in *Moses, Man of the Mountain.* In her chapter, "Religion," she shows herself even as a child aware of the inadequacies of this deity. While she masks it behind humor seemingly directed at her own childish brazenness, she exposes the incompetency she sees in the white father's Creation:

> I wanted to know, for instance, why didn't God make grown babies in-
> stead of those little measly things that messed up didies and cried all the
> time? What was the sense in making babies with no teeth? He knew
> that they had to have teeth, didn't He? So why not give babies their
> teeth in the beginning instead of hiding the toothless things in hollow
> stumps and logs for grannies and doctors to find and give to people? He
> could see all the trouble people had with babies, rubbing their gums and
> putting wood-lice around their necks to get them to cut teeth. (267)

Highlighting the hypocrisy she sees underlying the Judeo-Christian tradition with her seemingly naive, childish questions, she then on a more serious note questions its emphasis on repression, sin, and death:

> Why did God hate for children to play on Sundays? If Christ, God's
> son, hated to die, and God hated for Him to die and have everybody
> grieving over it ever since, why did He have to do it? Why did people
> die anyway?
>   It was explained to me that Christ died to save the world from sin
> and then too, so that folks did not have to die any more. That was a
> simple, clear-cut explanation. But then I heard my father and other
> preachers accusing people of sin. They went so far as to say that people
> were so prone to sin, that they sinned with every breath they drew. You
> couldn't even breathe without sinning! How could that happen if we
> had already been saved from it? So far as the dying part was concerned,
> I saw enough funerals to know that somebody was dying. (267–68)

In place of this wrathful deity, the youthful (already pagan) Zora adopts symbols of the exuberant life and love within her experience. Rejecting an unloving, transcendent "spirit away off who found fault with every-body all the time" (268), baffled by "the passionate declarations of love for a being nobody could see" (268), she embraces instead "[her] family, [her] puppy and the new bull-calf" (268), an echo of the Egyptian bull-god, Apis, frequently alluded to in *Moses, Man of the Mountain.*

In place of institutionalized Christianity, which Hurston describes as the religion of imperialism and one inimical to every value she holds dear, she expresses spiritual beliefs (echoing the religion practiced by Mentu and Moses while under his tutelage) grounded in worship of Nature and natural law.[21] Like Moses at his most insightful, she yearns only to ask Nature questions and to understand her mysteries: "I have made my peace with the universe as I find it, and bow to its laws. The ever-sleepless sea in its bed, crying out 'How long?' to Time; million-formed and never motionless flame; the contemplation of these two aspects alone, affords me sufficient food for ten spans of my expected lifetime" (278). The love of life, energy, and pleasure, an understanding of immortality (like that of Mentu) grounded in the continuity of natural processes—all associated with the Osirian faith—informs Hurston's passionate and poetic conclusion to her chapter on religion:

> The springing of the yellow line of morning out of the misty deep of dawn, is glory enough for me. I know that nothing is destructible; things merely change forms. When the consciousness we know as life ceases, I know that I shall still be part and parcel of the world. I was a part before the sun rolled into shape and burst forth in the glory of change. I was, when the earth was hurled out from its fiery rim. I shall return with the earth to Father Sun, and still exist in substance when the sun has lost its fire, and disintegrated in infinity to perhaps become a part of the whirling rubble in space. Why fear? The stuff of my being is matter, ever changing, ever moving, but never lost; so what need of denominations and creeds to deny myself the comfort of all my fellow men? The wide belt of the universe has no need for finger-rings. I am one with the infinite and need no other assurance. (279)

The invocation of a "cosmic" Zora here is thus no reactionary denial of harsh political and social realities but rather central to Hurston's rejection of the spiritual values underpinning the oppression blacks have experienced in a world controlled by whites. Refusing to worship this oppressive power or to pray to this white father, she originally planned to end *Dust Tracks on a Road* with a bow to a mother goddess, asking Nature not for power, military victory, or forgiveness but for natural wisdom:

> I know that destruction and construction are but two faces of Dame Nature, and that it is nothing to her if I choose to make personal tragedy out of her unbreakable laws.
>
> So I ask of her few things. May I never do good consciously nor evil unconsciously. Let my evil be known to me in advance of my acts, and my good when Nature wills. May I be granted a just mind and a timely death. (348)

Isis, Erzulie, Marie Leveau, and Amazon warriors are thus the real foremothers of Big Sweet, Aunt Caroline, Ethel Waters, and Hurston herself. Defying white norms for black women in embracing such titanic women, Hurston originally planned to end her autobiography in this spirit. The manuscript chapter, "Seeing the World As It Is," included as an appendix in Hemenway's edition of *Dust Tracks,* was designed to round out this portrait by showing Hurston taking a much more combative stance toward Jim Meserve's world. Had it made it into the published version as the last chapter, it would have completed a much more radical portrait of Hurston, for it contains the most open and extended critiques of American and European imperialism she ever tried to publish through white-controlled periodicals or publishing houses. Although it is certainly the case that Hurston's comments on Hitler and Japan would have elicited harsh response had they been published at the time, nowhere is the attempt to silence Hurston's defiant voice clearer than in the version of that chapter published as the final chapter to her autobiography. Even though her publishers may have felt merely pragmatic in requiring her to remove these comments, what is also erased in the published version (in response to an editorial "suggestion" to eliminate "international opinions as irrelevant to autobiography" [JWJ]) are much broader, scathing attacks on the discrepancy between American principles and actions:

> There was the dignity of man. His inalienable rights were sacred.
> Man, noble man, had risen in his might and glory and had stamped out
> the vile institution of slavery. That is just what they said. But I know
> that the principle of human bondage has not yet vanished from the
> earth. I know that great nations are standing on it. I would not go so far
> as to deny that there has been no progress toward the concept of liberty.
> Already it has been agreed that the name of slavery is very bad. No civi-
> lized nation will use such a term any more. Neither will they keep the
> business around the home. Life will be on a loftier level by operating at
> a distance and calling it acquiring sources of raw material, and keeping
> the market open. It has been decided, also, that it is not cricket to en-
> slave one's own kind. That is unspeakable tyranny.
>
> But must a nation suffer from lack of prosperity and expansion by
> lofty concepts? Not at all! If a ruler can find a place way off where the
> people do not look like him, kill enough of them to convince the rest
> that they ought to support him with their lives and labor, that ruler is
> hailed as a great conqueror, and people built monuments to him. The
> very weapons he used are also honored. They picture him in unforgetta-
> ble stone with the sacred tool of his conquest in his hand. Democracy,
> like religion, never was designed to make our profits less. (338–39)

Laying down her crooked stick to take up her sword, Hurston wields it even more broadly in arguing that the concept of slavery still exists in

U.S. foreign economic policy. In Big Sweet fashion, she "gives a read-ing" on this subject, explicitly announcing her intention to "lay a hear-ing on it" (333): "The idea of human slavery is so deeply ground in that the pink-toes can't get it out of their system. It has just been decided to move the slave quarters farther away from the house" (343).

In this original chapter, Hurston not only speaks openly and often venomously about American imperialism; she also makes unabashed and threatening demands for action. With a directness often lacking in her other public political writing (but echoing the anger expressed in letters written to black figures during World War II), she announces her dissat-isfaction with token benevolent gifts bestowed by the white establish-ment.[22] Beneath her folksy and charming metaphors lie both awareness and defiance of the contemporary black's economic slavery: "You can-not arouse any enthusiasm in me to join in a protest for the boss to provide me with a better hoe to chop his cotton with. Why must I chop cotton at all? Why fix a class of cotton-choppers? I will join in no pro-tests for the boss to put a little more stuffing in my bunk. I don't even want the bunk. I want the boss's bed" (345). Sounding a radical note in suggesting that many reforms simply perpetuate a more comfortable form of slavery, she announces: "So I can get no lift out of nominating myself to be a peasant and celebrating any feasts back stairs. I want the front of the house and I am going to keep on trying even if I never satisfy my plan" (345–46). In addition to this threat to white supremacy, Hurston, in Amazonian fashion, openly embraces violence to fight it: "If the leaders on the left feel that only violence can right things, I see no need of fingernail warfare. Why not take a stronger position? Shoot in the hearse, don't care how sad the funeral is. Get the feeling of the ban-tam hen jumping on the mule. Kill dead and go to jail. I am not blood-thirsty and have no yearning for strife, but, if what they say is true, that there must be this upset, why not make it cosmic?" (346).[23]

A comparison of this manuscript chapter and the published version reveals the power of her publishers not only to alter Hurston's words but also, in fact, to mutilate the "cosmic" self Hurston claims for herself in her autobiography. The change in title from "Seeing the World as it is" to "Looking Things Over" accurately reflects the constriction of scope and trivialization of theme that results in the published version's focus on personal issues. When the pages of criticism of American imperialism are erased, what remains is a very short and comparatively bland chapter. Without Hurston's broadened definition of slavery (criticism of how

America has moved the slave quarters farther away from the house), her remaining depiction of American slavery as a finished chapter of history looks naive and even reactionary. In the manuscript version, Hurston's purpose in softpedaling slavery of the past is to urge her readers to action against the broader, more insidious forms of slavery in the present. Instead of spending her energy berating the grandchildren of slave owners, she stresses the importance of correcting current injustices: "The present is upon me and that white man's grandchildren as well. I have business with the grandson as of today. I want to get on with the business in hand. Since I cannot pry loose the clutching hand of time, I will settle for some influence on the present" (332). From this point Hurston launches into her analysis of world affairs, directing her sword at contemporary injustice, rather than at the immutable past. The version of slavery that was published (282–84) is, by contrast, much more insipid, the threat of social, political—even revolutionary—action replaced by a statement that makes Hurston appear blithely indifferent to past or present injustice: "While I have a handkerchief over my eyes crying over the landing of the first slaves in 1619, I might miss something swell that is going on in 1942" (284).

Hurston has, however, learned the efficacy of the "crooked stick," and there is evidence of it even in the published version of this chapter.[24] Both her critique of white America and her defiance of it find a way into that version, though in much abbreviated and thickly veiled form. When Hurston deletes the large sections of critique, she inserts a conversation between herself and a slave owner's grandson (ostensibly intended to show how futile it is to blame white folks for slavery) in which she "foolishly" chides him for his responsibility for the past. He responds that he "was not able to get any better view of social conditions from [his] grandmother's womb than [she] could from [her] grandmother's" (282–83) and continues with this interesting comment:

Are you so simple as to assume that the Big Surrender . . . banished the concept of human slavery from the earth? What is the principle of slavery? Only the buying and selling of human flesh on the block? That was only an outside symbol. Real slavery is couched in the desire and the efforts of any man or community to live and advance their interests at the expense of the lives and interests of others. All of the outward signs come out of that. Do you not realize that the power, prestige and prosperity of the greatest nations on earth rests on colonies and sources

of raw materials? Why else are great wars waged? If you have not
thought, then why waste up time with your vapid accusations? (283)

As the unpublished version of this chapter indicates, Hurston certainly
had "thought" about this matter and had, in fact, tried to write about it
at length. Although it is much abbreviated here, Hurston smuggles the
gist of her argument into the published version by putting it into the
mouth of a powerful white male. What appears to be a vindication of
his personal guilt is, in fact, a much broader political indictment of his
world.

Recognizing the ways Hurston is forced to speak in *Dust Tracks on a
Road* is crucial to understanding its complexity. The mutilation of her
views—and her persona—that results in the published version remains a
statement to a black woman's lack of power as tragic as Hurston's childhood failure to find a voice for her mother. That we see the powerful
hand of the white publisher in a black woman's attempt to tell her own
story is a telling irony repeatedly corroborated in the work itself. The
price for veiling one's ideas, evident in the history of its reception, is also
sobering: the Anisfield Prize for the Improvement of Race Relations
and positive white reviews paid for by the harshest of criticism from
black reviewers.[25] Nevertheless, while Hurston was unable to adopt the
voice of Big Sweet at the end of her autobiography and "specify" as
she might have liked, what she was able to express, however circui-
tously, remains a testament to the survival powers of the black female
self Hurston trusted and to her own persistent desire—even when "doubleteened"—to "smite 'em hip and thigh."

7 The "Trials" of Black Women in the 1950s: Ruby McCollum and Laura Lee Kimble

As THE COMPLEXITY OF *Dust Tracks on a Road* and the fuller picture of her writings during the 1940s (including letters, manuscripts, and articles directed at a black readership) suggest, Hurston was not so much conflicted about her evaluation of Jim Meserve's world as she was forced to different methods of critiquing it, depending on the audience she addressed. Although Hurston faced even greater difficulties publishing her work in the last decade of her life, she never abandoned her fundamental concern with black people's struggle for dignity and independence in a white-dominated world. Having shown in nearly every piece of fiction she wrote that black cultural autonomy could—with tragic results for the racial and gender identities of black women and men—be lost in a world of "mules and men," she struck a note in some of her last articles (nearly always seen as confirmation of her conservatism) out of tune with the more integrationist aspirations of some of her contemporaries. Her conviction that self-hatred and internal conflict often resulted when blacks moved into a white world led her to distrust desegregation as a panacea for racial inequality.[1] Seeing the unacknowledged adoration of whites that had motivated some of her fictional characters played out in the actions of some contemporaries, she continued to argue, in a variety of venues and genres, against the validity of white standards for black people. For instance, in an article in the *Orlando Sentinel* (reprinted in the *Dallas Morning News*), she satirized what she called the "white mare" phenomenon—the mule mindlessly following a white mare and the black person seeking a white spouse—to raise the larger issue of cultural independence: "Growth from within. Ethical and cultural desegregation. It is a contradiction in terms to scream race pride and equality while at the same time spurning Negro teachers and self-association.

That old white mare business can go racking on down the road for all I care" (October 19, 1955, HC).[2]

With even fewer avenues for self-expression open to her during the 1950s, Hurston published where she could, finding it perhaps even more necessary during that conservative decade to camouflage her message in mainstream publishing circles. Nevertheless, the thematic integrity of Hurston's oeuvre and the subtlety of her craft even late in her career (contrary to a general perception of her waning talent) are evident in her treatment of two black women, Ruby McCollum and Laura Lee Kimble.[3] Echoing earlier works in her series of journalistic writings on Ruby McCollum and in her short story, "The Conscience of the Court," Hurston exposes the forces of oppression in these black women's lives in ways that are neither politically naive nor discursively simple. Writing about the trial of Ruby McCollum in the black newspaper, *The Pittsburgh Courier,* and about that of Laura Lee Kimble in a short story published in *The Saturday Evening Post,* Hurston dealt with these two women's assaults on and "trials" in a white-dominated world in quite different ways that can best be understood in relation to the audiences she was addressing.

Clearly fascinated with the story of Ruby McCollum, Hurston wrote extensively about her during the 1950s, covering the sensational trial of a black woman accused of murdering her prominent white lover for the *Pittsburgh Courier* in almost daily columns, writing a series on her life story for the same paper after McCollum's conviction, and finally urging William Bradford Huie to write a book about the subject, a part of which included her own discussion.[4] As Hurston describes it, much about Ruby McCollum's situation recapitulates the racism and sexism she had seen in the lives of black women she had written about earlier in her career. Directing this story to a black readership, Hurston portrays a black woman's defiance much more openly than she was often able to when addressing a white one, depicting McCollum as a titan rather than a trickster and wielding her own writing sword with similar power.

Although Hurston's interpretation of McCollum's act is ultimately unequivocal, the actual trial proceedings (warped by both racism and sexism) leave McCollum's motives open to wild speculation by both black and white observers. McCollum is never allowed to tell her story in court, one that would have focused on her sexual relationship with Dr. Adams and revealed her motives for killing him. Further, despite clear evidence of her long-standing affair with Dr. Adams, the judge forbids the defense to call Ruby's light-skinned daughter she claims is his or to produce the child's birth certificate signed by Adams as the father. With McCollum's silence leaving her story radically open for interpretation, Hurston could have shaped the contradictory "facts" presented during the trial to develop a tragic tale of the contemporary black woman's plight as a modern-day slave, a story casting McCollum as a defenseless black woman, forced to submit to a white man. This is not Hurston's theme, however, even though McCollum—with "nothing out of the ordinary in her. Always quiet with little to say and utterly absorbed in ordinary domestic affairs" ("Life Story," Feb. 28, 1953)—seems an unlikely character to be involved in any violence, much less the murder of a white man.

As she does with most of her seemingly subservient black female characters, Hurston immediately complicates this appearance. In stark contrast to the conventional image McCollum's diminutive stature and conservative dress convey, Hurston emphasizes—in "specifying" rather than "signifying" language for a black audience—the premeditation and violence in McCollum's murderous act: her killing of Dr. Adams, as Hurston here shapes it, is no accidental shooting, but a "slaying" in which the large, prominent white man "f[alls] before the blazing gun of . . . [a] slightly built, soft-spoken Negro woman" ("Life Story," Feb. 28, 1953). Despite the mask McCollum presents in her everyday life or at her trial, Hurston throughout her reporting underscores this contrast between "The quiet, restrained matron whom Live Oak had known prior to Aug. 3 . . . and the intensely emotional woman who had gone to Dr. Adams' office on that Sunday morning with a gun, and had shot him down with one bullet, then stepped over his body and fired others into his body in her rage" ("Victim of Fate!"). She dispels rumors suggesting McCollum killed Adams over a doctor's bill and those casting her as a lover scorned to create a female character as powerful and defiant as Big Sweet of *Mules and Men* and *Dust Tracks on a Road,* a lover as intense and potentially dangerous as the goddess, Erzulie, of *Tell My Horse.* Her story, as Hurston tells it for a black audience, is that of a rebellious black woman who breaks fundamental taboos underlying a racist and sexist social order, "no ordinary mortal, no cringing victim inadequate in its fate" but "an extraordinary personality," "a woman, a Negro woman with the courage to dare every fate, to boldly attack every tradition of her surroundings and even the age-old laws of every land" ("Life Story," Feb. 28, 1953).

In the series she wrote about Ruby McCollum's life story after her conviction, Hurston even more deftly crafts her character. Finding the seeds of this iconoclastic self in her childhood (one that echoes much she had emphasized in her own autobiography), Hurston describes McCollum as an independent young girl who defied the passive female role assigned her, becoming a spunky "tom-boy" who "gave a good account of herself in a fight with [the boys]" ("Life Story," March 7) and who "took her licking[s] with fewer tears and less noise than any of the others." Like the young Zora who "changes words" with nearly every authority figure in her youth, Ruby defied the ban of silence imposed on her, verbally fighting back and "defend[ing] herself with a few well-chosen words" that, Hurston claims, were "insight then into the type of woman she was to later develop into" ("Life Story," March 7).

Describing her growth into womanhood with images and phrases drawn from *Their Eyes Were Watching God,* Hurston again chronicles in her story of McCollum the black woman's difficult journey toward independence and sexual fulfillment. Growing up in a repressive environment, a religious family that forbade any expression of sexuality (even in the form of dancing ["Life Story," March 7, 1953]) and that "trained [her] to despise and fight against physical pleasures and desires as sinful things inspired by the devil" ("Life Story," March 14, 1953), Ruby, who "did not walk in footprints," is unwilling to cram her soul into society's confining pigeonholes: "Secretly she saw no reason why her life must follow the pattern of her surroundings" ("Life Story," March 21, 1953). Like Janie and the young Zora herself, the youthful Ruby inchoately yearns for possibilities beyond the narrow ones offered her, for adventure and sexual fulfillment; she

> live[d] at her front gate, ready for departure. Internally, she had outgrown the confines of Martin, Florida.
> The horizon of the world was her hatband. Ruby longed for fulfillment of her natural desires, and so she was restless beneath her always outward calm. Neither relatives nor friends suspected the intense fires that raged within her. ("Life Story," March 21, 1953)

Possessed with sexual energy of mythic proportions, "a singular power over men" that made her "one of those females who appear now and then in human history" ("Life Story," March 14, 1953), Ruby (like Janie) searches for a man equally vigorous and passionate, someone "around whom she could drape her intense feelings, her great capacity for love" (March 14, 1953). Feeling like "a blossom on the bare limb of a pear tree in the spring . . . opening her gifts to the world" and seeking "the bee for her blossom" ("Life Story," March 14, 1953), she seeks the spiritual and physical communion in marriage so critical in Janie's quest. Her husband, Sam, seems the answer to her dreams and her companion to the horizon; however, like Joe Starks, he proves false, gradually strangling her with the same restraints she had struggled to escape and ultimately becoming not a companion who travels beside her on the road to self-fulfillment but a tyrannical god who demands her subservience and self-denial. When Ruby complains about his numerous affairs with young girls, his retort—"she had the big house and had charge of all his money; she had servants and anything she wanted, so why should she care?" ("Life Story," March 28, 1953)—not only betrays a basely materialistic attitude toward their marriage that desecrates the "pear tree," but even more seriously, a denial of Ruby's own sexuality. Like Starks who feels Janie should be satisfied as Mrs. Mayor, Sam sees Ruby's role as wife as that of sexless, subservient appendage of her husband. Not surprisingly, he echoes Joe Starks (*Eyes*, 69) when he brags to other men about Ruby: "'I wouldn't even put up with the kind of wife you got. My wife is always at home no matter when I get there. She's home and acting like a wife ought to act. Clean in her living and looking after her husband and children'" ("Life Story," March 28, 1953). Final proof that their marriage is not that between pear blossom and bee occurs one night when Ruby complains about some of Sam's drinking companions and the damage they do to their home. In an act that makes visible both Sam's notion of marriage and the violence to Ruby's selfhood that he represents, Sam beats her and forces her to clean up after his friends ("Life Story," April 4, 1953). Their marriage effectively dissolved, Ruby now recognizes Sam as a false idol: "An image—something sacred and precious—[falls] off the shelf in Ruby's heart" ("Life Story," April 4, 1953) at that moment.[5]

Although Hurston's description of Ruby and Sam's marriage highlights sexism in the black community and confronts Sam's oppressive behavior more directly than Hurston often felt free to do before a white readership, her characterization of Ruby's relationship with Adams explodes myths created by both black and white communities. Depicting Adams as a "a broad-shouldered six-footer with magnificence of body and an irresistible smile, a handsome white man whom women of both races seemed unable to resist" ("Life Story," Feb. 28, 1953), Hurston describes him as overwhelmed by Ruby's sexual energy even in their first meeting: "Something electric passed between Ruby McCollum and Dr. Adams the very first time they met. A few minutes after the introduction in her living room, Ruby happened to lift her eyes to find the big handsome white man studying her with a look that she knew only too well. It was so intense it flustered her" ("Life Story," April 4, 1953). In a way that strikes deep into white and black stereotypes of black women, Ruby, sexually spurned and spiritually thwarted by Sam, finds in Adams (at least temporarily) a physical bee for her blossom; with this white man, she was "a riot of passion. She was wanted as she had always yearned to be wanted" ("Life Story," April 11, 1953). Placing Ruby's murder of Adams in this psychobiographical context, Hurston ultimately suggests that she kills him, not because he tries to collect a bill or even because he spurns her, but because he also proves a false god, a threat to her autonomy in his insistence that she move out to his farm ("Life Story," April 25, 1953). Suggesting in Ruby's enigmatic metaphor for her motive the threat both Sam and Adams now present to her self-hood—"'I was between two guns'" ("Life Story," April 25, 1953)—Hurston depicts the murder of Adams as a profound act of self-affirmation: Ruby shoots him to protect the freedom and independence she has fought to attain.

"A woman who ruled the lives and fate of two strong men, one white, the other colored" ("Life Story," May 2, 1953), Ruby McCollum thus becomes a mythic character in the "world-shaking drama" ("Life Story," April 18, 1953) Hurston describes.[6] It is repeatedly the titanic proportions of her character—as awesome as Big Sweet or the supernatural figures of the folktales in *Mules and Men*—that Hurston emphasizes in the images used to describe her. As she suggests in describing Ruby's seemingly passive demeanor, McCollum is no "mule" or "seraph" but a power that when thwarted "bursts forth like an awesome Niagara or Victoria Nyansa" ("Life Story," Feb. 28, 1953). Hurston's story of Ruby McCollum recounts the triumph of an oppressed black woman who has used her power not merely to manipulate but to assault the racial and gendered hierarchies of Jim Meserve's world. This black female power—both its awesome creative and (if threatened) its destructive capacity—is finally what Hurston glimpses through Ruby's mask at the trial.

Despite their varied public stories about Ruby, even the black community gleans this theme from her tale. Among them, she is "enshrined in legend and folk-lore even before the trial begins. Something on the order of Jesse James, the very boldness of her act and the mystery surrounding it, have made of her a heroine" ("Ruby McCollum Fights for Life"). Predicting her execution, several people have visions in which she appears as a wandering black spirit, as vengeful as Kanty in Hurston's short story, "Spunk": "Several claim to have already seen her spirit in one form or another wandering around free from her imprisoned body. She had appeared in the bedroom of a couple one night in the form of a cat-like animal, and was crying piteously" ("Ruby McCollum Fights for Life"). Another woman's dream draws significantly on the mythic symbols of black women's power Hurston had used in *Dust Tracks on a Road*. The Ruby she dreams of and the character Hurston creates for a black audience echo the "cosmic" sword-wielding persona she had evoked in her autobiography; the character is finally "a woman with the head of an eagle with a flaming sword in her hand in flowing robes, circling their house for three nights running and crying out in defiance" ("Ruby McCollum Fights for Life").

Ruby McCollum, a sister to Big Sweet, Aunt Caroline of *Dust Tracks on a Road,* Amy of *Jonah's Gourd Vine,* and the formidable black women of men's nightmares, seems a stark contrast to the deferential and helpless black woman portrayed in "Conscience of the Court." Although Hurston's last published piece of fiction initially seems an embarrassing story of black subservience to white authority, it demonstrates Hurston's ability, even when writing in 1950 for the predominantly white audience of the *Saturday Evening Post,* to address contentious issues of race and gender. Because she was forced yet again "to hit a straight lick with a crooked stick," the story is a deceptively complex one: just as the white judge finds the black defendant, Laura Lee Kimble, to be "a riddle," so too the story is enigmatic, open to two quite different interpretations.

On the surface the story seems a valorization of the American legal system in which an ignorant black woman, on trial for beating up a white man, is saved by the conscience of a white male judge. Although Laura Lee Kimble does not deny the act, she argues that Beaseley was trying to steal the possessions of the white woman she has adored and served throughout both their lives. Despite the suggestion early in the story that she will surely be convicted (the only evidence is the word of the white male plaintiff against that of the black female defendant), Kimble is ultimately acquitted, thanks to a benevolent white judge and a set of ideals of justice that transcend racial prejudice. These values are most clearly articulated by the judge at the end of the trial: "The protection of women and children, he said, was inherent, implicit in Anglo-Saxon civilization, and here in the United States it had become a sacred trust. He reviewed the long, slow climb of humanity from the rule of the club and the stone hatchet to the Constitution of the United States. The English-speaking people had given the world its highest concepts of the rights of the individual, and they were not going to be made a mock of and nullified by this court" (122).

As the title suggests, the judge can be seen as both the embodiment of these lofty ideals and the hero of the story, a man with a profound sense of fairness despite the racist society in which he lives. When, at an early stage, Kimble fatalistically refuses a lawyer because "'[she] don't reckon it would do . . . a bit of good'" (23), the judge is moved by the contradiction between the racism alluded to in Laura's comment and nobler ideals of universal justice:

> The implications penetrated instantly and the judge flushed. This unlettered woman had called up something that he had not thought about
> for quite some time. The campus of the University of Virginia and himself as a very young man there, filled with a reverence for his profession
> amounting to an almost holy dedication. His fascination and awe as a
> professor traced the more than two thousand years of growth of the concepts of human rights and justice. That brought him to his greatest hero,
> John Marshall, and his inner resolve to follow in the great man's steps,
> and even add to interpretations of human rights if his abilities allowed.
> No, he had not thought about all this for quite some time. (23)

With his conscience awakened, he takes pity on Kimble and her ignorance, treating her with kindness, translating legal terms for her "in a gentle voice" (23), and making it possible for her to get a fair trial.

Kimble, however, seems to be the helpless beneficiary of white justice, generally bewildered by the courtroom proceedings, so befuddled by legal language that she cannot answer even simple questions; when asked how she pleads, she can only respond: "'Plead? Don't reckon I make out just what you all mean by that'" (23). Even after the judge translates into simpler language, she is still confused: "'Deed I don't know if I's guilty or not. I hit the man after he hit me, to be sure, Mister Judge, but if I'm guilty I don't know for sure. All them big words and all'" (23). Even beyond her passive and helpless relation to the white judge, Kimble is a discomfitting character, a stereotypical faithful retainer (complete with "head-rag" and a husband named Tom), concerned only with serving her white mistress. This devotion has not only landed her in jail; she clings to Miss Celestine and defends her throughout her trial, even when her employer does not answer letters asking for help. Always servile in court, smiling at the judge and thanking him for every "kindness," Kimble seems to accept her subservient role with enthusiasm. Acquitted by the white jury and relieved to learn that Miss Celestine never received her pleas for help, Kimble returns home at the end of the story to serve and to worship in the sacred temple of her white mistress:

> Back at the house, Laura Lee did not enter at once. Like a pilgrim before a shrine, she stood and bowed her head. "I ain't fitten to enter. For a time, I allowed myself to doubt my Celestine. But maybe nobody ain't as pure in heart as they aim to be. The cock crowed on Apostle Peter. Old Maker, please take my guilt away and cast it into the sea of forgetfulness where it won't ever rise to accuse me in this world, nor condemn me in the next."
>
> Laura Lee entered and opened all the windows with a ceremonial air. She was hungry, but before she would eat, she made a ritual of atonement by serving. She took a finely wrought silver platter from the massive old side-board and gleamed it to perfection. So the platter, so she wanted her love to shine. (122)

On the surface, then, "The Conscience of the Court," offering to a white audience in 1950 a comforting picture of race relations grounded in inequality, seems another of Hurston's stories an admirer might wish she had not written. With its approbation of the American legal system, depicted as color-blind in the justice it dispenses, and its nonthreatening portrait of blacks, however, it is little wonder that Hurston could get this story placed in a prestigious white magazine when little else of her material was being accepted.

This interpretation is initially complicated, however, by remembering what Hurston had written about American political and judicial ideals earlier in her career. Speaking specifically about "justice," for instance, she had voiced a more cynical attitude about eloquent expressions of noble ideals, emphasizing the contradiction between "abstractions about justice" and "the cold hardness to the black individual" (Hurston to Douglas Gilbert, quoted in *Dust Tracks,* xxx). As Hurston had suggested in the manuscript chapter on world affairs of her autobiography, while she might like to imagine her country more just than others, "now and then the embroidered hangings blow aside, and I am less exalted. I see that the high principles enunciated so throatedly are like the flowers in spring—they have nothing to do with the case" (337).

Despite Hurston's seeming reverence for the white judge and the ideals he espouses, she similarly undercuts his eloquent "high principles." In the rural South at the beginning of the 1950s, the trial of a black woman accused of assault against a white man would have been, as Hurston well knew, an exercise not in legal abstractions but in concrete racial realities. With Kimble facing her jury in a trial more accurately seen as "The [White] People versus Laura Lee Kimble" (23), Hurston deflates the judge's abstract rhetoric early in the story by emphasizing the racist prejudice Kimble faces, "The hostility in the room" (23) and the condemnation that "crawled all over [her] like reptiles" (23). The proceedings brisk—"twelve names called, and just like that the jury box was filled and sworn in" (23)—and the verdict assured, "this here so-called trial was nothing to [Laura] but a form and a fashion and an outside show to the world" (23). While Kimble seems merely confused by the legal terminology, there is unwitting folk wisdom in her analysis that "The People was a meddlesome and unfriendly passel and had no use for the truth" (23); for, as she realizes, her fate seems sealed (23).

Hurston also blows aside the embroidered hangings of the judicial system through Kimble's "unlearnt" responses to courtroom rhetoric:

> "Charged with felonious and aggravated assault. Mayhem. Premeditated attempted murder on the person of one Clement Beaseley. Obscene and abusive language. Laura Lee Kimble, how do you plead?"
>
> Laura Lee was so fascinated by the long-named things that they were accusing her of that she stood there tasting over the words. *Lawdy me!* she mused inside herself. *Look like I done every crime excepting habeas corpus and stealing a mule.* (23, emphasis in original)

Echoing folktales (such as "The First Colored Man in Massa's House" narrated in *Mules and Men*) that deflate white circumlocution, Hurston satirizes legalese in the different versions of the crime that are given. The doctor "told how terribly Clement Beaseley had been hurt. Left arm broken above the elbow, compound fracture of the forearm, two ribs cracked, concussion of the brain and various internal injuries" (23). Kimble's version, rich in folk idiom, lampoons the insipidity of that language and reduces her crime (and Beaseley's suffering) to slapstick:

"All I did next was to grab him by his heels and frail the pillar or the
porch with him a few times. I let him go, but he just laid there like
a log."

"'Don't you lay there, making out you's dead, sir!' I told him. "'Git
on up from there, even if you is dead, and git on off this place!'"

"The contrary scamp laid right there, so I reached down and muscled
him up on acrost my shoulder and toted him to the gate, and heaved
him over the fence out onto the street. None of my business what become of him and his dirty mouth after that." (114, 116)

Hurston also surrounds the judge's final speech with irony that undercuts his pompous self-righteousness. Although he concludes that
Kimble should be found innocent of the "crimes" with which she
is charged, he displays a disconcerting arrogance and racial superiority
toward Kimble throughout the story that is summed up in his final reference to her as a "faithful watch-dog who bit [Beaseley]" (122). Furthermore, despite his "big words" about Anglo-Saxon civilization, the
Constitution of the United States, and the concepts of individual rights,
the ideals of justice he appeals to "have nothing to do with the case."
Perhaps the judge, enraptured with his own abstract rhetoric, momentarily forgets racial realities, but Hurston certainly possessed no illusions
about the "protection" offered black women by either Anglo-Saxon
civilization or the American Constitution. In fact, Hurston's story makes
it clear that Kimble is saved not by American judicial ideals or the benevolence of the white judge but by her own wits. Crafting her story
in the fashion of many black folktales with a servile, even racist overt
theme, Hurston ultimately conveys a message with much more subversive implications. In fact, "The Conscience of the Court" was Hurston's
final trickster tale, one in which Kimble masterfully manipulates her
white audience in the court for her own benefit.

The apparent moral is seriously undermined by a closer examination
of Kimble's motive in attacking Beaseley. Whereas she claims repeatedly
in her testimony that allegiance to Mrs. Claiborne forced her physically to prevent Beaseley from stealing the white woman's possessions,
her version of why she stayed on—even when her husband, Tom, wanted
to move—points to financial arrangements indicating a less servile motive for her assault. As Mrs. Claiborne's promise that, should she die first,
"Anything she left was willed to [Laura] to do with as [she] saw fit"
(120) suggests, Kimble acts not out of selfless devotion but out of self-
interest to save her own possessions. When Beaseley states that he was

simply trying to collect collateral on an overdue loan, it is extremely difficult to tell whether Kimble is more upset at the slur against Mrs. Claiborne's character or at his ridiculous undervaluing of her future inheritance: "Laura Lee was no longer a spectator at her own trial. Now she was in a flaming rage. She would have leaped to her feet as the man pictured Miz' Celestine as a cheat and a crook, and again as he sat up there and calmly lied about the worth of the furniture. All of those wonderful antiques, this man making out that they did not equal his minching six hundred dollars! That lie was a sin and a shame!" (23). For a woman who has risked death by beating up a white man to protect her belongings, Beaseley's lie about their value *is* a greater "sin and shame" than offense to one's employer.

Once this motive for her actions is acknowledged, Kimble's behavior in court appears not as mindless servility, but as conscious manipulation of her audience for self-preservation. Although her testimony seems spontaneous and her demeanor unaffected, Hurston hints at a mind able to assess a situation quickly and to form an appropriate response. When asked if she wants the court to appoint an attorney, for instance, Kimble does not reply immediately but swiftly "cover[s] a lot of ground" before answering (23). Aware that she faces the possibility of a long jail term or mob violence, she draws on the folk wisdom of High John, who knows his white folks and uses this knowledge to beat them at their own game. Like John, Kimble relies on white stereotypes of blacks, consciously developing an image of herself as an ignorant, deferential faithful retainer, both to encourage sympathy and to camouflage her astute maneuvering. Throwing her white judge and jurors off their guard by her early feigned confusion and helplessness, she reinforces this image at the beginning of her testimony by depicting herself as "'a unlearnt woman'" "'ignorant about a whole heap of things'" (112). Her helpless look at the judge "with bewilderment in her eyes" (23) is merely part of her masking strategy, as Hurston's careful phrasing hints: she may feign bewilderment with her eyes, but as her behavior suggests, there is none in her mind.

Even her apparent blunders are in actuality brilliant maneuvers. Her refusal of a court-appointed attorney, which the judge sees as a grave "mistake" (112), is a masterful ploy with two significant results. By refusing this help, she not only pricks the judge's conscience in alluding to the futility of it but also frees herself of the encumbrance of ponderous

legal abstractions. Refusing the lawyer not because she fails to understand the gravity of her situation or because she is fatalistic about her
chances for a fair trial (as she claims) but because she wants to be in
control of her own story, she begins manipulating her audience from the
very beginning of her testimony. Acting reluctant to tell her "unlearnt"
tale before such an august body, she sits (apparently dumbfounded) for
"nearly a minute" (112) when called on to testify—long enough and
helpless enough to disarm the judge, who entreats her to begin: " 'Believe it or not, Laura Lee, this is a court of law. It is needful to hear both
sides of every question before the court can reach a conclusion and
know what to do. Now, you don't strike me as a person that is unoblig-
ing at all. I believe if you knew you would be helping me out a great
deal by telling your side of the story, you would do it' " (112). While the
judge's patronizing tone reflects his pompous analysis of the power relation here, Kimble's response suggests another and more accurate one.
Delighted at the tactical success of her first maneuver, she smiles "involuntarily" and responds with the trickster's veiled assessment of who is
in control: " 'Yes, sir, Mister Judge. If I can be of some help to you, I sure
will. And I thank you for asking me' " (112).

Kimble now has her opportunity to tell the tale she has planned
for this occasion. She develops a story that for her white audience is
both familiar and reassuring, one of romanticized plantation relations in
which the main characters, the white aristocrat and her "pet Negro,"
mutually (but appropriate to their station) love and support one another.
With Beaseley's bashed body displayed in the courtroom "on [a] hospital
cot swaddled up in bandage rags" (23), this strategy allows Kimble to
tackle an extremely difficult rhetorical task. Unable to deny her violence
against a white man, she can only make this act appear not an act of
aggression against whites but a selfless act in defense of them. She embellishes the elements of this nostalgic tale so well that, as the audience's changed response from "anger" (23) to "approval" (116) suggests,
she would have probably been acquitted even if the loan note exposing
Beaseley's lies had not been produced.

Kimble's emphasis on her husband, Tom, seemingly another of her
logical irrelevancies, serves an important function for her portrayal of
herself as faithful retainer. By inserting him as a character into her tale
and by carefully crafting his words, she is able to inject a characterization
of herself that appears objective rather than self-serving:

"Tom claimed that he ever loved me harder than the thunder could
bump a stump, but I had one habit that he ever wished he could break
me of. Claimed that I always placed other folks's cares in front of my
own, and more expecially Miz' Celestine. Said that I made out of myself
a wishbone shining in the sun. Just something for folks to come along
and pick up and rub and pull and get their wishes and good luck on.
Never looked out for nothing for my ownself." (116)

Tom also serves the important function of proving the tenacity of
Kimble's love for Miz' Celestine. Repeatedly referring to her defiance
of his wishes to leave, even when he "'rear[ed] and pitch[ed] like a mule
in a tin stable'" (120), she is able to underscore her own faithfulness
to Miz' Celestine's wishes. By stressing Tom's feelings of self-interest
(he always felt they should "'grab the cash'" and look out for themselves [120]) and his scorn of the faithful retainer role (he thought she
was "'wrong'" (116) to do so much for Miz' Celestine), Kimble creates through him a powerful symbolic threat to white supremacy and a
stark contrast to the persona she presents in her summation to the jury:
"'Maybe I is guilty sure enough. I could be wrong for staying all them
years and making Miz' Celestine's cares my own. You gentlemens is got
more book-learning than me, so you would know more than I do. So far
as this fracas is concerned, yeah, I hurted this plaintive, but with him
acting the way he was, it just couldn't be helped. And 'tain't nary one of
you gentlemens but what wouldn't of done the same'" (120, 122). By
this point Kimble has subtly managed to redefine the notion of guilt.
The issue of whether she has committed the crimes of which she is
accused has evaporated, and in its place is left the issue of whether the
role of faithful retainer is right or wrong. Having been brainwashed by
Kimble's repeated equation of right and black subservience—she "'fig-
gered [she] done right not to leave [Beaseley] come in there and haul
off Miz' Celestine's things which she had left there under [her] trust
and care'" (116) and she "'felt right and good, looking out for Miz'
Celestine's interest and standing true and strong'" (116)—the jury is
thus left with a choice: they may vote for the racist status quo and find
Kimble innocent; or they can follow Tom's logic, find her selfless adoration wrong, and return a guilty verdict. To do so, as Kimble well knows,
would require them to accept the symbolic challenge to white supremacy that Tom has come to represent.

Whatever white people's opinion, Kimble emerges from the story as
a formidable power, more nearly the "savage queen" and "man-killing

bear cat of a woman" (23) that the judge initially believes than the "faithful watch-dog" he finally labels her. As Beaseley's bruised body hilariously images, she defends herself and her possessions as vigorously and successfully as Hurston's other "lionesses." As astute in her analysis and flexible in her response to power as many of Hurston's black women, however, she takes another tact when "doubleteened" in court: aware that "The People" may be "a meddlesome passel with no use for the truth," she proves through her rhetorical acumen that they can nonetheless be manipulated by a good story. Kimble's ultimate triumph over the entire white cast arrayed against her is suggested in the story's final, initially discomfitting, scene of her return home. With an awareness that Kimble polishes her own silver in a fine house that will someday be hers, that final image acquires a quite different significance, one in which Hurston wins for a black woman what she had claimed as her goal in *Dust Tracks on a Road*—not a bunk, but "the boss's bed" (*Dust Tracks*, 345); not the "back stairs," but "the front of the house" (*Dust Tracks*, 346).

In these final stories of black women's "trials," Hurston treats two very different responses to power that, read in conjunction with her earlier works, demonstrate the kind of thematic and symbolic reverberations that echo throughout her oeuvre. The trickster (from Isie Watts to Laura Lee Kimble) and the titan (from Big Sweet to Ruby McCollum) appear throughout her writing, as they do in her depiction of these women, not as opposites but as aspects of black female identity (including Hurston's) and modes of resistance to be called upon in different social or discursive contexts. Given Hurston's literary project—exposing relations of power and subordination from a subordinate position— she was most often thwarted in her attempts to write as Big Sweet and forced to adopt Kimble's strategy, a position that for a woman who loved to "change words" and "call names," who kept her "oyster knife" ("How It Feels to Be Colored Me") sharpened (and not merely for mussels), must have rankled. Although Hurston invariably put the best face possible on her response to subordination, depicting herself as gleefully emerging with the spoils, her own laughter must have often been as complex as much of that she describes, for the trickster figure as a discursive strategy was not without its problems and its price.

While Hurston's use of the trickster strategy, like John's, was a way of "making a way out of no-way" ("High John," p. 70), it was—as she well knew—a survival tactic, a manipulation of power relations rather than a frontal assault or radical reorganization of them, a strategy used (even in *Mules and Men*) by necessity rather than choice. Her consistent resort to the trickster's approach in her mainstream published works should be taken, however, not as evidence of her naiveté about the kind of victories tricksters win, so much as her profound awareness—learned from decades of experience trying to express herself in other ways— of the weighty overlapping hierarchies pressing down on black women writers. To suggest that Hurston should simply have wielded her sword against racism and sexism (however one might wish she could have) is itself a naively romanticized and ahistorical demand that denies the social context in which she wrote. Her approach to writing in a world of "mules and men," despite its limitation, made possible the more modest but critical victory she claimed for High John stories, the survival of the black woman's soul "So [s]he could use it afterwards" ("High John," p. 70), to fight another day in perhaps a more direct way and to imagine more autonomous and less oppressive alternatives.

Even this achievement was not without its aesthetic and personal costs. Hurston's frequent expressions of dissatisfaction with individual works and her blanket statement in her autobiography—"I regret all of my books" (212)—perhaps signals both Hurston's frustration with the constraints on tricksters and her awareness of the scars that strategy sometimes left in her work. Veiling and masking did, in fact, sometimes result in jarring or contrived metaphors to convey a message (the underwear motif of *Seraph on the Suwanee* approaches the border of bathos while the details of Arvay's bathroom habits cross it), and occasionally (as in the "Herod the Great" manuscript Hurston was trying to publish almost until her death) both cryptic and less than compelling narratives.

Hurston's trickster strategy had personal costs as well. Despite the early enthusiasm and optimism she had expressed for it in "Drenched in Light," decades of experience trying to negotiate power in that manner must have revealed the sheer difficulty of keeping "the soul whole and free" ("High John," p. 70) and the psychic toll of the project. The condescension and exploitation Hurston often encountered (so pronounced in comments written to her and about her during her life) were often experiences less like those of "Isis the Joyful" and more like those of Belinda in *Seraph on the Suwanee*, "the greatest artist of her day," whose performances were degrading and whose rewards for her efforts were often appropriated by a middle-man.

As Belinda's experience suggests, gender also played a role in complicating Hurston's "performances." The trickster's mask, which works, of course, because a segment of the divided audience recognizes it *as* a mask, can only be rhetorically effective when donned by a figure of some status within the subordinate audience, one who commands enough respect to be acknowledged as a subversive rather than a dupe. John, for instance, may get no respect from white people, but that he commands in his own community allows him to be embraced by them, not as a fool but as a hero. As Mae Henderson ("Speaking in Tongues") argues is often the case for African American women writers, Hurston could not count on such a unified black audience. Invading traditional male territory in adopting a trickster discursive strategy, she was simply not recognized by black male literary figures of her day (as the tone even more than the substance of their comments on her work suggests) as a figure of such stature. Her sharp retorts to a number of them reveal not simply the pettiness or legendary "difficulty" of Hurston's personality but her angry recognition of and sword-wielding response to their condescension.[7]

In complex ways Hurston's solution to the problem of audience had its own difficulties, not the least of which was the absence of a visible and powerful black female readership during her day. Just as black women's voices were noticeably absent in response to Janie's testimony at her trial and just as their powerlessness to "pass judgment" on her case may have influenced her testimony, the same void in Hurston's career profoundly affected not only her discursive strategy but also for decades her place in literary history. Hurston's discursive tactic did, however, function as a textual survival strategy, one that made it possible for her to "save the text"—however sometimes mutilated and unsatisfactory for the author—for a later generation of African American women readers and writers who have claimed her as a foremother. Like Nanny who was not able to preach *about* black women "sitting on high," Hurston was rarely able to preach *as* such a woman, but her trickster strategy was one that achieved her literary survival and that allowed her, like Laura Lee Kimble, to enter the "big house" of *The Saturday Evening Post* and other mainstream publishing concerns, no doubt aware that her mask would often be mistaken by blacks and whites as the whole self, that the public portrait of her as the "perfect book of entertainment" (*The Big Sea,* 238) would affect interpretation of her work and appreciation of her artistry. Even though hitting a straight lick with a crooked stick would surely not have been Hurston's preferred tactic, it produced a literary craft both subtly complex in its treatment of race and gender and, in its deft handling of a heterogenous readership, seasoned with more than a pinch of craftiness.

Conclusion

DESPITE THE IMAGE OF Hurston as a "unique character" and a writer whose work fits into no "pigeonhole," her career underscores the important role that the social position of African American women writers as gendered and racial outsiders in a patriarchal white American society has played both in their discursive practice and in reception of their work. As Carole Boyce Davies emphasizes in *Black Women, Writing and Identity,* for instance, the silencing and censorship black women writers have historically faced (and so striking in Hurston's career) are directly related to this fact, for it is the politics of location that "allows one to speak or not speak, to be affirmed in one's speech or rejected, to be heard or censored" (153) and that also affects artistic strategies and choices. The difficulties Hurston faced thus represent just one specific case of the complex discursive dilemmas facing African American women writers, who as black women, have possessed the power to control neither publication of their work nor the context in which it is interpreted.

Mae Henderson's more detailed analysis of the ways in which black women's positionality creates quite different relationships with various segments of a heterogenous audience sheds light on the difficulties of reception Hurston and other African American women writers encounter:

> [Black women] writers enter simultaneously into familial, or *testimonial*
> and public, or *competitive* discourses—discourses that both affirm and
> challenge the values and expectations of the reader. As such, black
> women writers enter into testimonial discourse with black men as
> blacks, with white women as women, and with black women as black
> women. At the same time, they enter into a competitive discourse with
> black men as women, with white women as blacks, and with white men

as black women. If black women speak a discourse of racial and gendered difference in the dominant or hegemonic discursive order, they
speak a discourse of racial and gender identity and difference in the sub-
dominant discursive order. This dialogic of difference and dialectic of
identity characterize both black women's subjectivity and black
women's discourse. (20–21)

The discursive position of black women is thus similar to Janie's at her
trial and the literary courtroom in which black women writers speak an
equally complex affair, affecting both how they *can* speak and how their
words are interpreted. Henderson's analysis further suggests reasons why,
as was the case with Janie's testimony, the folktales in *Mules and Men,*
and every one of Hurston's books, different segments of black women
writers' heterogenous audience may, in fact, "hear" quite different tales
in their work.

The story of Hurston's struggle with this fractured audience, her
efforts to address complex issues of race and gender in a social and literary context shaped by race and gender, is far from unique. As several
critics have emphasized, other black women writers during the Harlem
Renaissance who addressed both race and gender issues also found
themselves forced to masking and other subtextual narrative techniques. In *Women of the Harlem Renaissance,* Cheryl Wall, for instance, has
pointed out how heightened race consciousness of the period—a race
consciousness that gendered the "New Negro" as male—often made it
extremely difficult for black women writers to address issues of sexism
directly: "Amid the effort to forge a revised racial identity, a woman
who persisted in raising such concerns might see them dismissed as irrelevant or trivial; she might herself be perceived as disloyal to the race"
(7). As a result, Nella Larsen and Jesse Fauset, for instance, quite different
in many critical ways from Hurston, nevertheless also struggled with the
complex interaction of racism and sexism in their relations with publishers, patrons, and critics and also developed indirect ways to address
volatile issues in their work.[1] The profound—and ultimately negative—
effect that such strategies of indirection had on reception of their work
certainly applies equally in Hurston's case. Like Hurston's, Nella Larsen's
"readers were so sure they knew the story Larsen was telling they misread the story she actually told. . . . [S]he set forth a vision far more
complex and daring than even her most enthusiastic critics imagined.
She paid a price. Her success was measured by those who *knew* what they
were seeing and thereby missed the point" (Wall, *Women,* 138).

Whereas Hurston's struggles with black male readers and her misin-
terpretation by many white ones suggest affinities with African American women writers of her own era, the reading of Hurston's work I
have offered also underscores her close relationship with contemporary
African American women writers. Many critics have rightly emphasized
thematic similarities between Hurston and African American women
writers, such as Toni Morrison, Gloria Naylor, Toni Cade Bambara,
Ntozake Shange, Audre Lorde, Paule Marshall, and Alice Walker, who
since the 1970s have directly addressed issues of race *and* gender in
their work. Hurston is appropriately proclaimed a "foremother" of these
writers because of similarities, for instance, in her treatment of black
women's particular problems in their search for identity. Like many of
her literary descendants, Hurston also repeatedly addressed intraracial
aspects of black women's oppression and critiqued traditional notions of
masculinity that perpetuated it while never forgetting the racial context
in which relationships between black women and men were embedded.
In fact, the current term, "womanist," embraced by many contemporary black women to highlight the interaction of race and sex in black
women's experience and the inadequacy of exclusive focus on either,
also captures central themes that recur in Hurston's work. As Chikwenye Ogunyemi defines it, womanism is "a philosophy that celebrates
black roots, the ideals of black life, while giving a balanced presentation
of black womandom. It concerns itself as much with the black sexual
power tussle as with the world power that subjugates blacks. Its ideal is
for black unity where every black person has a modicum of power and
so can be a 'brother' or 'sister' or a 'father' or a 'mother' of the other" (82).
This too was Hurston's ideal, one that involved not only the critique of
white America and of black women and men who failed to embrace
alternative ideals but also the vision of a broad social transformation that
would make possible, in Alice Walker's definition of "womanism," the
"survival and wholeness of entire people, male *and* female" (*In Search,*
xi).[2] This set of values, which I have argued informed not just *Their Eyes
Were Watching God* but all of Hurston's books, suggests even more
strongly her connection to contemporary African American women
writers.

What separates Hurston most sharply from these contemporary African American women writers is the directness with which they often
address themes that she was forced to mask. As Cheryl Wall suggests,
this change in discursive practice is a major difference between black

women writers of the Harlem Renaissance and contemporary African American women writers, one that can obscure important thematic
similarities:

> Individually and collectively, the biographies of the women of the
> Harlem Renaissance offer both models and cautionary tales. But if these
> literary foremothers were sometimes unable to *live* their dreams and con-
> victions, they left a legacy in their art. Their literary legatees critique, re-
> vise, and extend the themes, forms, and metaphors that they employed in
> their poetry and fiction. Perhaps the most telling act of recuperation
> and revision is the determination of this new generation to bring to the
> surface those themes and plots that their precursors masked. The subtext
> has become the text. (*Women,* 204)

Whereas Wall here emphasizes important historical changes in discursive practice, the public response to many contemporary African
American women writers suggests that simply translating the subtext to
text has not been an unproblematic solution to the discursive dilemma
faced by Hurston and other African American women writers. In fact,
critical reception to contemporary "specifying" underscores that, despite social changes that make it more possible for contemporary black
women to speak directly, the overarching dynamics of race and sex so
striking in the history of Hurston's reception are still operative today.
In fact, the "trials" of contemporary African American women writers
sometimes sound distressingly familiar and suggest that the "courtroom" in which they "testify" today is not entirely different from that
in which Janie spoke or Hurston wrote.[3]
    As Deborah McDowell points out, critical response to contempo-
rary African American women writers underscores the fact that their
texts often "take shape in the minds of readers and critics who form dis-
parate interpretive communities" ("Reading," 75), communities often
based on racial and gendered social position. McDowell goes on to discuss differences in the response of various segments of black women's
readership, chronicling in detail the vituperative response of some black
men to contemporary black women writers, who see in much of their
work not an affirmation of black women but an assault on black men.[4]
Like the male auditors at Janie's trial, who heard her testimony from a
narrow, unexamined position as black males and consequently misinter-
preted her experience, a group of contemporary black male readers, according to McDowell, "brings to the reading of black women's texts
a complex of powerful assumptions, not the least of which is the equa-

tion of textuality with masculine subjectivity and masculine point of view" ("Reading," 83). Hearing only the "competitive" or "contestatorial" register in black women's work, these critics

> have lumped all black women writers together and have focused on one tiny aspect of their immensely complex and diverse project—the image of black men—despite the fact that, if we can claim a center for these texts, it is located in the complexities of black female subjectivity and experience. In other words, though black women writers have made black women the subjects of their own family stories, these male readers/critics are attempting to usurp that place for themselves and place it at the center of critical inquiry. ("Reading," 84)

Although McDowell focuses on the fractures along gender lines among black readers of African American women writers, she raises important concerns about the larger courtroom in which this conflict is played out. As was the case with Sop and his friends, who turned against Janie at her trial, readers approaching black women's texts from this limited perspective not only misread those texts but also fail to see the larger racial context in which conflicts between black women and men are embedded: "While these male gazes are fixed on the texts of black women in which they seek to find idealized reflections of themselves, they fail to see the highest mountain, the meta-structure who has the naming power and in whose name and interests that power is secured. It is this looming, distant structure that orchestrates and dominates this literary battle royal, this already fixed match betweeen black men and black women" ("Reading," 96).

Apprehension about the politics of reception at this "meta-level" and the response of white readers to direct portrayal of intragroup conflicts has led to other criticisms of contemporary African American women writers. Just as Janie, John, and Hurston recognized that white listeners represented no disinterested segment of their audience and could misappropriate overt treatment of conflicts between black people, Trudier Harris, for instance, has voiced concern that "spectator readers" may, like Janie's white audience at her trial, hear stories that reassure rather than challenge them. She critiques Alice Walker's *The Color Purple* from this perspective because of concern that Walker's treatment of "degradation, abuse, dehumanization . . . invites spectator readers to generalize about black people in the same negative ways that have been going on for centuries" ("On *The Color Purple*," 142).[5]

Although response to contemporary African American women

writers highlights important continuities in the "trials" of black women writers, what has changed perhaps most significantly in reception of Hurston and other African American women writers is the presence, since the 1970s, of more black women in the literary "courtroom" and their role in redefining the terms in which interpretations are framed and "verdicts" rendered. Redrawing the boundaries of critical theory and addressing the inadequacies of mainstream (male) African American and (white) feminist perspectives to deal with black women writers, black feminist critics have been instrumental in developing our understanding of both thematic nuances in the work of black women writers and the complex discursive positions from which they write. Although, as Deborah McDowell's discussion of black feminist criticism suggests, this perspective represents no "unitary essence" defined solely by race or sex of the critic or even by one methodology in the 1990s, it is unified around the principle that "black women's experience must be comprehended simultaneously in sexual, class, and racial terms" ("Boundaries," 53).[6] Using this perspective to explore "ways in which the experience of race affects the experience of gender . . . [and] ways in which the culturally constituted experience of gender, specifically of womanhood, affects the experience of race" (Valerie Smith, "Gender," 484), black feminist critics have reshaped the literary courtroom and profoundly transformed the "trials" of black women writers. It is such a set of "judges" and "jurors" that Hurston acutely realized she lacked in her own day, but it is also the audience her work has helped to create.

Notes

Introduction

1. Rambeau has, for instance, argued that Hurston works by a white aesthetic rather than a black one. Ikonné's claim that Hurston actually hated the black world and felt strongly the superiority of the white one (183–84) is perhaps most damning. Accepted by whites both as an individual and as a writer, she was "helpless before an understandable subconscious urge to gratify the ego of her white friends" (187). The result evident in her work was "contempt for the Negro race and, since she was a member of the 'mean' Negro race, respect for the white race whose feeling of superiority she gratified by acting out demeaning stereotypes attributed to the Negro" (184).

2. In an article for *Opportunity* titled "Our Literary Audience," Sterling Brown similarly decried the demands placed on black authors by black readers. Like Johnson he criticized some black readers for demanding only "idealistic optimistic tracts for race advertisement" (42), pointing out the implications of these literary values in a satirical anecdote: "According to this scale of values, a book about a Negro and a mule would be a better one than one about a muleless Negro; about a Negro and a horse and buggy a better book than about the mule owner; about a Negro and a Ford, better than about the buggy rider; and a book about a Negro and a Rolls Royce better than one about a Negro and a Ford. All that it seems our writers need to do, to guarantee a perfect book and deathless reputation is to write about a Negro and an aeroplane" (44).

Johnson's point about the black writer's dilemma was echoed by Harlem Renaissance figures on into the 1940s. According to Sterling Brown in "The Negro Author and His Publisher," white readers were still demanding the familiar old stereotypes: "When we cease to be exotic, we do not sell well" (15). Many black readers, he argued, still demanded universally flattering portraits of black characters; authors straying from this image could expect to be accused of "'selling the race down the river'" (18). J. Saunders Redding in "The Negro Author: His Public and His Purse" also reiterates Johnson's point, stressing necessity for a black author to recognize the power of a white audience. A black author who "say[s], in effect, the devil with a white audience . . . runs the risk of publishing the book himself and peddling it from door to door" (1288).

3. In *Tell My Horse,* Hurston delights in describing another trickster figure—Guedé—the Haitian god of the poor and powerless. "A hilarious divinity and full of the stuff of burlesque" (232), Guedé is "the deification of the common people of Haiti" (232). "Bit[ing] with sarcasm and slash[ing] with ridicule the [upper] class" (233), he "burlesque[s] the society that crushe[s]" (233) the dispossessed. In that work Hurston also refers several times to stories of the tricksters Ti Malice and Anansi. In "God and the Pintards" (273–75) she narrates a trickster tale that recapitulates the dynamics of many African American ones.

4. Numerous critics have written about the centrality of masking in the Afro-American literary tradition. Houston Baker, for instance, argues that "the mastery of the minstrel mask by blacks . . . constitutes the primary move in Afro-American discursive modernism" (*Modernism and the Harlem Renaissance,* 17), whereas Constance Rourke suggests that masking is crucial in black literature before the 1940s. Nathan Huggins has discussed its importance specifically in the Harlem Renaissance (*Harlem Renaissance,* 261–301). For related discussions, see Eric Lott's *Love and Theft,* Henry Louis Gates, Jr.'s "'Dis and Dat': Dialect and Descent" in *Figures in Black: Words, Signs, and the "Racial" Self* (167–95), Ostendorf's *Black Literature in White America* (14–94), Roberts's *From Trickster to Badman: The Black Folk Hero in Slavery and Freedom,* Thomas's *From Folklore to Fiction* (81–110), and Cooke's introduction to *Afro-American Literature in the Twentieth Century.* For discussions of "signifying," see Geneva Smitherman, Thomas Kochman, Alan Dundes, Claudia Mitchell-Kernan, and Henry Louis Gates, Jr. (*The Signifying Monkey*).

5. In her introduction to an edition of *Quicksand and Passing,* Deborah E. McDowell suggests that Nella Larsen also responded in a complex way to the constraints placed upon her as a black woman writer: "In *Passing,* she uses a technique found commonly in narratives by Afro-American and women novelists with a 'dangerous' story to tell: 'safe' themes, plots, and conventions are used as the protective cover underneath which lie more dangerous subplots" (xx). In a similar vein, Carolyn Sylvander argues that Jessie Redmond Fauset's *Plum Bun* is a "Skillfully disguised feminist critique of male and female roles" (182). For a discussion of the trickster figure in these and other black women writers, see Mary Dearborn's discussion in *Pocahontas's Daughters: Gender and Ethnicity in American Culture.* For a discussion of the "trickster aesthetic" as used by women of color to challenge ethnocentric as well as phallocentric traditions, see Jeanne Smith's *Writing Tricksters.*

6. Her defiance of Grandma's notion of womanhood is starkest in the shaving episode, one of quite complicated significance. Just to handle such a "male" instrument involves defiance of gender expectations, as her brother haughtily reminds her when they struggle over it: "'Aw, Isie, you doan know nothin' 'bout shavin' a-tall—but a *man* lak *me*—'" (13). Retaining control of the razor, however, Isis soon forgets her original project of shaving Grandma. She focuses instead on the razor itself, as if she recognizes it as the embodiment of the power denied to women: "Isis stood on one side of the chair with the razor clutched cleaver fashion. The niceties of

razor-handling had passed over her head. The thing with her was to *hold* the razor—sufficient in itself" (13).

7. In *Down Home* Robert Bone offers a very different reading of this dream and of the story. He sees evidence "that in Hurston's unconscious mind, having access to experience was tantamount to being white. . . . It is clear from 'Drenched in Light' that one of her most potent fantasies—imaged as a princess, wearing stately robes and riding on a white horse to the horizon—was that of being white" (*Down Home*, 146). For my own interpretation, the fact that Hurston sees herself as riding on the backs of whites is a crucial one, showing a desire not to be like whites but to use them for her own purposes. Margaret Perry has criticized this short story for reasons similar to Bone's: "The major weakness of the story derives from the author's acquiescence to a need to accept white appreciation even if it casts Isis in the role of " 'happy darkie' " (122).

8. That "race" as a significant category for Hurston involved cultural identification rather than skin color is clear in Hurston's manuscript version of "My People! My People!" in *Dust Tracks on a Road,* in which she repeatedly lampoons black people who, she claims, are actually "white folks passing for colored" (295).

1. "Fractious" Mules and Covert Resistance in *Mules and Men*

1. Her contemporary reviewers in mainstream peridocals (for instance, Chubb, MacGowan, Daniels, and Brickell), universally responding to the work enthusiastically, appreciated its light-hearted exterior. For Sterling Brown, however, these apparent qualities indicate Hurston's lack of critical awareness. In his view the humor Hurston conveys in describing "a land shadowed by squalor, poverty, disease, violence, enforced ignorance, and exploitation" is only one side of the story. *Mules and Men,* he concludes, "should be more bitter; it would be nearer the total truth" (quoted in Hemenway's introduction to *Mules and Men,* xxv–vi).

2. See, for instance, letters from Boas to Hurston dated May 3, 1927 (APS) and May 17, 1927 (APS) for evidence of Boas's control of Hurston's work. Boas, like Mason, also inserted himself into Hurston's financial arrangements (Boas to Hurston, March 24, 1927, APS), an intrusion Hurston responded to with an "apology" both humorous and satirical (Hurston to Boas, March 29, 1927, APS).

Hurston was not the only one of Boas's female protégés to note his powerful control. Margaret Mead, for instance, comments on his "authoritative and uncompromising sense of what was right" (4) and the "austerity of his fundamentally paternal relationship to his students" (9).

3. Despite Boas's admonitions, Hurston managed to smuggle her views on fire and water symbolism into *Mules and Men.* At the beginning of Part II, she states that Hoodoo "adapts itself like Christianity to its locale, reclaiming some of its borrowed characteristics to itself. Such as fire-worship as signified in the Christian church by the altar and candles and the belief in the power of water to sanctify as in baptism" (193). The correspondence between Hurston and Boas (Boas to Hurston

[September 12, 1934, APS] and Hurston to Boas [October 23, 1934, APS]), indicating that Boas was originally sent only the folklore section to read before deciding whether to write a preface, raises the possibility that Hurston did not want him to see parts she knew he would find problematic.

4. Most reviewers, including Brock, MacGowan, Stoney, Gannett, Fallaize, Chubb, and Moon, made this explicit comparison in discussing Hurston's work. For a scholarly discussion of Hurston's persona in *Mules and Men,* see D. A. Boxwell's article, "'Sis Cat' as Ethnographer: Self-Presentation and Self-Inscription in Zora Neale Hurston's *Mules and Men.*"

5. Many reviewers, including Chubb, Moon, MacGowan, Brickell, and Stoney, expressed their delight in being brought "inside" black folklife. Some even felt free to evaluate Hurston's own firsthand knowledge; for instance, MacGowan commented that "those who know their Negro will scarcely doubt a line of [*Mules and Men*]."

6. The anthropological significance of the social context in which Hurston embedded her tales has only really begun to be appreciated recently. John Roberts, reviewing *Mules and Men* for the *Journal of American Folklore* in 1980, argues that Hurston's "narrative structure" "provided her with a unique opportunity to present storytelling context. In the process, she demonstrated a folkloristic sophistication and sensitivity to folklore processes shared by few of her contemporaries" (464). Specifically, he suggests that the dialogue is central, for from it, "one also gains insights into how the participants viewed the role of the tales within their own experience" (464). Dana McKinnon Preu has also stressed the importance of social context for interpreting tales in *Mules and Men.*

7. Hurston worked hard to convince Boas of her scientific rigor. Despite her claims to have meticulously transcribed folktales (Hurston to Boas, October 20, 1929, APS), Hurston most likely took some literary license in recasting the tales she heard. A comparison with her version of traditional tales in other anthologies often shows how much more unified and artistically developed Hurston's versions are. In his review, Roberts questions the absolute "authenticity of the transcription," finding it quite unlikely that Hurston could have transcribed tales in some of the "tense situations" described (464). Evidence of how widespread and traditional most of the tales narrated in *Mules and Men* are and how Hurston's versions differed from others can be seen by examining such black folktale anthologies as those by Botkin (*Lay My Burden Down*), Courlander (*A Treasury of Afro-American Folklore*), Puckett (*Folk Beliefs of the Southern Negro*), Dorson (*Negro Folktales in Michigan* and *American Negro Folktales*), Jones (*Negro Myths from the Georgia Coast*), Brewer (*Dog Ghosts and Other Texas Negro Folk Tales* and *American Negro Folklore*), Fauset ("Negro Tales from the South"), Dance (*Shuckin' and Jivin'*), Hughes and Bontemps (*The Book of Negro Folklore*), and Lester (*Black Folktales*).

It is also interesting that a number of the stories in *Mules and Men* also appear in unpublished material of the Florida Writers Project on which Hurston worked. Hemenway ("Folklore Field Notes") has reprinted a number of these tales.

8. For discussion of this traditional figure in black folklore, see Oster, Brewer ("John Tales"), Weldon, Anderson, and Dorson (*American Negro Folktales,* 124–70).

9. Another tale, "The First Colored Man in Massa's House" (85–86), one that also demonstrates how central mimicry of the master's language is for effective masking, has been discussed by Hemenway in his Introduction to *Mules and Men* (xxii–xxiii). As he argues, the tale not only lampoons white pretensions but also shows the slave, despite his subservient behavior, as not at all duped by them.

10. Hurston reinforces this lampooning of whites by including two tales, "How the Negro Got His Freedom" (88–90) and "God an' de Devil in de Cemetery" (93–95), that depict the white master as more superstitious than the slave.

11. Susan Willis has given a detailed reading of one tale, "How Jack Beat the Devil" (51–58), to show how Hurston's tales often reflect economic realities (*Specifying*, 40–44). This one, she argues, highlights Jack's oppression, revealing that "everything Jack does is contained by the system of capital that is in no way influenced or affected by the forms of exchange employed by Jack" (40).

12. The ludicrous portrait of the white master, indistinguishable from a deer when adorned "'wid a pack of chairs on his head'" (82), is also an important element in the subversive humor of this tale.

13. In *Shuckin' and Jivin'* Daryl Dance provides numerous examples of self-degrading tales built on white stereotypes of blacks (77–100).

14. Both Mikell ("The Anthropological Imagination of Zora Neale Hurston") and Willis (*Specifying*) have pointed to feminist elements in *Mules and Men*. Mikell argues, for instance, that Hurston portrays women in her anthropology as both subject and object (31), whereas Willis points out that many women in Hurston's tales are not "stereotypically subservient" (43) but intelligent and clever. Mary Katherine Wainwright, Benigo Sanchez-Eppler, Barbara Monroe, and Cheryl Wall ("*Mules and Men* and Women") have also discussed the battles between the sexes in *Mules and Men*.

15. Hurston's contribution to anthropological understanding of black women's folklore was significant and original. Ferris has pointed out the lack of women's stories in the literature and attributes it to the fact that most collectors have been male.

16. Dance provides examples of many black folktales about women (110–42) and discusses the sexist stereotypes on which they are built.

17. Drawing from black folklore and blues depictions of men as dogs, Hurston often uses the dog in her fiction and in *Mules and Men* to symbolize oppressive masculinity. See Dance's *Shuckin' and Jivin'*, Chapter 15, "Risqué Tales" (262–305), for numerous examples of the male represented as a dog in black folk culture.

18. As Hurston often does, she also here hints at the complexity of cow/mule image. The man in the tale "rides" (136) the woman, but she is a "fractious" beast and takes off with her rider, who is hardly in control of the situation.

19. The strength and compassion evident in Big Sweet's character are important features of Hurston's ideal black woman. Marie Leveau, for instance, the famed two-headed doctor described in the hoodoo section of *Mules and Men,* is powerful and god-like, yet loving (201–4).

20. As Dundes points out, the mule metaphor in black folklore is a richly complex one, symbolizing the black person's slavish existence but also his or

her "mother wit," strength, and stubbornness (37n). Despite the obvious allusion, Hurston's title has prompted some interesting comments. Missing the metaphorical significance entirely, MacGowan suggests that "The few mules that appear in the pages supply the comic relief and the alliteration for a snappy title" and uses the mule metaphor as the basis for a condescending conclusion about black life: "If voodoo, or hoodoo, does persist with the force that Miss Hurston claims, it is evidence that a race will cling for generations, even in a changed environment and under benign influences, to the beaten tracks of the past. Therein men are mules." In a scathing critique of the book, Harold Preece points to the title as evidence of Hurston's racial self-hatred. He understands the "resentment of some Negro circles toward the work of Miss Hurston," for "when a Negro author describes her race with such a servile term as 'Mules and Men,' critical members of the race must necessarily evaluate the author as a literary climber" ("The Negro Folk Cult," 37).

2. "Natural Men" and "Pagan Poesy" in *Jonah's Gourd Vine*

1. It is difficult to overstate the popularity of black religion during the Harlem Renaissance: whites flocked to Harlem to hear black preachers; scholars wrote studies of black religion; and black writers (including Charles S. Johnson in *Shadow of the Plantation* and James Weldon Johnson in *God's Trombones*) immortalized the sermons of black preachers. Behind much of this interest lay a view of black religion, offered as early as W. E. B. Du Bois's in *The Gift of Black Folk,* as possessing a "wilder spiritualism" (331), "a certain spiritual joyousness; a sensuous, tropical love of life, in vivid contrast to the cool and cautious New England reason" (320).

2. Most of Hurston's contemporary reviewers expressed enthusiasm for her rich use of folk language in *Jonah's Gourd Vine.* In her introduction to the first edition, Fannie Hurst praises the novel in strangely racist language: "A brilliantly facile spade has turned over rich new earth. Words lift up, the hottish smells of soil rise, negro toes dredge into that soil, smells of racial fecundity are about" (7). Josephine Pinckney, in "A Pungent, Poetic Novel about Negroes," expresses an opinion (suggested even in the title) that is representative: "The story unfolds in pages and pages of talk, and delighting talk it is—the pungent, expressive idiom of the country Negro, full of humor and folk-notions; poetic, whether on the secular side or transposed into the biblical phraseology required by the many country scenes." In his review in *North American Review,* Herschel Brickell also praised "its fine, juicy and eminently natural humor, and its record of curious folkways" (95). Similarly, the reviewer in *The Nation* found "The atmosphere . . . rich and highly affecting" and "the cotton-country speech . . . laden with humor, ancient poetry, and folk wisdom" (683). Martha Gruening praised Hurston's own "touch of 'pagan poesy'" (244), a quality also commented on by Margaret Wallace, who noted the "rhythm and balance of the sentences" (6) and "warm artlessness of the phrasing" (6).

The two exceptional reviews were by William Plomer, who found the dialect "trying," and Andrew Burris, who argued in *The Crisis* that "She has used her characters and the various situations created for them as mere pegs upon which to hang their dialect and their folkways. She has become so absorbed with these phases of her craft that she has almost completely lost sight of the equally essential elements of plot and construction, chracterization and motivation."

More recent critical evaluations of Hurston's language have been mixed. Whereas Arthur Davis praises Hurston's skillful use of folk speech (*From the Dark Tower,* 115) and Kirkland Jones emphasizes the humor in the speech of Hurston's characters, most literary critics have found Hurston's use of folk material overdone. Bell, for instance, argues that Hurston "subordinates plot and character to the illustration of black folklore" (120) and that "frequently the use of metaphor, invective, and folksayings are inappropriate and improbable for the dramatic mood, indicating either a lack of control of the aesthetic distance between author-narrator and material or the exploitation of language as an end in itself" (121). In a similar vein, Robert Bone suggests that "*Jonah's Gourd Vine* has style without structure, a rich verbal texture without dramatic form, 'atmosphere' without real characterization" (*The Negro Novel in America,* 127). Finding Hurston's use of folk sayings too extravagent, he concludes that they are "too nonfunctional, too anthropological, and in the end merely exotic" (127). Gloster (236), Rambeau (63), Harris ("Our People," 38), and Wall ("Zora Neale Hurston," 382) have offered similar assessments.

3. Although Hurston's description of John as a pure African American poet (Hurston to James Weldon Johnson, April 16, 1934, JWJ Yale) has often been taken as straightforward evidence that she considered John the hero of the novel, a fuller picture of the correspondence between Hurston and Johnson sheds more light on her words. As an earlier letter indicates, Hurston had a quite specific motive for explaining her characterization of John: hoping to persuade Johnson to write a positive review of the work, she pleads: "May I place your name on the [publisher's] list? I *want* to do it very much. It is a story of Florida life. You *ought* to have something to say. *Please*" (January 22, 1934, JWJ). Convincing him in her April letter that she is following in his tradition, she wins the praise she sought (Johnson to Hurston, April 20, 1934, JWJ).

4. Finding this work "hopelessly incompetent" (*Down Home,* 144), Robert Bone sees it as Hurston's "recoil from the black metropolis" (148), a story that "depicts the self in jeopardy from false, urban values" (148).

5. Drawing from black folklore and blues depictions of men as dogs, Hurston uses the dog in other works (most notably in *Their Eyes Were Watching God*) and in *Mules and Men* [133]) to symbolize dangerous masculinity. See Dance's *Shuckin' and Jivin',* Chapter 15, "Risqué Tales" (262–305), for numerous examples of the male represented as a dog in black folk culture.

6. Lillie Howard sees very different implications in the story's conclusion: "That Muttsy has returned to his gambling does not particularly bode ill. Pinkie will probably have to modify her 'likes,' but a happy marriage between Muttsy and Pinkie still seems possible" (*Zora Neale Hurston,* 66).

7. In his review Lewis Gannett, for instance, interpreting the symbol straightforwardly, argues that John "flourished like a gourd vine . . . but God prepared a worm, and it smote him, and he withered." Darwin Turner, on the other hand, finds the title inappropriate: "The image of 'jonah's gourd vine' does not seem to repre-

sent John effectively because no Jonah exists. The fact that John Buddy is created by God and is smitten by God furnishes merely a strained analogy" (*In A Minor Chord*, 105). Lillie Howard is one of the few critics to see Lucy as the symbolic gourd vine, "rescuing and protecting [John] from the harsh realities of life" (*Zora Neale Hurston*, 81).

8. Most of Hurston's contemporary reviewers responded positively to the character of John. The facts one must overlook in arriving at such an evaluation are clearest, perhaps, in the review published in the *Times Literary Supplement*: "In spite of a long series of adventures with other women, mostly not of his own choosing, he remains faithful in spirit to Lucy, at any rate while the children are still young" (716). Wallace, too, excuses John's behavior: "John really loved Lucy and intended to be true to her, but he was totally unable to resist the open and insistent blandishments of other women" (7).

Sympathetic analyses of John by literary critics include those of Howard in *Zora Neale Hurston* and Larry Neal in his introduction to the novel. Howard, for instance, sees John as a "man in conflict with himself and with society" (75), a victim of "a christian society where to follow his natural bent is immoral" (76). Neal too provides a sociological rather than a moral explanation of John's behavior. He sees in John a conflict of "two distinctly different *cultural* attitudes toward the concept of spirituality. The one springs from a formerly enslaved communal society, non-Christian in background, where there is really no clean-cut dichotomy between the world of spirit and the world of flesh. The other attitude is clearly more rigid, being a blend of Puritan concepts and the fire-and-brimstone imagery of the white evangelical tradition" (6–7).

Other critics have offered less complimentary interpretations of John's character. Nigel Thomas has noted his shallowness and weakness (51). Addison Gayle reaches conclusions concerning the relationship between John and Lucy similar to my own. Arguing that John is unable to break free from white conceptions of black men, he sees Lucy as the hero of the novel, for she "succeeds in breaking free of the images which circumscribe her as a Black and a woman and, in so doing, presents a positive image of black women" (140). Seeing Hurston's letter to James Weldon Johnson as no accurate indicator of the novel's theme, he suggests that the "implications of Miss Hurston's statement and the actions that unfold in the novel contradict one another; for to suggest that the preacher, outside the pulpit, should be free to 'follow his bent as other men' means to condone the actions which lead Pearson along the road to his tragic end—a tragedy manifested by his inability to move beyond the terms which circumscribe him" (140). John's behavior in the novel demonstrates, he concludes, his belief "that the black man's route to manhood lay in the exploitation of black women" (143). Wall has also argued that "John remains bound by the slaveholder's conception of black men" (381) while "Lucy is, by contrast, a new black woman" ("Zora Neale Hurston," 382). For a discussion of Hurston's treatment of black men, see Stanford.

9. Although Hurston includes details that seem to make Mehaley's wedding humorous—she is married to her barefoot husband by an illiterate, self-ordained

preacher holding an almanac (83)—she ironically suggests that Mehaley marries a better man than Lucy. When Mehaley asks Pomp to take her away, he agrees in words of devotion: " 'M'haley, you might not know it, but youse gittin' uh do-right man. Whenever you needs somebody tuh do uh man's part Ah'll be 'round dere wakin' heavy over de floor' " (82). Unlike John, who offers Lucy only promises, Pomp is true to his word when payday comes (84).

10. Hurston expresses the underlying problem in John and Lucy's marriage through the symbol of their bed. Significantly, Lucy has difficulty keeping one: she loses her first to Bud in payment of John's debt and is thwarted in her desire to leave her second to Isis when Hattie usurps it. Although family members refer to Lucy's "making her bed hard" (78, 98) in marrying John, it is symbolically the white world that does so. Lucy and John's first bed is a wedding present from Alf Pearson (81) (certainly an ominous beginning for their sexual relationship) and the second is from " 'uh white woman over in Maitland' " (130). By contrast, during the happiest period in their marriage, immediately after Lucy joins John in Eatonville, they sleep on the floor (109).

11. For another view of the beast imagery in the novel, see Alan Brown.

12. Darwin Turner has also briefly discussed Hurston's use of the train as an image of John's sexual awareness (105).

13. Hurston reiterates these aspects of the train in *Dust Tracks on a Road*. She, too, in her youth sees it as "a fearsome thing" (111) and becomes fascinated by "the plush and metal of the inside of that coach" (113). Her discussion concludes tellingly, "The inside of that train was too pretty for words. It took years for me to get over loving it" (113).

14. In a letter to Alain Locke, Hurston alluded to the seductive symbolic power of trains by suggesting that stories of the Underground Railway led many Southern blacks to idolize white conductors and to expect a degree of freedom in the North that was simply not offered there (July 23, 1943, AL). Benjamin Brawley, C. Vann Woodward, Carter G. Woodson, and Emmett J. Scott have also discussed the racism and economic hardships faced by blacks during the Great Migration.

15. Throughout the novel, Hurston emphasizes that John's pulpit oratory tells us more about himself than about his religious beliefs. His preaching, for instance, is temporally and thematically related to John's betrayal of Lucy's trust, for his first "calling" to preach arises after his initial act of infidelity. Horrified to see Mehaley arrive at church one morning after a night of love-making, he immediately "fell to his knees and prayed for cleansing" (52). The spiritual emptiness and dishonesty of the prayer are clear. Like Lucy's mother's ludicrous prayer that John and Lucy stay five feet apart, which "bumbl[es] 'round 'mong de rafters" (74), John's plea never leaves the room: "He prayed aloud and the empty house threw back his resonant tones like a guitar box" (52). The captivated audience for his own eloquence, much more aware of his impressive words than of his contrite feelings, he exults in the sound of his voice: " 'Dat sho sound good. . . . If mah voice sound *dat* good de first time Ah ever prayed in de church house, it sho' won't be de las' ' " (52).

Throughout John's preaching career, it is the voice rather than the sentiment, the words rather than the substance, that are important. He has "'uh good strainin' voice'" and "'plenty fire in 'im'" (89), but there is no evidence that he believes a word he says; he is, in fact, just as eloquent when mimicking someone else's style (107) as when speaking "from the heart."

Karla Holloway has also pointed to the duplicity and manipulation characterizing John's language: "The prayers uttered by John Pearson should, by rights be prayers for others—it is for his congregation that his words are meant. His role, ancient or contemporary, is to give life to the community by the enlivening of their spirits. But John is a contradiction" (*The Character of the Word,* 38).

16. Hurston's contemporary reviewers appreciated the power of this final sermon. Brickell called it "magnificent" (96) and Burris, "the most poetic rendition of this familiar theme that we have yet encountered in print." Several (including Gannett and the reviewer in *The Boston Chronicle*) favorably compared it to sermons in *God's Trombones.* Although admiring the sermon's artistry, Hemenway finds its eloquence at odds with Hurston's narrative:

> No passage demonstrates the book's contradiction more sharply than the
> long sermon that John preaches on the same communion Sunday when he
> will renounce his pulpit. It is a linguistic tour de force; traditional metaphors
> and similes well known in the black communicity are skillfully improvised.
> In fact, the language is so powerful that the reader forgets that the sermon is
> intended as a climax to the novel. As we become captured by John's lan-
> guage, his personal crisis—whether to remain as a man of God—fades to
> the background. John's crisis is not important to the sermon; only his lan-
> guage compels, and it is this separation of confused self from inspired utter-
> ance that frustrates him. (*Zora Neale Hurston,* 196)

His conclusions are quite different from my own: "the sermon itself is the important literary event at this point in the novel—not the fact that it is John's final sermon before his congregation. One could remove the sermon, place it in another context, and the language would command virtually the same response: the power of the passage is in the text, not the context" (197).

17. Slightly different versions of this traditional courtship conversation are reported in Banks and Smiley's "Old-Time Courtship Conversation" (255) and Talley's *Negro Folk Rhymes* (135). In his article, Hemenway offers a very different interpretation of this courting ritual (134–47). Lucy's response indicates, he suggests, that she does not know the answer:

> Her reference to the jaybird jeopardizes the relationship, for it reveals that
> perhaps she is too young, as well as too far removed from John's shared
> knowledge, to enter into marriage. The emotional demands of both are in
> great peril at this point, endangered by Lucy's inability to participate in the
> more adult ceremonies of her culture. She is vaguely aware of the folkloric
> context of John's riddle, but she is without access to the correct responses to
> participate in the performance. (139–40)

Wall basically agrees with Hemenway's interpretaion of this scene ("Zora Neale Hurston," 380–81).

18. For discussion of the verbal strategies black women use to "negotiate respect" in their interactions with men, see Abrahams.

19. Talley cites both of these traditional rhymes in his collection, *Negro Folk Rhymes:*

If you sees a mule tied up to a tree,
You mought pull his tail and think about me.
For if a Nigger don't know de natcher of a mule,
It makes no difference what 'comes of a fool. (108)

As shore as de grass grows 'round de stump,
You is my darlin' sugar lump. (128)

Hurston may have modified Lucy's vow slightly to fit in with the novel's vine imagery.

20. Hurston often uses feline imagery as a positive symbol of female power. For instance, in *Dust Tracks on a Road,* Hurston describes herself as "a tiger" (100) in defending her sister against her cruel stepmother and Big Sweet as "a lioness" (190) protecting Hurston against her enemies.

21. Lionnet has argued that Lucy's request to leave the mirror uncovered represents her desire to leave an imprint on her daughter's memory (117–18). Speisman has seen Lucy's deathbed demands as an attempt to prevent the townspeople from practicing voodoo on her.

22. Catherine Starke's discussion of the "brute" (61–65), a stereotype of black men as oversexed animals in fiction written by whites, helps explain why Hurston avoided a straightforward indictment of John in *Jonah's Gourd Vine.*

3. "Mink Skin or Coon Hide": The Janus-faced Narrative of *Their Eyes Were Watching God*

1. John Lowe has discussed the numerous parallels between Janie and the Roman god, Janus.

2. Significantly, these nonthreatening and apparently apolitical features of the novel were responsible for its popularity with most reviewers in mainstream publications, who often praised Hurston's language, "its raciness, its rich invention, and its music" (Stevens, 3) and the "refreshingly pagan undercurrent of the joy of life" in the novel (Brickell). (For similar comments, see also reviews written by Tompkins and Thompson.) Often lapsing into racially stereotypical language to express their enthusiasm, white reviewers sometimes linked their enthusiasm for Hurston's primitivism with approval for her apparent avoidance of The Race Problem. One reviewer, for instance, breathed a sigh of relief that Hurston had written "a simple and unpretentious story" that "never comes to the verge of conscious, sentimen-

tal sympathy" (Stevens, 3). Another admired Hurston's picture of black life "in its naturally creative and unself-conscious grace" and found the book (thankfully) "unlimbered of the clumsy formality, defiance and apology of a Minority Cause" (Ferguson).

For a number of her black contemporaries, those features of the novel were precisely the source of criticism. Disillusioned with white voyeuristic response to primitivism during the Harlem Renaissance, both Alain Locke and Richard Wright felt that *Their Eyes Were Watching God* reinforced white stereotypes of blacks. Locke found the novel's poetic dazzle superficial and its primitive joyousness simple-minded:

> But as always thus far with this talented writer, setting and surprising flashes of contemporary folk lore are the main point. Her gift for poetic phrase, for rare dialect and folk humor keep her flashing on the surface of her community and her characters and from diving down deep either to the inner psychology of characterization or to sharp analysis of the social background. It is folklore fiction at its best, which we gratefully accept as an overdue replacement for so much faulty local color fiction about Negroes. But when will the Negro novelist of maturity who knows how to tell a story convincingly,—which is Miss Hurston's cradle-gift, come to grips with motive fiction and social document fiction? Progressive southern fiction has already banished the legend of these entertaining pseudo-primitives whom the reading public still loves to laugh with, weep over and envy. Having gotten rid of condescension, let us now get rid of over-simplification! ("Review of Negro Books," 10)

Definitely the most damning review was that published by Richard Wright in *New Masses*. Like Locke, he found Hurston's mastery of language and the story's apparent primitive simplicity most problematic. Her language, "cloaked in . . . facile sensuality," "manages to catch the psychological movements of the Negro folk-mind in their pure simplicity, but that's as far as it goes." The book is all surface dazzle; its "sensory sweep . . . carries no theme, no message, no thought." Wright's most scathing remarks were directed at what he saw as Hurston's capitulation to white demands for harmless images of blacks: "Miss Hurston *voluntarily* continues in her novel the tradition which was *forced* upon the Negro in the theater, that is, the minstrel technique that makes the 'white folks' laugh. Her characters eat and laugh and cry and work and kill; they swing like a pendulum eternally in that safe and narrow orbit in which America likes to see the Negro live: between laughter and tears."

Of reviews written by her black male contemporaries, the most sympathetic was an unenthusiastic one by Sterling Brown. In less vitriolic language than Wright, he too notes the apparent lack of social commentary in *Their Eyes Were Watching God:* "Living in an all-colored town, these people escape the worst pressures of class and caste. There is little harshness; there is enough money and work to go around. The author does not dwell upon the 'people ugly from ignorance and broken from being poor' who swarm upon the 'muck' for short-time jobs" ("Luck is Fortune"). In a final, undeveloped thought, he points to an aspect of the novel overlooked by other—black or white—reviewers, what he called a "bitterness," sometimes explicit, but often "oblique, in the enforced folk manner" (Brown 110). Although Hurston would have disliked Brown's term, "bitterness," he accurately points to the novel's underlying attack on the white world and to her strategy for making it.

Hurston's oblique method in the novel has also been commented on by Wilentz, who argues that *Their Eyes Were Watching God* is "a novel of resistance" in which Hurston "tricks the white readership by her own positive resistance— her ability to negate the values of the dominant culture . . . without once saying it outright" (291). Crabtree's discussion of the ways Hurston uses folk material self-consciously and symbolically to develop her themes is also an important one for my own. Echoing the sentiments of Hurston's contemporary reviewers, various critics, including Ford, Gloster, and Byrd, have argued that Hurston ignored race in *Their Eyes Were Watching God*. Those focusing on her treatment of race include Wilentz, Benesch, Washington, and Giles.

3. The manuscript provides evidence that Hurston gradually developed the mule metaphor in writing the novel. This speech by Nanny is inserted in the manuscript, and the story of Matt Bonner's mule (81–85, 86–99) is not in the handwritten manuscript.

4. The limitations of Nanny's vision have been noticed by numerous critics, including Giles (52), Awkward ("'The Inaudible Voice,'" 68) and Crabtree (62). One of the few who stresses the value in her remarks is Lillie Howard, who argues that "Nanny's vision is clearer than Janie's" ("Nanny and Janie: Will the Twain Ever Meet?" 407).

5. The contrast between this metaphor for male/female sexual relationships and that described in *Seraph on the Suwanee* is striking. When Arvay is raped by her future husband under the mulberry tree, Hurston images this phallic rapaciousness in her description of the tree, its "new green leaves, punctuated by tiny fuzzy things that looked like green stubby worms" (34).

6. Critics who have discussed Starks's symbolic whiteness include Washington, Crabtree, Wilentz, Awkward ("'The Inaudible Voice,'" 75), Wall (385), Benesch, and Giles.

7. That Jody sees his act in this way is evident in his comparison of the lamp to the power of "de Sun-Maker" (72). That at least some members of the community accept this interpretation is revealed in the hymn Mrs. Bogle sings at the celebration, "Jesus, the light of the world" (73). The story of Starks's installation of the light post was not part of Hurston's original conception of the novel, for it is absent in the manuscript version of the novel.

8. This complex symbol is also absent in the handwritten manuscript.

9. Darwin Turner has criticized this chapter of the novel: "Digressive and unnecessary, the chapter merely suggests that Miss Hurston did not know how to integrate the folk material which she considered essential for local color" (107).

10. Hurston made Mrs. Robbins's character more ambiguous in the published version of the novel, leaving us with only the men's comments about her. In the manuscript version, her bizarre habit of begging is explained in a sympathetic way that makes the men's response seem even more cruel: "Somehow she had felt like

telling Janie about her half-starved childhood and the fear that it might happen to her own children. A little 'off' on the subject of food." See "Eatonville Anthology" for another version of this woman's behavior (*I Love Myself When I Am Laughing*, 177–78).

11. In contrast to Turner's argument that Janie's act is unnecessarily cruel (108), McCredie, Lupton, and Ferguson have discussed its role in freeing Janie.

12. The emptiness of this love talk is obvious when they actually scrape together enough money to buy Daisy a pickled pig's foot (109).

13. The ease with which she can be banished from the community is clear when she flees after the men stage a mock fight that destroys her restaurant. Dealing with her as black tricksters do whites, Tea Cake orchestrates the destruction while appearing to be Mrs. Turner's ally (233). Thoroughly duped by Tea Cake's smiling mask, "Mrs. Turner beamed on Tea Cake" (223) before returning to Miami.

14. Critical opinion is divided on the ultimate evaluation Hurston makes of Tea Cake's character in the novel. Those who see him as an ideal include Bone, Wilentz, Carr, Thornton, Naylor, McCredie, and S. Jay Walker. Especially revealing of the way an emphasis on race alone slights Tea Cake's faults is the argument put forth by Benesch. Acknowledging the traditional sex roles Tea Cake's beating reinstitutes, he dismisses its significance: "However, according to my argument, Janie's development is above all a function of her meaningful participation in black folk traditions, and only secondarily depends on the opposition of a woman to gender-related expectations" (634). Critics who do emphasize shortcomings in Tea Cake toward the end of the novel include Hooks ("A Subversive Reading"), Pondrom, Ferguson, Lloyd Brown, Saunders, Lupton, Curren, Kathleen Davies, and Awkward (" 'The Inaudible Voice' ").

15. Tea Cake's respect for money is repeated after the storm. The danger of his false values is evident in his comment to Janie reassuring her that it is safe for him to venture out into Palm Beach: " 'Ah got money on men, Janie. Dey can't bother me" (250). While he seems to think money erases his blackness, his capture and forced labor by white men reveals how misguided Tea Cake is. This comment, not present in the handwritten manuscript, represents another instance of Hurston strengthening the depiction of Tea Cake's whiteness.

16. Hurston added many of these details that suggest Tea Cake's acceptance of white values in the process of writing the novel. Neither of the comments about the superior judgment of white people appear in the handwritten version. Tea Cake's abandonment of his guitar is inserted in that version.

17. For other discussions of the storm's significance, see Curren, Hubbard, Kathleen Davies, and Gordon Thompson.

18. See Chapter 15, "Risqué Tales," in Dance's *Shuckin' and Jivin'* (262–305) for numerous examples of the male as dog in black folk culture.

19. Hurston's description of her own relationship with A. W. P., which was, she asserts, the basis for *Their Eyes Were Watching God,* underscores the seduction and the hazards of such a conception of masculinity. Her lover's desire to "be a *man!*" (*Dust Tracks on a Road,* 253) strong and independent, easily slipped over into something more deadly: "That very manliness, sweet as it was, made us both suffer" (253), she

discovered, for it involved a concomitant notion of womanliness in conflict with Hurston's independence. As he becomes more and more "the master kind" (257) and she "his slave" (258), she finally had to "fight [her]self free from [her] obsession" (260) by escaping to Jamaica and work.

20. Most critics, including Carr, Kubitschek, Naylor, Wolff, Wilentz, and Ferguson, have argued that Janie achieves liberation in the novel. Those painting a more qualified portrait of Janie include Reich, Awkward ("'The Inaudible Voice'"), Jordan, duCille, Krasner, Levecq, and Lloyd Brown.

21. For other discussions of Janie's trial, see DuPlessis (102–6), Callahan (140–41), Brigham (416–17), Lowe (190–94), Kaplan (127–31), and Henderson (21–22).

22. Stepto (166), Bell (123), Turner (109), and Hemenway (*Zora Neale Hurston*, 233) have all found the third-person narrative in the novel problematic.

23. Gates, for instance, has argued that Hurston's multivocal narrative voice "echoes and aspires to the status of the impersonality, anonymity, and authority of the black vernacular tradition, a nameless, selfless tradition, at once collective and compelling, true somehow to the unwritten text of a common blackness" (*The Signifying Monkey*, 183). In a similar vein, Awkward, rather than viewing third-person narrative as a flaw, sees it as confirmation of Janie's status "as a communally oriented, culturally informed Afro-American woman" ("'The Inaudible Voice,'" 100). Callahan has emphasized the narrative's relation to the "rhetoric of intimacy," a relationship between Hurston's voice and Janie's characterized by cooperation and support (119). Critics who have also examined the narrative's multivocal quality include Brigham, Racine, and Kalb. For an excellent review of criticism on the novel's narration, see Awkward's discussion.

24. Awkward ("'The Inaudible Voice'") suggests a very different view of Janie's silence in response to Tea Cake's beating, which he sees as "an application of the strategic self-division that she had employed in her second marriage. She withdraws, when Tea Cake beats her, into voiceless absence. She no more accepts his abuse 'without flinching' than she accepts Starks's mistreatment. Rather, her silence indicates that she employs what has been her only means of protest throughout the entire text of the novel" (85).

25. Critics who see Janie's shooting of Tea Cake as a blow for freedom include Saunders, Ferguson, Lupton, Lloyd Brown, Sadoff, and Willis, who describes it as "the book's strongest statement" (71). Alice Walker has argued that Tea Cake's beating of Janie is "the reason Hurston *permits* Janie to kill Tea Cake" (305). Thomas Cassidy has also argued that "events of the hurricane leading to Tea Cake's death after being bit by a mad dog can be read as an eruption of Janie's unconscious turmoil and rage" (261).

4. The Ways of White Folks in *Seraph on the Suwanee*

1. In her review of Richard Wright's *Uncle Tom's Children* ("Stories of Conflict"), Hurston explained the popularity of "poor girl marries rich boy" stories. Hatred, she argued, is the "favorite Negro theme just as how the stenographer or

some other poor girl won the boss or the boss's son is the favorite white theme." She expected her own treatment of this theme to be a popular success: in a letter to Burroughs Mitchell (December 5, 1947, SC), she expressed hopes for her novel to be sold to the movies or to a book club.

2. Hurston actually wrote the novel in British Honduras, where she had gone with the hopes of discovering an ancient Mayan city. As a letter to her editor, Burroughs Mitchell, suggests, she was out of money during this time and desperate for the novel to do well financially so that she could actually undertake her expedition (July 31, 1947, SC). For a detailed discussion of this period, see Hemenway (*Zora Neale Hurston,* 301–7).

3. Ingratiating Hurston certainly was with Rawlings. After reading *Cross Creek,* Hurston wrote to Rawlings praising the book: "You did a thing I like in dealing with your Negroes. You looked at them as they are instead of slobbering over them as other authors do. You have written the best thing on Negroes of any white writer who ever lived" (Silvertone, 232).

Despite Rawlings's respect for some blacks as "faithful retainers" in *Cross Creek,* Hurston could not have missed Rawlings's racism sugared over by affectionate humor throughout the book. Describing one "disastrous" attempt to train a young maid, after buying her from her father, Rawlings writes in the vignette, "Catching One Young": "A five-dollar-bill sealed the bargain. Two months of life with her made me wonder why he [the father] had not given her to the first passing gypsy caravan, or drowned her decently" (77). Rawlings ends the chapter with an amused thought and revealing metaphor: perhaps "I had pulled from too early a litter" (77–78).

At times Rawlings drops her picturesque humor in depicting blacks as shiftless and irresponsible. In "Black Shadows" she describes her one mistake in dealing with blacks: "I have expected that, given justice and kindness, a reasonable attitude toward their problems, and wages higher than the customary ones, they could carry considerable responsibility and learn to discipline themselves. I should have known better. I should have understood that only in rare instances can a Negro work for long on his own initiative" (181). Hurston was honest in one respect: Rawlings did not "slobber" over black people in her work.

Hurston parades her outspoken brashness in an interesting exercise of self-presentation delightedly related by Rawlings in a letter: "She discussed lynching with the Kleagle of the Ku Klux Klan! Remarked to him that the individual didn't matter—a man has to die sometime—but a wise and practical system of law was built up by the Greeks and Romans, taken to England, from England here, and when you go against that you're undermining something valuable that has taken thousands of years to build. She said he took his feet off his desk and said, 'Zora, there's something in that'" (Bigelow and Monti 223). The rhetoric of this anecdote—apocryphal or not—is fascinating not only for its revelation of Hurston's strategy in arguing with such a person (she avoids the whole issue of racism) but also for the clever and spunky self it presents to Rawlings.

4. As she consistently did with white patrons, Hurston often told Rawlings what she wanted to hear. Silvertone gives an account of another such instance:

"when Zora Neale heard that Marjorie was working on her new book at Cross Creek, she wrote that if she were not working on a book of her own, she would come and be a 'buffer' for Marjorie's housekeeper, Idella, who had left her to work in Harlem. Zora Neale told her that if things got too awful 'give a hoot and a holler' and she would drop her own work to come help her friend. Marjorie took her up on the offer and she came and spent ten days" (Silvertone, 233). When Rawlings became involved in a libel suit brought by Zelma Carson, Hurston wrote to a mutual friend (who passed the letter on to Rawlings), expressing her loyalty to Rawlings. Referring to the suit, Hurston writes:

> I could have saved all kinds of trouble if she had let me just plain kill that poor white trash that she took up so much time with, and who paid her for it by suing her for defamation of character. Marjorie Baskin does not even know the kinds of words that it would take to defame that woman. *Everybody* around Cross Creek says that the creature has a filthy mouth. You have no idea how good and kind M. K. R. is to everybody. The folks who work for her are really in soft. She no way deserves what she got from that trash. She as a woman is big wood while that strumpet is not even good brush. If you hear of the tramp getting a heavy load of rock salt and fat-back in her rump, and I happen to be in Fla. at the time, you will know who loaded the shell, but you need not get confidential with the police. (Bigelow and Monti, 313–14)

Needless to say, Rawlings was, as she said, "enchanted" by this passage (313).

Part of what is disturbing about this relationship is the price Hurston had to pay to maintain it. Despite Rawlings's fascination with Hurston's personality, she, at least initially, could not overcome her racism in her response to Hurston. (Silvertone does argue, however, that Rawlings later changed her racial attitudes, partly as a result of her friendship with Hurston.) At the end of the letter describing Hurston's visit, she writes that she "should accept this woman as a human being and a friend—certainly an attractive member of society acceptable anywhere," but admits that she "feels rather small" and "is a coward" (Bigelow and Monti, 223).

Years later, when Hurston was suffering from being accused of sexual assault on a young boy, Rawlings's response was callous and flippant. In an afterthought at the end of a letter to Carl Van Vechten, she writes, "Charles Scribner reported that our Zora had been in trouble on a mild sex charge. This is idiotic. Sex is never mild" (Bigelow and Monti, 325).

5. Rawlings wrote a letter on April 30, 1947, to Maxwell Perkins of Scribner's saying she was "delighted" they were going to publish *Seraph on the Suwanee*. She goes on to praise Hurston's work: "I feel that she has a very great talent. You really should read her 'Moses, Man of the Mountain.' She has not only the Negro gift of rhythm and imagination, but she is proud of her blood and her people, and presents her stories from the Negro point of view" (Bigelow and Monti, 293). An undated letter from Hurston to Rawlings in the Rawlings Collection at the University of Florida also indicates that Rawlings lent Hurston money while she was working on *Seraph on the Suwanee*.

6. One episode in *Seraph on the Suwanee,* the scene of Arvay's fits and Jim's response, is drawn from Hurston's collection of anecdotes, *The Eatonville Anthology:*

Jim Merchant is always in good humor—even with his wife. He says he fell in love with her at first sight. That was some years ago. She has had all her teeth pulled out, but they still get along splendidly.

He says the first time he called on her he found out that she was subject to fits. This didn't cool his love, however. She had several in his presence.

One Sunday, while he was there, she had one, and her mother tried to give her a dose of turpentine to stop it. Accidentally, she spilled it in her eye and it cured her. She never had another fit, so they got married and have kept each other in good humor ever since. (*I Love Myself,* 176)

7. Rawlings's attraction for males and their world has been noticed by critics of her work. See, for instance, Samuel I. Bellman's discussion in *Marjorie Kinnan Rawlings* (54–80). This characteristic was apparently noticed by Hurston. In the letter referred to earlier that Rawlings passed on in one of hers, Hurston comments that she considers it "a triumph" to be among Rawlings's friends "because the justly celebrated Marjorie K. R. does not usually take to women" (Bigelow and Monti, 313).

8. Hurston was able to gauge white response to her book even before its publication. Her extensive correspondence with her editor and agent indicates that they liked the novel for similar reasons. Jean G. Parker, for instance, responded to it with enthusiasm: "I like the sudden shifts into high speed . . . the rape under the mulberry tree, the fight with Hawley, the hunt for Earl in the swamps" (June 7, 1947, SC). Ann Watkins, too, found it to be "powerful, fast moving stuff" (June 20, 1947, SC), and Burroughs Mitchell praised its "fine vigor and humor" (August 18, 1947, SC).

Literary critics have been less generous. Darwin Turner, for instance, finds Hurston's "constant adjustment to the tastes of a new generation of readers" (111) a shortcoming; Robert Bone, similarly, feels that Hurston "betrayed her talent by adopting a new tone [in the novel]. To write a best seller for the forties, she added sex and sensation to her usual fare" (*The Negro Novel in America,* 115). Both Hemenway (*Zora Neale Hurston,* 311–15) and Howard (*Zora Neale Hurston,* 146) also find major shortcomings in the work. Most critics (including Rayson, Carl Milton Hughes, Hemenway, Coleman, Lowe, and Howard) echo the predominant view of Hurston's contemporaries that Arvay is a neurotic who moves toward self-awareness and Jim is the healthy man who helps her. One of the few who have emphasized Jim's domination of Arvay is duCille, who argues that the novel is a parody of *Gone with the Wind* (139–42).

9. Suggesting a similar idea, Bone has argued that in the novel Hurston "plunged her readers into the deep and bitter emotions of a sick world." He sees this, however, as a serious weakness: "it is regrettable that Miss Hurston did not restrict her tours to the world of the healthy" (*The Negro Novel in America,* 115).

10. The black world Hurston depicts in her other works also serves as an ironic backdrop against which Hurston develops *Seraph on the Suwanee.* In the place of

John Pearson and his powerful sermons, for instance, we are shown a white preacher, Carl Middleton, who "never did say anything that had not been already said," and whose "repetitions were not very dramatic" (12). If that were not bad enough, he could not "raise a tune if you put a wagon-load of good compost under him and ten sacks of commercial fertilizer" (12).

11. As Howard has noted, "Unflattering attitudes about women occupy a more prominent position in this novel than in any of the other Hurston novels" (*Zora Neale Hurston,* 144).

12. An indication of the sexual mores of Hurston's time is the description of this scene by one reviewer as a "seduction" (Hedden).

13. White male attitudes toward rape are consistent in the novel, even between two figures who seem as different as Jim and Arvay's father, Brock Henson. Both respond to the rape of their daughters with pragmatic aplomb. When Arvay overhears Hatton "lovingly" threaten to rape Angeline, she impulsively runs for the gun to save her daughter. She is prevented from killing Hatton by Jim, whose pragmatic response is to do a little investigating into Hatton's background and financial situation to see "if he will in any way do" (181). Sensing what has happened between Jim and Arvay under the mulberry tree, Maria (like Arvay) wants to save her daughter: "'If you was any man at all, you'd take that shot-gun and get on your horse and overtake 'em'" (55). Brock's response, however, echoes Jim's: "'Better let well enough do. . . . Far as I can see, things is coming along just fine as it is. Don't reckon Jim Meserve is the kind to back out now, with the wedding all set and all. It would take a mighty heap of gall'" (55).

14. A deleted sentence in the manuscript description of the rape scene makes this idea explicit: "She was passive in defeat" (65, HC). Hurston associates the mulberry tree with death later when Arvay returns to Sawley. Sitting underneath the tree, she hears the cry of the screech owl (134), a folk symbol for death that Hurston alludes to in several of her works. As she often does, Arvay misses this ominous symbolism.

15. Arvay's subconscious senses the parallels between Earl and his father. She twice expresses irrational worries that Earl might be bitten by a snake (138, 180) and dreams that he drowns, "his poor body . . . hung on a snag under the water" (138). Both, however, are dangers Jim, not Earl encounters: Jim is nearly bitten in the snake-handling scene and risks drowning when he tries to approach Earl in the swamp (152–53). These parallels between father and son are starkly evident in Arvay's vacillating thoughts after Earl's death:

> Passionate pictures formed on her eyelids and faded and were instantly replaced by others. Earl lying dead there at the front steps. That first time she had seen Jim Meserve, his broad felt hat shoved back from his tumbling curls and his white teeth flashing in a laugh as he talked with two other young men in Sawley. Their first visit to the mulberry tree. Earl as a newborn infant and her pangs of pain at the sight of him. Coming down the courthouse steps the day of her marriage. The moment that she knew that she was pregnant for her Jim. (168)

16. The symbol of the dog, associated with males, is pervasive in the novel. Even before this encounter, Arvay worries that Earl will "die like a dog" (138) at her mother's. Sensing Hatton's dangerous sexuality when she sees him about to rape Angeline, she runs for the gun, to "shoot him like a mangy dog" (180). Even Carl, who is reduced to a sexless buffoon toward the end of the novel, expresses his feelings of inadequacy with the statement that Arvay treats him like "'some old throwed-away dog'" (285).

17. In both *The Yearling* and *Seraph on the Suwanee* an afflicted boy stands for the author's ultimate evaluation of that culture. While Earl symbolizes in purest form the perversion of male sexuality in white society, Rawlings's treatment of Fodder-wing reflects her idealization of that culture. Even though Fodder-wing is "witless" (50), he is a "gentle mind in [a] twisted body" (138), injured in an attempt to fly with fodder tied to his arms. In Jody's mind, he represents the idealism of the human spirit: he understands Fodder-wing's "longing for flight; for lightness; for a moment's freedom from his body, earthbound and bent and stumbling" (51).

18. In a letter to Hurston (September 26, 1947, SC) Burroughs Mitchell suggested that he read this scene and the earlier snake episode very differently. He advises Hurston that she "must use episodes to express Arvay's condition just as effectively as the snake scene reveals the crisis of her weakness, and the scene crossing the bar expresses her victory."

19. Both Hemenway and Howard have noticed some ambiguity in this ending. Howard, for instance, discussing the emphasis on mothering as the sum of happiness, notes, "Where Hurston stands on all this is unclear" (*Zora Neale Hurston,* 146). Hemenway suggests, "It is possible that Zora meant this last scene to be semitragic, Arvay descending into the trap of her marriage forever; but if so, it fails for lack of preparation" (*Zora Neale Hurston,* 313).

20. Sun imagery is so central in the novel that Hurston toyed with reinforcing it in two of her early possible titles—*Good Morning Sun* (Hemenway, *Zora Neale Hurston,* 306) and *Sign of the Sun.* She uses this imagery in extremely ironic ways to highlight the danger Jim represents to Arvay and to Nature. For instance, she stresses Jim's oppressive power over the "plants" around him: Arvay thinks of the mulberry tree as "the servant of the sun" (307) and expresses her own powerlessness in her marriage in similar terms: "the call of Jim could no more be resisted than the sunflower can help turning to the sun" (136). This dynamic underlies many of Arvay's quaint, colloquial expressions. At another point, she thinks: "Her resolutions against Jim Meserve were just like the lightning-bugs holding a convention. They met at night and made scorning speeches against the sun and swore to do away with it and light up the world themselves. But the sun came up the next morning and they all went under the leaves and owned up that the sun was boss-man in the world" (200). The sun, consistently associated in the novel with Jim, is not a nurturer but a deadly "boss-man." The seemingly optimistic use of this imagery in the sunrise at the end of the novel portends Arvay's future servitude: she "met the look of the sun with confidence. Yes, she was doing what the big light had told her to do. She was serving and meant to serve. She made the sun welcome to come on in, then

snuggled down again beside her husband" (351). The manuscript version of the ending, although not as elegantly phrased, also revolves around sun imagery: "She was a servant, it was true, but she saw herself now as an humble servant to light and hold lamps for those she loved. . . . To love meant to bring some light. Then she could look upon herself as the servant of the sun, tending it's [*sic*] pulpit and serving light" (412, HC).

21. This relationship between the color of Arvay's eyes and her sexual arousal is reiterated in a later "romantic" interlude:

> But Jim was concentrating on her eyes. Once again he saw that greenish infusion creep in and mingle with the sky blue of her eyes. That peculiar thing about Arvay's eyes that he had a momentary glimpse of the first time that he had encountered her on the street of Sawley. He had seen it more fully when he had kissed her for the first time that Sunday at the table when they had become engaged. It had been daringly out in the open that flaming hour under the mulberry tree. (219)

22. The violence of male response to female resistance is depicted in Hurston's one instance of revolt in this depressing allegory. One pregnant female shark (significantly, a "man-killing" one [338]) fights back, cuts the nets, and almost manages to free the other creatures. This shark (as if aware of her enemy) strikes out at Jim, nearly biting his leg (298). When the female retaliates in self-defense, the male response is swift and brutal mutilation. After "blaspheming the honor of female sharks" (338), swearing that "Never had a shark's mother been married or begot a shark in a decent bed" (338), the men attack the shark, bludgeoning it to "a bloody mess in no time" (338).

23. In a number of ways, Hurston symbolically stresses Arvay's internalization of Jim's values at the end of the novel. She not only wears clothes like his (345), but she also becomes associated with the phallic snake imagery (343, 344) earlier reserved for Jim.

24. In "The Dilemma of the Negro Author" Johnson makes a similar argument about white appropriation: "White America has for a long time been annexing and appropriating Negro territory, and is prone to think of every part of the domain it now controls as originally and aboriginally its own" (479). Hurston had to argue with her editor and agents to keep this section from being deleted. In response to suggestions to omit it, she wrote a letter to Burroughs Mitchell (October, 1947, SC), providing a lengthy explanation for its inclusion.

5. "Crossing Over" and "Heading Back": Black Cultural Freedom in *Moses, Man of the Mountain*

1. As Sheffey points out, the connection between Moses and Africa goes back to ancient times and Flavius Josephus, who argues in *Antiquities of the Jews* that Moses was an Egyptian general. Josephus's idea was repeated by many Egyptologists of the

late nineteenth and earlier twentieth centuries as well as by writers such as Freud in *Moses and Monotheism*. In making Moses Egyptian, Hurston was thus tapping into a long and widespread tradition.

Hurston's translation of Moses to a black context was the focus of many reviews of the novel and of some disagreement about how effective this innovation was. Carmer, Hutchinson, and Blyden Jackson, for instance, enthusiastically approved of Hurston's approach. Others (including Slomovitz and Untermeyer) have not been so complimentary of what Blyden Jackson has praised as the book's cultural "cross-pollenation" (105). Alain Locke also criticized the work ("Dry Fields and Green Pastures"). Certainly the most damning review was that written by Ralph Ellison in "Recent Negro Fiction." Ellison found *Moses, Man of the Mountain* full of "the blight of calculated burlesque" and concluded vituperatively that "for Negro Fiction [*Moses*] did nothing" (24). Robert Hemenway has called the novel a "noble failure" because, in his view, Hurston "could not maintain the fusion of black creative style, biblical tone, ethnic humor, and legendary reference that periodically appears" (270–71).

2. Hurston alludes to this tradition in several of her other works. In *Tell My Horse*, for instance, she discusses the Haitian equation of Damballah and Moses (139–40) and alludes to the tradition of Moses as hoodoo man in *Jonah's Gourd Vine* (147).

3. Hemenway (*Zora Neale Hurston*, 258–60), Sheffey, and Howard have discussed the African American tradition of Moses as black liberator in America. Sheffey sees the book as a successful novel of liberation, "a positive scenario for black leadership" (217). Lillie Howard has also seen the novel as a positive picture of liberation (*Zora Neale Hurston*, 113–32).

4. Hurston has clearly read widely about the reign of Rameses II; she refers, for instance to his building projects (27, 58) and the militarism that characterized his reign (78). She also refers numerous times to the invasion of the Hyksos (31, 33, 67, 68, 69, 118) that preceded it. As a student of anthropology, Hurston was probably aware of the work of such noted Egyptologists as Budge (*The Book of the Dead, The Dwellers on the Nile, Egyptian Magic, Egyptian Religion, From Fetish to God in Ancient Egypt, The Gods of the Egyptians, History of Egypt, Osiris*), Breasted (*Ancient Records of Egypt, The Dawn of Conscience, Development of Religion and Thought in Ancient Egypt, A History of Egypt, from the Earliest Times to the Persian Conquest, A History of the Ancient Egyptians*), Frazer (*Adonis, Attis, Osiris, The Golden Bough*), Mackenzie (*Egyptian Myth and Legend*), Moret (*The Nile and Egyptian Civilization*), Petrie (*Egypt and Israel, Egyptian Tales, A History of Egypt, The Religion of Ancient Egypt, Religion and Conscience in Ancient Egypt*), and Weigall (*The Glory of the Pharaohs, A History of the Pharaohs*).

5. For discussion of this idea, see Moret (253), Budge (*The Gods of the Egyptians*, I. 334); Breasted (*Development of Religion*, 14–43); Breasted (*A History of the Ancient Egyptians*, 148); Breasted (*Dawn of Conscience*, 243).

6. Pondrom discusses how indebted *Their Eyes Were Watching God* is to myths of Isthar/Tammuz and Isis/Osiris, which show the regenerative power of the fe-

male. She discusses at length the parallels between Janie and Isis and between Tea Cake and Osiris in the novel.

7. For the historians and anthropologists of the day, the set of social values associated with the myth of Isis and Osiris and echoed by Mentu and Moses after his apprenticeship were explicitly defined as matriarchal ones. The most extensive discussions of matriarchy, ones that an anthropology student of the 1930s who was interested in ancient religions would certainly have encountered, were those of Bachofen and Briffault. In *The Mothers*, published in 1927 and indebted to Bachofen's earlier work (as the author acknowledges), Briffault, using Egypt as a primary example, points out important differences between matriarchy and patriarchy:

> It is assumed that in a matriarchal type of society the women exercise a
> domination over the men similar or equivalent to the domination exercised
> by the men over the women in a patriarchal social order, and that the two
> types of society thus differ merely in the sex which exercises dominant
> power in each. But such a conception is very far from accurate. The charac-
> teristics of societies of a matriarchal type are by no means a simple inver-
> sion of the parts respectively played by the sexes in a patriarchal society. In
> the most primitive human societies there is nothing equivalent to the domi-
> nation which, in advanced societies, is exercised by individuals, by classes,
> by one sex over the other. The notion of such a domination is entirely for-
> eign to primitive humanity; the conception of authority is not understood.
> (I. 433)

In addition to this fundamental equality between male and female and rejection of hierarchy, matriarchal cultures were also seen as ones close to Nature and respectful of natural law. See, for instance, Bachofen (91–92) and Diner (65). Associated with natural law rather than civil law, matriarchies develop a set of symbols in direct contrast to those of patriarchies, a preference for the left side over the right, night over day, and the moon over the sun.

8. Hurston was not the only one to see parallels between Moses and Osiris. The ancient Jewish historian, Josephus, whose story of Moses was universally referred to, gives an account of Moses' life that explicitly identifies him with Osiris (*Life and Works*, p. 875).

9. Hurston quotes extensively from this tale in other parts of her story as well. For instance, Mentu's comment on the source of his knowledge about the book—"It was told by the father of the father of my father to the father of my father and the father of my father has told it to my father" (73) echoes the source of "Setna and the Magic Book": "'It was told by the father of the father of my father to the father of my father, and the father of my father has told it to my father'" (II. 117). After Moses reads the book, "Light went before him and Darkness after" (154) just as "there went a Light before [Setna], and Darkness behind him" (111) after he read it. Similarly, the ritual Moses performs after reading the book is drawn from the Egyptian tale: "When he had read the book, he took a new piece of pa-

pyrus and copied the words of the book on it. Then he washed off the writing with beer and drank the beer for then he knew he would never forget what he had read" (154). In "Setna and the Magic Book," Naneferkaptah "called for a new piece of papyrus, and wrote on it all that was in the book before him. He dipped it in beer, and washed it off in the liquid; for he knew that if it were washed off, and he drank it, he would know all that there was in the writing" (II. 101–2). Finally, the mysterious sign of having read the book, a " 'forked stick in [Moses'] hand and a fire pan on [his] head' " (*Moses*, 149) is the same as the " 'forked stick in [the] hand' " and " 'fire-pan on [the] head' " (*Tales*, 112) of the character in the Egyptian story.

10. Mackenzie argues, for instance, that Moses became "mighty in word and in deed" while he was being educated at Helopolis (xviii). Like many other writers, Budge quotes the Bible as proof that Moses knew Egyptian magic (Budge, *Egyptian Magic*, 5).

11. See Budge, *Egyptian Magic*, 5. Hurston herself offers a similar explanation of this miracle in *Tell My Horse*:

> At any rate, concerning Moses' rod and the serpent, they say that many witch doctors in Africa can so hypnotize a snake that it can be made rigid and seemingly lifeless and carried as a cane and brought to life again at the will of the witch doctor. They contend that that was why the rod of Aaron, which was none other than the rod of Moses, was such a cane thrust into the hand of Aaron at the right moment. Such were the "rods" of the magicians of the Pharaoh. But Moses knew that his "rod" fed on the variety that the king's men of magic used, so he knew what would happen the moment that the magicians turned their "rods" into snakes. (140)

12. The indebtedness of Moses' new religion to an Egyptian predecessor was commented on by many writers Hurston might have encountered. See, for instance, Budge (*The Gods of the Egyptians,* I. 279), Breasted (*Dawn of Conscience,* 320–22, 353–54), Petrie (*Egypt and Israel,* 61), and Weigall (*The Paganism of Our Christianity,* 118–27).

13. Hurston's development of the change from Egyptian religion to Judaism as a cultural move to patriarchy was also a common one among the writers she would have read. Freud's argument in *Moses and Monotheism* is perhaps the best known expression of this argument in our day. Having suggested in *Totem and Taboo* that maternal gods were replaced in human history by paternal ones, Freud drew on the work of other writers in *Moses and Monotheism* to suggest that the change from the concrete female and male deities of Egyptian religion to the invisible, father figure of Judaism constituted an advance in intellectuality for humankind. Although Hurston was most probably not able to read any part of *Moses and Monotheism* before she finished *Moses, Man of the Mountain,* she could certainly have encountered this basic argument in the work of other writers.

Bachofen, for instance, who had written in the nineteenth century (but who, as Joseph Campbell points out in his introduction to Diner's *Mothers and Amazons,* was discovered during the 1920s) had made a very similar argument. He, too, argued that mother right preceded father right and took as his mission "to restore the picture of a cultural stage which was overlaid or totally destroyed by the later development of the ancient world" (70). Although he admits the idea has fallen into academic disrepute by 1927, Briffault, acknowledging his debt to Bachofen, repeats this argument about the historical primacy of matriarchies. In discussing the move to Judaism and its patriarchal character, Briffault argues that it replaced an older religion (III. 77) centered on worship of the moon, whose most general name was Sinn and who was associated with Mount Sinai, the Mountain of the Moon (III. 107). The struggle within Judaism, Briffault argues, was to abolish the idea of a female deity traditionally associated with moon worship: "The Jewish god had, in fact, but one real and formidable rival . . . the Goddess, the Queen of Heaven, who, from being a subsidiary aspect of the primitive male moon-deity, had, among the agricultural populations, come to displace him well-nigh entirely" (III. 114). Purging Judaism of this female aspect was an intense battle, one both religious and social:

> One aspect of the contexts was neither purely religious nor political. The religious Hebrew opposition to the Great Goddess was also a struggle of patriarchal principles against the survivals of matriarchal society. The chief opponents of the Yahwistic priests and prophets through the old prophetic reformation, the opponents whom the reformers recognized as their true enemies, and against whom they never wearied of hurling their invectives, were the women. It was the women who answered them by refusing to give up their allegiance to the Queen of Heaven and their mother lamentations over the Dying God. (III. 114–15)

Two women writing about matriarchies and their usurpation by patriarchy may have been known to Hurston. In *Mothers and Amazons,* published in German in the early 1930s, Helen Diner draws on Bachofen and Briffault but gives their analysis a decidedly feminist twist, implicitly praising the values of matriarchies. Esther Harding's *Women's Mysteries, Ancient and Modern* also presents very positively the values of matriarchal religions, the "worship of nature, of her creative and fecund powers and of the wisdom that lies inherent in instinct and in the at-one-ness with natural law" (220).

14. Hurston's details repeatedly identify Jehovah as Jethro's and later Moses' voice. At an early stage, Jethro is always conveniently "out of town" when Moses encounters Yahweh (276). Moses too apparently engages in ventriloquism, such a masterful act that "the voice of the unseen Moses speaking behind the altar seem[ed] like the voice of God" (150), only questioned much later by Miriam, who " 'Sometimes . . . thought God's voice in the tabernacle sounded mighty much like [Moses']' " (321).

15. Beneath his apparent affection for Joshua lies a concern for power that mirrors Jethro's attraction to Moses. Moses embraces Joshua because " 'I can use you' " (187) and is "absolutely satisfied with him" because he is so eager "to anticipate the wishes of Moses so he could hurry to do them" (200). Instead of an egalitarian, nonhierarchical relationship like the one Mentu fosters with the young Moses, Moses uses Joshua for his own purposes, seeing him as "the perfect instrument to his hand" (200).

16. In detailing Moses' destructive use of his powers, Hurston suggests his betrayal of Isis's magic. As Budge points out, Isis's magic was associated with life and
healing, for she brought "'with her her words of magical power, and her mouth was
full of the breath of life; for her talismans vanquish the pains of sickness, and her
words make to live again the throats of those who are dead'" (*Egyptian Magic,* 139).
Hurston stresses the contrast between Isis's healing magic and Moses' destructive
force quite subtly in her frequent references to the right hand that holds his rod.
From the Burning Bush (162) through his terrible acts against the Egyptians, Moses
always uses his right hand to inflict fear and pain (221, 301). As both Diner (71) and
Bachofen (77) have stressed, the left hand of Isis was the one that supposedly possessed magical powers and restored Osiris. The right hand, they point out, is symbolically associated with patriarchy.

17. Hurston also stresses this idea earlier when Moses tells Aaron about their
"'big project'": it is, he says, "'too big for us to be mere people. We've got to give
up being people and feel like the tools of destiny'" (173).

18. The ethical system of Egyptian religion (and its contrast to the Judeo-
Christian one) was commented on by many Egyptologists, most extensively perhaps by Breasted in *The Dawn of Conscience* and Petrie in *Religion and Conscience in
Ancient Egypt.* As several noted, the Egyptian concept of justice—the idea of Nature as the basis of moral law—was quite different from that developed in the Old
Testament. With ethical behavior defined not just as following rules but as caring for
human feelings, the Egyptian equivalent of the Decalogue—the Negative Confes-
sion—which souls recited at their judgment, included vows that one had oppressed
no other human being, had clothed the naked, and fed the hungry.

19. In the manuscript version of the novel, Hurston makes Moses' words more
harshly cruel: "'You know better than I who the leaders and agitators of this thing
are. Take 'em boys. Fall in behind Joshua. There just can't be no nation with folks
like that around. Do the most hurting thing you can do to a man—tell him his
dying day. That's no later than right now. Go ahead boys and clean up the camp'"
(127, JWJ).

20. Hurston imagined several scenarios surrounding Moses' death. Alluding to
this same moment in her manuscript "Just Like Us," she asks the telling question,
"Did the angels bury Moses on Nebom or was he expelled by the people?" (4, SC).
In "The Fire and the Cloud" Hurston also captures Moses at this time but without
the feeling of rejuvenation suggested in the end of the novel.

6. "With a Harp and a Sword in My Hand": Black Female Identity in *Dust Tracks on a Road*

1. In addition to the direct assaults on Western imperialism Hurston expressed in her manuscript chapter on world affairs, "Seeing the World as It is," she
also planned in her original version of "My People, My People!" much more overt
criticism of those black people who merely recreated a white world among themselves.

2. More recent readers have also focused on Hurston's treatment of race and her engagement of a white readership in *Dust Tracks*. Darwin Turner, for instance, concludes that the book demonstrates Hurston's "artful candor and coy reticence, her contradictions and silences, her irrationalities and extravagant boasts which plead for the white world to recognize and respect her" (*In A Minor Chord*, 91). Even two of Hurston's most stalwart supporters, Robert Hemenway and Alice Walker, express deep reservations about her autobiography. Hemenway also finds her treatment of race here "discomfiting" because "Like much of her career, it often appears contradictory. Zora seems to be both an advocate for the universal, demonstrating that this black woman does not look at the world in racial terms, and the celebrant of a unique ethnic upbringing in an all-black village" (276). Walker is also troubled by Hurston's obvious ingratiation in dealing with whites:

> For me, the most unfortunate thing Zora ever wrote is her autobiography.
> After the first several chapters, it rings false. One begins to hear the voice of
> someone whose life required the assistance of too many transitory "friends."
> A Taoist proverb states that *to act sincerely with the insincere is dangerous*. (A mis-
> take blacks as a group have tended to make in America.) And so we have
> Zora sincerely offering gratitude and kind words to people one knows she
> could not have respected. But this unctuousness, so out of character for
> Zora, is also a result of dependency, a sign of powerlessness, her inability to
> pay back her debts with anything but words. (*In Search*, 91)

Contemporary critics examining Hurston's autobiography from sympathetic (but differing) standpoints include Plant, Rayson, Lionnet, and Raynaud. Plant, for instance, points out parallels between *Dust Tracks* and black folk sermons and sees Hurston's autobiography as "a unified work with a unitary voice" (17). Rayson, arguing that Hurston's treatment of race is that of a traditional conservative, concludes that Hurston defines her character "as what Melville called an 'isolato,' playing an individual who refuses to be typecast in any Negro or intellectual role" ("*Dust Tracks*," 41). In a quite different vein, Lionnet, disputing Hemenway's critique of *Dust Tracks* as "camouflage" and "escape," suggests that Hurston's style in the work artfully "*exemplifies* the 'paradoxes of her personality'" (103). In discussing her treatment of race, she draws interesting parallels between Hurston's approach and Franz Fanon's denial of race as an abstract concept (105). Raynaud sees *Dust Tracks* as a "signifying" (128) text, one in which Hurston plays with a white audience and masks her real message. Finally, Kathleen Hassall also stresses the importance of seeing *Dust Tracks* as "a set of glimpses into the character of an inventive, resourceful, spirited, effective warrior—in disguise" (160). Other discussions of the influence of audience on Hurston's autobiography include those of Fox-Genovese and Robey.

3. Part of the reason for the difficulty interpreting Hurston's autobiography is its marked difference from many other black autobiographies. As Hemenway points out, *Dust Tracks on a Road* shares few features of black autobiography that Butterfield describes in *Black Autobiography in America* (*Zora Neale Hurston*, 278). Many of the criticisms leveled against *Dust Tracks on a Road* echo those made against women's autobiographies. As Estelle C. Jelinek points out in her introduction to *Women's*

Autobiographies: Essays in Criticism, women's autobiographies are often judged by an implied critical standard drawn from male autobiographies. Unlike those written by men, women's autobiographies "rarely mirror the establishment history of their times. They [women] emphasize to a much lesser extent the public aspect of their lives, the affairs of the world, or even their careers, and concentrate instead on their personal lives—domestic details, family difficulties, close friends, and especially people who influenced them" (7–8).

4. In the handwritten manuscript of the chapter, "My People! My People!" Hurston describes a similar kind of flexible adaptation to power as characteristic of blackness:

> Then, too, I do not worry about the future of my people because I know
> that our mamas gave us something that will take us anywhere. Call it charm
> if you want to, or adaptation, which is the highest genius of the species, we
> will survive. You will remember that the saurians once dominated the earth,
> but some other species who did not cover so many acres are here while they
> are gone. It is true that the big lizards licked up quite a fog while they were
> straw-bossing the job, but if you look around, you will notice that they are
> fine sights in museums now, but they are no trouble at all to the descendants
> of smaller animals who played it close to the vest. Call it whatever you will,
> but there is something which will save the brother in black from destruc-
> tion. (12, JWJ)

5. Hurston makes it clear that "truth" in the sense of historical accuracy is not her aim when she says, "anybody whose mouth is cut cross-ways is given to lying, unconsciously as well as knowingly" (265). Rebecca Chalmers Barton, in her introduction to *Witnesses for Freedom: Negro Americans in Autobiography,* gives a more sociological explanation for the reticence evident in some black autobiographies, one that also applies to Hurston's: "Undoubtedly, the Negro autobiographer especially has layer upon layer of consciousness that he may or may not choose to expose to the casual reader, while his unconscious omissions and distortions further complicate the presentation of reality" (xii).

6. Hurston was quite aware of how contact with white culture could sever black people from their own roots. As she points out, when she returns home— aglow with the "glamor" (174) of Barnard and its "marble halls" (175), people refuse to tell her folktales.

7. Hurston's assertion of her freedom to assign her own meanings, often in defiance of cultural norms, is also evident in her "interpretation" of Leviticus, a favorite of hers for its information on the "facts of life" (55).

8. Hurston also subtly lampoons this white man's handiwork; he may be proud of his expertise, but Aunt Judy is (rightfully) unimpressed: "He got no thanks from Aunt Judy. She grumbled for years about it. She complained that the cord had not been cut just right, and the belly-band had not been put on tight enough. She was mighty scared I was going to have a weak back, and that I would have trouble holding my water until I reached puberty. I did" (30).

9. In nearly every story of her interaction with whites, Hurston complicates

what appears initially to be her dependence and adoration. For instance, when (working as a manicurist near Capitol Hill) she learned political secrets from one man and refused to divulge them to another, her motives included not only respect for the politician but also awareness that his friendship was valuable to her: he was a good Greek scholar who helped her with her homework (160).

10. The descriptions of Fannie Hurst and Miss M—are strikingly parallel. Hurston stresses Miss M—'s strange mood swings: "At times she was playful as a kitten. At others, she would be solemn and moody" (139). Her inclusion of the story about the "game" Miss M— invented also stresses her childishness: "She would take rouge and paint her face all over a most startling red. Then I must take eye-shadow and paint myself blue. Blue Jake and Red Jake would then chase each other into closets, across beds, into bathrooms, with our sheet-robes trailing around us and tripping us up at odd moments. We crouched and growled and ambushed each other and laughed and yelled until we were exhausted" (140).

11. Despite differences in their backgrounds, Waters in her autobiography develops a similar picture of black womanhood. She presents herself as a headstrong child and a woman who stands up for herself, even whipping one unfaithful lover. She, too, often softpedals the issue of race while at the same time stressing her pride in being black. She discusses her problems with love, detailing how she often was "caught on the well-baited hook called love" (115). Women, especially her grandmother, play an important supportive role in her life; in fact, the climax of her autobiography is a reunion with her mother. Finally, visions and psychic experiences also play a crucial role.

12. Hurst's childishness also surfaces in Hurston's sketch, "Fannie Hurst," published in *Saturday Review.* One anecdote in that article is even less complimentary than her portrait in *Dust Tracks:*

> Then I have seen her annoyed by some petty incident, drop everything and
> rush to the telephone to tell her husband all abut it. And the way she says
> "Jack" it is the most helpless sound in the whole world. "Jack, they did this
> and thus to me. What must I do now, Jack? When are you coming home,
> Jack?" You can just hear him on the other end of the wire figuratively pat-
> ting her curls and wiping her eyes, and she is all mollified again. She returns
> to her desk with the air of "There, now! I told Jack on you and I bet he'll
> fix you good. Goody, goody, goody!" (16)

Years later, Hurst wrote "Zora Hurston: A Personality Sketch," published in *Yale University Library Gazette.* Discussing these articles and the correspondence between the two women, Wilentz ("White Patron") has offered an analysis of Hurston's treatment of Hurst quite different from my own.

13. Raynaud has briefly discussed the relationship of *Dust Tracks* to the traditional Cinderella story (124).

14. Regina Blackburn points out that one of the most common issues dealt with in black women's autobiographies is what she calls the "bind of double jeopardy, being both black and female, with sexism displayed by black males toward black females" (136).

15. Hurston also tells these stories in "The Jook" section of "Characteristics of Negro Expression" (*Sanctified Church,* 65).

16. In her article, "Hoodoo in America," Hurston also discusses similar aspects of Marie Leveau (326) and her hoodoo initiation (359).

17. Plant has discussed Hurston's portrayal of herself in her autobiography as "a righteous militant" akin to David.

18. This desire to portray a black woman with "some meat on her bones" colors much of Hurston's interpretation of her life and is partly responsible for her downplaying of social forces and her emphasis on personal initiative. Rebecca Barton, who interprets Hurston's treatment of race in a different way, discusses her in relation to a larger group of black autobiographers of the 1930s and 1940s whose memoirs downplay the problem of race and focus on more personal issues. As she analyzes the reason for this shift, "It could be claimed that these men and women are undergoing a reaction to the 'race uplifting' ideals of their predecessors. Weary of being a part of a problem, they seem to seek escape into more fruitful fields" (87–88). Regina Blackburn finds that a positive sense of self and a downplaying of color are both common features in black women's autobiographies.

19. Demetrakopoulos argues that the Demeter/Kore myth underlies many women's autobiographies (181).

20. Lionnet has made a similar point about Hurston's relation to Isis in *Dust Tracks.* Stressing Isis's "re-membering" powers, she sees Hurston as "the wanderer who conducts her research, establishes spatiotemporal connections among the children of the diaspora, and re-members the scattered body of folk material so that siblings can again 'touch each other'" (119).

21. The underlying ethical similarities between the religious beliefs of Mentu, Hurston, and Mother Catherine (a hoodoo doctor Hurston wrote about) are striking. Mother Catherine, for instance, practices a religion Hurston explicitly labels as "matriarchal" (*Sanctified Church,* 28), one based not on fear, law, and repression but on "individual[ity]," "originality," "gaiety," and "tenderness" (25). In the place of a phallic, deadly rod, Sister Catherine posits the womb as a central symbol: "It is right that a woman should lead. A womb is what God made in the beginning, and out of that womb was born Time, and all that fills up space" (26). Hers is no abstract, faceless god but one intimately connected with this life; as she says, "There is no heaven beyond dat blue globe" (26). Worship of Nature and the search for natural wisdom rather than obedience to law form the core of this matriarchal religion. Just as Hurston conceives of an afterlife as simply a return to Nature, Sister Catherine tells her congregation, "When we die, where does the breath go? Into trees and grass and animals. Your flesh goes back to mortal earth to fertilize it" (26). Embracing Nature rather than priestly authority as her gauge of truth, she urges people not to "teach what the Apostles and prophets say. Go to the tree . . . and find out whether they were right" (26).

22. Despite her image as a writer unconcerned with race or duped by whites, she wrote extensively and often scathingly during the 1940s about the racist "false foundation" ("My Most Humiliating Jim Crow Experience" [164]) of the white world, decrying the racism of whites and expressing her eagerness to overthrow

white supremacy in correspondence to Alain Locke (July 23, 1943, AL) and to Claude Barnett (February 1943, CHS). She expresses similar strong feelings in a letter to Countee Cullen (March 5, 1943): "I know that the Anglo-Saxon mentality is one of violence. Violence is his religion. He has gained everything by it, and respects nothing else" (Borders, 91). In this letter Hurston explains that her disaffection with liberal "race leaders" stems, not from their call for equal rights, but from their tentative, nonthreatening methods: "When I suggest to our 'leaders' that the white man is not going to surrender for mere words what he has fought and died for, and that if we want anything substantial we must speak with the same weapons, immediately they object" (Borders, 91). She demands, instead, direct and—if necessary, violent—confrontation: "My stand is this: either we must do something about it that the white man will understand and respect, or shut up. No whiner ever got any respect or relief. If some of us must die for human justice, then let us die. For my own part, this poor body of mine is not so precious that I would not be willing to give it up for a good cause. But my own self-respect refuses to let me go to the mourner's bench" (Borders, 92). Hurston's allegiance is clear: "If any of our leaders start something like that [violent insurrection] then I will be in it body and soul. But I shall never join the cry-babies" (Borders, 92).

Not silenced when her white editors forced her to delete such comments from her autobiography, Hurston repeated some of the main ideas in an article, "Crazy for this Democracy," originally published in the December 1945 issue of *Negro Digest*. With venomous satire, she announces, "The Ass-and-All of Democracy has shouldered the load of subjugating the dark world completely" (*I Love Myself*, 166). Such a stance is not recognized as the economic exploitation that it is but legitimated as divine call: "The inference is that God has restated the superiority of the West. God always does like that when a thousand white people surround one dark one. Dark people are always 'bad' when they do not admit the Divine Plan like that" (166).

American actions toward the end of World War II did nothing to soften Hurston's attitude. Writing to Barnett in July 1946 (CHS), she not only attributed Truman's postwar treatment of the Japanese and Chinese to racism but also linked the racism she saw in American foreign policy to treatment of blacks within the country.

23. The proverbial elements in the middle of this passage, which seem to defuse the violent threat in these lines by making Hurston sound like a quaint "character," actually strengthen their subversive import. Tremendous irony is buried in her statement "Kill dead and go to jail": when her white male midwife and mentor had told her to "'kill dead and go to jail'" (42) when anyone spit on or kicked her, he certainly never intended for her to direct her violence against whites or to express it in revolutionary rhetoric.

24. When she donated the manuscript of *Dust Tracks* to Yale University, Hurston penned a note on the title page that invites comparison of the two versions: "Parts of this manscript were not used in composition for publisher's reasons" (JWJ).

25. In an interview printed after the publication of her autobiography,

Hurston openly discusses the way she had to tailor her ideas at times to get them published: "Rather than get across all of the things which you want to say you must compromise and work within the limitations [of those people] who have the final authority in deciding whether or not a book shall be printed" ("Zora Neale Hurston Reveals Key to Her Literary Success." *New York Amsterdam News,* November 18, 1944; clipping at Howard University). In speaking specifically about *Dust Tracks on a Road,* Hurston emphasizes a feeling of disappointment about it probably attributable, at least in part, to the ways she was forced to veil her controversial opinions: "I have the feeling of disappointment about it. I don't think that I achieved all that I set out to do. I thought that in this book I would achieve my ideal, but it seems that I have not yet reached it. . . . it still doesn't say all that I want it to say" (Hemenway's introduction to *Dust Tracks,* xxxviii).

7. The "Trials" of Black Women in the 1950s: Ruby McCollum and Laura Lee Kimble

1. In a letter written during the mid-1950s, Hurston decried the condescension she saw behind much white acceptance of integration (Hurston to Madame Soblonière, December 3, 1955, HC).

2. Similarly, although her article, "Mourner's Bench, Communist Line: Why the Negro Won't Buy Communism," sounded a patriotic theme popular enough in the 1950s to be published in *American Legion Magazine,* her reasons for rejecting it fail to fit neatly into a "conservative" pigeonhole. Lambasting so-called friends of the Negro, who felt American blacks "were so downtrodden, they deeply pitied our case," she rejects such condescension: "Right then and there they lost one black sheep. I was poor, but I certainly did not feel pitiful" (15). Behind professions of compassion, she sensed racism, a view of blacks as "dumb, but useful tool[s]" (15) and "dumb black brutes" (55). For an excellent discussion of the relationship between Hurston's poetics and politics, see Wald.

3. Kevin McCarthy has discussed Hurston's treatment of these two trials in relation to her own traumatic experience of being falsely charged with child molestation in 1948.

4. Hurston's coverage of the trial was reported in the following articles: "Zora's Revealing Story of Ruby's First Day in Court," "Victim of Fate," "Ruby Sane," "Ruby McCollum Fights for Life," "Bare Plot against Ruby," "Trial Highlights," "McCollum-Adams Trial Highlights," "Ruby Bares Her Love," "Doctor's Threats, Tussle over Gun Led to Slaying," and "Ruby's Troubles Mount." Her series, *The Life Story of Mrs. Ruby J. McCollum,* ran on February 28, March 7, 14, 21, 28, April 4, 11, 18, 25, May 2, 1953.

5. Hurston recreates images she had used to describe Janie and Starks's marriage to suggest the similar dynamics of Ruby and Sam's. Here she echoes Janie's realization about Starks when he strikes her (*Eyes,* 112). Later, echoing her description of Starks after his masculine ego is deflated by Janie (119–20), Hurston suggests

that Sam begins to die when he learns of Ruby's affair with Adams: His wife was "lost to him except in name only. So, he was not so lively about town, nor so full of wisecracks as he once had been. In quiet moments, the sides of his face looked limp and sagging, like wet-wash hung out to dry from his ears" (*Life Story,* April 18, 1953). Like Starks, he gets sick shortly after this time and never recovers.

6. Hurston repeatedly depicts Ruby as a powerful personality in her relationships with men. Hated by Sam's family because she handles the money and is "too possessive and domineering" (*Life Story,* March 21, 1953), Ruby (like Erzulie) has a "strong inner drive to dominate . . . [and] to possess" ("Ruby Sane"). As she hints early in her reporting of the trial, Hurston felt this character trait led to her murder of Adams: Ruby McCollum was "a very jealous woman under her own roof. She was possessive, and what was hers . . . or she considered hers . . . she must RULE! Could that be the explanation, in part, of what took place in the office of Dr. Adams on the Sunday morning of Aug. 3?" ("Ruby Sane").

7. Two of Hurston's angriest retorts were in response to reviews of *Their Eyes Were Watching God.* Hurston was furious at Alain Locke's criticism (see chapter 3, note 2) and wrote her venomous essay, "The Chick with One Hen," in retaliation. She vented some of her anger at Richard Wright's damning review (see chapter 3, note 2) in her own review of *Uncle Tom's Children,* in which she comments, "There is lavish killing here, perhaps enough to satisfy all male black readers." She concludes even more cynically: "One hopes that Mr. Wright will find in Negro life a vehicle for his talents" ("Stories of Conflict").

Conclusion

1. See discussions by Wall (*Women of the Harlem Renaissance,* 33–138) and McDowell ("The Neglected Dimension of Jessie Fauset," "'That nameless . . . shameful impulse': Sexuality in Nella Larsen's *Quicksand* and *Passing,*" and "On Face: The Masks of Identity in Jessie Fauset's *Plum Bun* or Getting Rich in the Harlem Renaissance."

2. The writings of Davies and Graves, Davies and Fido, Williams, and Steady suggest the range of emphases in this perspective. For an excellent overview of womanist theory, see Adell, 90–117.

3. Deborah McDowell has emphasized the constraints on self-expression still experienced by African American women writers. She cites, for instance, the comments of Gloria Naylor about how her concerns with reception of her work influenced the writing of *The Women of Brewster Place:* "'I bent over backwards not to have a negative message come through about the men. . . . I worried about whether or not the problems that were being caused by the men in the women's lives would be interpreted as some bitter statement I had to make about black men'" ("Reading," 94).

4. Various critics have discussed the significance of these debates. See, for instance, Deborah McDowell's "Boundaries: Or Distant Relations and Close Kin,"

Calvin Hernton's *The Sexual Mountain and Black Women Writers* (1–36), Valerie Smith's "Gender and Afro-American Literary Theory and Criticism" and "Black Feminist Theory and the Representation of the 'Other.'"

5. Emphasizing the broader dynamics of the "courtroom" in which Hurston is read today, Hazel Carby raises important—and discomfitting—questions about the cultural processes that have resulted in Hurston's inclusion in the academy. In response to the question, "How is she being reread, now, to produce cultural meanings that this society wants or needs to hear?" ("The Politics of Fiction," 72), she raises the possibility that Hurston's emphasis on rural community functions as a displacement of contemporary urban conflict: "Has *Their Eyes Were Watching God* become the most frequently taught black novel," she asks, "because it acts as a mode of assurance that, really, the black folk are happy and healthy?" (89–90).

6. This notion has been analyzed in depth by many theorists since Barbara Smith's call for a black feminist approach that "embodies the realization that the politics of sex as well as the politics of race and class are crucially interlocking factors in the works of black women writers" ("Toward," 412). For discussions of developments in black feminist critical theory since Smith's essay, see Deborah McDowell ("Boundaries") and Valerie Smith ("Gender" and "Black Feminist Theory").

Works Cited

Abrahams, Roger. "Negotiating Respect: Patterns of Presentation Among Black Women." In *Women and Folklore,* edited by Claire R. Farrer, pp. 58–80. Austin and London: University of Texas Press, 1975.

Adell, Sandra. *Double-Consciousness/Double Bind: Theoretical Issues in Twentieth-Century Black Literature.* Urbana and Chicago: University of Illinois Press, 1994.

Anderson, John Q. "Old John and the Master." *Southern Folklore Quarterly* 25 (1961): 195–97.

Awkward, Michael. "'The Inaudible Voice of It All': Silence, Voice, and Action in *Their Eyes Were Watching God.*" In *Studies in Black American Literature, Vol. III: Black Feminist Criticism and Critical Theory,* edited by Joe Weixlmann and Houston Baker, Jr., pp. 57–109. Greenwood, Fla.: Penkevill Publishing Co., 1988.

———, ed. *New Essays on "Their Eyes Were Watching God."* Cambridge and New York: Cambridge University Press, 1990.

Bachofen, Johan Jacob. *Myth, Religion, and Mother Right: Selected Writings of J. J. Bachofen.* Trans. by Ralph Manheim. Bollingen Series, LXXXIV. Princeton: Princeton University Press, 1967. (Originally published, in German, 1926.)

Baker, Houston A. *Blues, Ideology, and Afro-American Literature: A Vernacular Theory.* Chicago: University of Chicago Press, 1984.

———. *Modernism and the Harlem Renaissance.* Chicago and London: University of Chicago Press, 1979.

Banks, Frank D., and Portia Smiley. "Old-Time Courtship Conversation." In *Mother Wit from the Laughing Barrel: Readings in the Interpretation of American Folklore,* edited by Alan Dunes, pp. 251–57. Englewood Cliffs: Prentice, 1973. (Originally published in *Southern Workman* 24 [1895]: 14–15.)

Barton, Rebecca Chalmers. *Witnesses for Freedom: Negro Americans in Autobiography.* New York and London: Harper and Brothers Publishers, 1948.

Bell, Bernard. *The African-American Novel and Its Tradition*. Amherst: University of Massachusetts Press, 1987.

Bellman, Samuel I. *Marjorie Kinnan Rawlings*. New York: Twayne Publishers, 1974.

Benesch, Klaus. "Oral Narrative and Literary Text: Afro-American Folklore in *Their Eyes Were Watching God*." *Callaloo* 11:3 (Summer 1988): 627–35.

Bethel, Lorraine. "'This Infinity of Conscious Pain': Zora Neale Hurston and the Black Female Literary Tradition." In *All the Women Are White, All the Blacks Are Men, But Some of Us Are Brave,* edited by Gloria T. Hull, Patricia Bell Scott, and Barbara Smith. Old Westbury: Feminist Press, 1982.

Bigelow, Gordon, and Laura V. Monti, eds. *Selected Letters of Marjorie Kinnan Rawlings*. Gainesville: University Presses of Florida, 1983.

Blackburn, Regina. "In Search of the Black Female Self: African-American Women's Autobiographies and Ethnicity." In *Women's Autobiography: Essays in Criticism,* edited by Estelle C. Jelinek, pp. 133–48. Bloomington and London: Indiana University Press, 1980.

Bloom, Harold, ed. *Zora Neale Hurston's "Their Eyes Were Watching God."* New York, New Haven, and Philadelphia: Chelsea House Publishers, 1987.

Bone, Robert. *Down Home: Origins of the Afro-American Short Story*. New York: Columbia University Press, 1975.

———. *The Negro Novel in America*. New Haven: Yale University Press, 1958.

Bontemps, Arna. "From Eatonville, Florida to Harlem" [Review of *Dust Tracks on a Road*]. *New York Herald Tribune Books,* November 22, 1942, p. 3.

Borders, Florence Edwards. "Zora Neale Hurston: Hidden Woman." *Callaloo* 2:2 (May 1979): 89–92.

Botkin, B. A., ed. *Lay My Burden Down, A Folk History of Slavery*. Chicago: University of Chicago, 1945.

Boxwell, D. A. "'Sis Cat' as Ethnographer: Self-Presentation and Self-Inscription in Zora Neale Hurston's *Mules and Men*." *African American Review* 26:4 (Winter 1992): 605–17.

Boylan, Patrick. *Thoth, The Hermes of Egypt: A Study of Some Aspects of Theological Thought in Ancient Egypt*. London: Oxford University Press, 1922.

Brawley, Benjamin. *A Social History of the American Negro*. New York: Macmillan, 1921.

Breasted, James Henry. *Ancient Records of Egypt*. 5 vols. New York: Russell and Russell, 1962. (Originally published in 1906.)

———. *The Dawn of Conscience*. New York: Charles Scribner's Sons, 1933.

———. *Development of Religion and Thought in Ancient Egypt*. New York: Harper and Row, 1959. (Originally published in 1912.)

———. *A History of Egypt, from the Earliest Times to the Persian Conquest*. Second Edition. New York: Charles Scribner's Sons, 1909. (Originally published in 1903).

———. *A History of the Ancient Egyptians.* New York: Charles Scribner's Sons, 1908.

Brewer, J. Mason. *American Negro Folklore.* Chicago: Quadrangle Books, 1968.

———. *Dog Ghosts and Other Texas Negro Folk Tales.* Austin: University of Texas Press, 1958.

———. "John Tales." *Publications of the Texas Folklore Society* 24 (1959): 170–89.

Brickell, Herschel. "A Woman Saved" [Review of *Seraph on the Suwanee*]. *Saturday Review of Literature,* November 6, 1948, p. 19.

———. "A Negro Writer and Her People" [Review of *Mules and Men*]. *New York Post,* October 26, 1935, p. 7.

———. Review of *Jonah's Gourd Vine. North American Review* 239 (July 23, 1934): 95–96.

———. Review of *Their Eyes Were Watching God. New York Post,* September 14, 1937.

Briffault, Robert. *The Mothers: A Study of the Origins of Sentiments and Institutions.* 3 vols. New York: Macmillan, 1927.

Brigham, Cathy. "The Talking Frame of Zora Neale Hurston's Talking Book: Storytelling as Dialectic in *Their Eyes Were Watching God. College Language Association Journal* 37:4 (June 1994): 402–19.

Brock, H. I. "The Full, True Flavor of Life in a Negro Community." [Review of *Mules and Men.*] *New York Times Book Review,* November 10, 1935, p. 4.

Brogan, D. W. "Both Sides of the Medal" [Review of *Mules and Men*]. *The Spectator* 156 (March 6, 1936): 403.

Brown, Alan. "'De Beast' Within: The Role of Nature in *Jonah's Gourd Vine.*" In *Zora In Florida,* edited by Steve Glassman and Kathryn Lee Seidel, pp. 76–85. Orlando: University of Central Florida Press, 1991.

Brown, Lloyd W. "Zora Neale Hurston and the Nature of Female Perception." *Obsidian* 4 (1978): 36–45.

Brown, Sterling. "Luck is Fortune." *The Nation,* October 16, 1937, pp. 109–10.

———. "The Negro Author and His Publisher." *Negro Quarterly* (Spring 1942): 7–20.

———. "Our Literary Audience." *Opportunity* (February 1930): 42–46, 61.

———. Review of *Mules and Men.* 1936. JWJ. No publication information.

Budge, E. A. Wallis. *The Book of the Dead.* 2d Edition. New York: Barnes and Noble, 1909.

———. *The Dwellers on the Nile.* New York: Benjamin Blom, 1972. (Originally published in 1885; revised in 1925.)

———. *Egyptian Magic.* New York: University Books (n.d.). (Originally published in 1899.)

———. *Egyptian Religion: Egyptian Ideas of the Future Life.* London and Boston: Routledge and Kegan Paul, 1975. (Originally published in 1899.)

———. *From Fetish to God in Ancient Egypt.* New York: Benjamin Blom, 1972. (Originally published in 1934.)

————. *The Gods of the Egyptians, or Studies in Egyptian Mythology.* 2 vols. New York: Dover Publications, 1969. (Originally published in 1904.)

————. *History of Egypt.* 8 vols. London: Kegan Paul, Trench, Trubner and Co., 1902.

————. *Osiris, The Egyptian Religion of Resurrection.* New York: University Books, 1961. (Originally published in 1911.)

Burris, Andrew. Review of *Jonah's Gourd Vine. Crisis,* June 1934.

Butterfield, Steven. *Black Autobiography in America.* Amherst: University of Massachusetts Press, 1974.

Byrd, James. "Zora Neale Hurston: A Folk Novelist." *Tennessee Folklore Society Bulletin* 21 (1955): 37–41.

Callahan, John F. "'Mah Tongue Is In My Friend's Mouf': The Rhetoric of Intimacy and Immensity in *Their Eyes Were Watching God.*" In *Zora Neale Hurston's "Their Eyes Were Watching God,"* edited by Harold Bloom, pp. 87–113. New York, New Haven, and Philadelphia: Chelsea House Publishers, 1987.

Carby, Hazel. "The Politics of Fiction, Anthropology, and the Folk: Zora Neale Hurston." In *New Essays on Their Eyes Were Watching God,* edited by Michael Awkward, pp. 71–93. Cambridge and New York: Cambridge University Press, 1990.

————. *Reconstructing Womanhood: The Emergence of the Afro-American Woman Novelist.* New York: Oxford University Press, 1987.

Carmer, Carl. "Biblical Story in Negro Rhythm" [Review of *Moses, Man of the Mountain*]. *New York Herald Tribune Books,* November 26, 1939, p. 5.

Carr, Glynis. "Storytelling as *Bildung* in Zora Neale Hurston's *Their Eyes Were Watching God.*" *College Language Association Journal* 31:2 (December 1987): 189–200.

Cassidy, Thomas. "Janie's Rage: The Dog and the Storm in *Their Eyes Were Watching God.*" *College Language Association Journal* 36 (1993): 260–69.

Chamberlain, John. Review of *Dust Tracks on a Road. New York Times,* November 7, 1942.

Chubb, Thomas Caldecot. Review of *Mules and Men. North American Review* 241 (March 1936): 181–83.

Coleman, Ancilla. "Mythological Structure and Psychological Significance in Hurston's *Seraph on the Suwanee.*" *Publications of the Mississippi Philological Association* (1988): 21–27.

Cooke, Michael G. *Afro-American Literature in the Twentieth Century.* New Haven and London: Yale, 1984.

Courlander, Harold. *A Treasury of Afro-American Folklore.* New York: Crown Publishers, 1976.

Crabtree, Claire. "The Confluence of Folklore, Feminism and Black Self-Determination in Zora Neale Hurston's *Their Eyes Were Watching God.*" *Southern Literary Journal* 17:2 (Spring 1985): 54–66.

Crowley, Daniel J., ed. *African Folklore in the New World.* Austin and London: University of Texas Press, 1977.

Cunard, Nancy, ed. *Negro: An Anthology.* London: Wishart, 1934.

Curren, Erik D. "Should Their Eyes Have Been Watching God?: Hurston's Use of Religious Experience and Gothic Horror." *African American Review* 29:1 (1995): 17–25.

Dance, Daryl Cumber. *Shuckin' and Jivin': Folklore from Contemporary Black Americans.* Bloomington: Indiana University Press, 1978.

Daniel, Walter C. *Images of the Preacher in Afro-American Literature.* Washington: University Press of America, 1981.

Daniels, Jonathan. "Black Magic and Dark Laughter" [Review of *Mules and Men*]. *Saturday Review of Literature* 12 (October 19, 1935): 12.

Davies, Carole Boyce. *Black Women, Writing and Identity: Migrations of the Subject.* London and New York: Routledge, 1994.

Davies, Carole Boyce, and Elaine Savoy Fido, eds. *Out of the Kumbla: Caribbean Women and Literature.* Trenton, N.J.: African World Press, 1990.

Davies, Carole Boyce, and Anne Adams Graves, eds. *Ngambika: Studies of Women in African Literature.* Trenton, N.J.: African World Press, 1986.

Davies, Kathleen. "Zora Neale Hurston's Poetics of Embalmment: Articulating the Rage of Black Women and Narrative Self-Defense." *African American Review* 26:1 (1992): 147–59.

Davis, Arthur P. *From the Dark Tower: Afro-American Writers 1900 to 1960.* Washington, D.C.: Howard University Press, 1974.

Dearborn, Mary V. *Pocahontas's Daughters: Gender and Ethnicity in American Culture.* New York: Oxford University Press, 1980.

Demetrakopoulos, Stephanie A. "The Metaphysics of Matrilinearism in Women's Autobiography: Studies of Mead's *Blackberry Winter,* Hellman's *Pentimento,* Angelou's *I Know Why the Caged Bird Sings,* and Kingston's *The Woman Warrior,*" in *Women's Autobiography: Essays in Criticism,* edited by Estelle C. Jelinek, pp. 180–206. Bloomington and London: Indiana University Press, 1986.

Diner, Helen (pseudonym). *Mothers and Amazons: The First Feminine History of Culture,* edited and translated by John Philip Lundin, introduction by Joseph Campbell. New York: Julian Press, 1965.

Dorson, Richard M. *American Negro Folktales.* Greenwich, Conn.: Fawcett Publications, 1956.

———. *Negro Folktales in Michigan.* Cambridge: Harvard University Press, 1956.

Du Bois, W. E. Burghardt. *The Gift of Black Folk: The Negroes in the Making of America.* New York: AMS Press, 1971. (Originally published in 1924.)

DuCille, Ann. *The Coupling Convention: Sex, Text, and Tradition in Black Women's Fiction.* New York and Oxford: Oxford University Press, 1993.

Dundes, Alan. *Mother Wit from the Laughing Barrel: Readings in the Interpretation of American Folklore.* Englewood Cliffs, N.J.: Prentice, 1973.

DuPlessis, Rachel Blau. "Power, Judgment, and Narrative in a Work of Zora Neale Hurston: Feminist Cultural Studies." In *New Essays on "Their Eyes Were Watching God,"* edited by Michael Awkward, pp. 95–123. Cambridge and New York: Cambridge University Press, 1990.

Egan, Susanna. *Patterns of Experience in Autobiography.* Chapel Hill and London: University of North Carolina Press, 1984.

Ellison, Ralph. "Recent Negro Fiction." *New Masses,* August 5, 1941, pp. 22–26.

Fallaize, E. N. "Negro Folklore" [Review of *Mules and Men*]. *Manchester Guardian,* April 7, 1936, p. 7.

Fauset, Arthur Huff. "Negro Tales from the South." *Journal of American Folklore* 40: 157 (July–September 1927): 213–303.

Ferguson, Otis. Review of *Their Eyes Were Watching God. The New Republic,* October 13, 1937.

Ferguson, SallyAnn. "Folkloric Men and Female Growth in *Their Eyes Were Watching God." Black American Literature Forum* 21: 1–2 (Spring–Summer 1987): 185–97.

Ferris, William R., Jr. "Black Prose Narratives in the Mississippi Delta." *Journal of American Folklore* 85 (1972): 140–51.

"Folklore and Ethnology." *Southern Workman* 24:8 (Hampton, Va.; September 1895): 154–56.

Ford, Nick Aaron. *The Contemporary Negro Novel.* Boston: Meador Publishers, 1936.

Fox-Genovese, Elizabeth. "My Statue, My Self: Autobiographical Writings of Afro-American Women." In *Reading Black, Reading Feminist: A Criticial Anthology,* edited by Henry Louis Gates, Jr., pp. 176–203. New York: Meridian, 1990.

Frazer, James George. *Adonis, Attis, Osiris: Studies in the History of Oriental Religion* (Part IV of *The Golden Bough: A Study of Magic and Religion*). New York: University Books, 1961. (Originally published in 1906.)

———. *Folk-lore in the Old Testament: Studies in Comparative Religion, Legend and Law.* 3 vols. London: Macmillan, 1918.

———. *The Golden Bough: A Study in Magic and Religion.* 3rd Edition. 12 vols. London: Macmillan, 1925–30.

Freud, Sigmund. *Moses and Monotheism in the Origins of Religion.* In *The Standard Edition of the Complete Psychological Works of Sigmund Freud,* translated and edited by James Strachey. London: The Hogarth Press, 1964. Vol. XXIII.

———. *Totem and Taboo: Resemblances between the Psychic Lives of Savages and Neurotics.* In *The Standard Edition of the Complete Psychological Works of Sigmund Freud,* translated and edited by James Strachey. London: The Hogarth Press, 1955. Vol. XIII.

Gannett, Lewis. "Books and Things" [Review of *Mules and Men*]. *New York Herald Tribune,* October 11, 1935, p. 27.

———. "Books and Things" [Review of *Jonah's Gourd Vine*]. *New York Herald Tribune,* May 3, 1934.

Gates, Henry Louis, Jr. *Figures in Black: Words, Signs, and the "Racial" Self.* New York and Oxford: Oxford University Press, 1987.

———. *The Signifying Monkey: A Theory of Afro-American Literary Criticism.* New York: Oxford University Press, 1988.

Gayle, Addison, Jr. *The Way of the New World: The Black Novel in America.* Garden City, N.Y.: Anchor Press, 1975.

Giles, James R. "The Significance of Time in Zora Neale Hurston's *Their Eyes Were Watching God." Negro American Literature Forum* 6 (1972): 52–53.

Gloster, Hugh M. *Negro Voices in American Fiction.* New York: Russell and Russell, 1948.

Gruening, Martha. "Darktown Strutter" [Review of *Jonah's Gourd Vine*]. *New Republic* 74 (July 11, 1934): 244–45.

Harding, M. Esther. *Women's Mysteries, Ancient and Modern.* London and New York: Longman, Green and Co., 1935.

Harris, Trudier. "On *The Color Purple,* Stereotypes, and Silence." *Black American Literature Forum* 18 (1984): 155–61.

———. "Our People, Our People." In *Alice Walker and Zora Neale Hurston: The Common Bond,* edited by Lillie P. Howard. Westport, Conn., and London: Greenwood Press, 1993.

Hassall, Kathleen. "Text and Personality in Disguise and in the Open: Zora Neale Hurston's *Dust Tracks on a Road."* In *Zora in Florida,* edited by Steve Glassman and Kathryn Lee Seidel, pp. 159–73. Orlando: University of Central Florida Press, 1991.

Hedden, Worth Tuttle. "Turpentine and Moonshine" [Review of *Seraph on the Suwanee*]. *New York Herald Tribune Book Review,* October 10, 1948, p. 2.

Hemenway, Robert. "Are You a Flying Lark or a Setting Dove?" In *Afro-American Literature: The Reconstruction of Instruction,* edited by Dexter Fisher and Robert Stepto, pp. 122–52. New York: MLA, 1979.

———. "Folklore Field Notes from Zora Neale Hurston." *Black Scholar,* 7 (1976): 39–47.

———. *Zora Neale Hurston: A Literary Biography.* Urbana: University of Illinois Press, 1977.

Henderson, Mae Gwendolyn. "Speaking in Tongues: Dialogics, Dialectics, and the Black Woman Writer's Literary Tradition." In *Changing Our Own Words: Essays on Criticism, Theory, and Writing by Black Women,* edited by Cheryl A. Wall, pp. 16–27. New Brunswick and London: Rutgers University Press.

Hernton, Calvin C. *The Sexual Mountain and Black Women Writers: Adventures in Sex, Literature and Real Life.* New York: Doubleday, 1987.

Holloway, Karla F. C. *The Character of the Word: The Texts of Zora Neale Hurston.* New York: Greenwood Press, 1987.

———. *Moorings and Metaphors: Figures of Culture and Gender in Black Women's Literature.* New Brunswick: Rutgers University Press, 1992.

Hooks, Bell. *Yearning: Race, Gender, and Cultural Politics.* Boston: South End Press, 1990.

———. "Zora Neale Hurston: A Subversive Reading." *Matatu* 3:6 (1989): 5–23.

Howard, Lillie. "Nanny and Janie: Will the Twain Ever Meet?" *Journal of Black Studies* 12 (1982): 403–14.

———. *Zora Neale Hurston.* Boston: Twayne Publishers, 1980.

Howard, Lillie P., ed. *Alice Walker and Zora Neale Hurston: The Common Bond.* Westport, Conn., and London: Greenwood Press, 1993.

Hubbard, Dolan. "' . . . Ah said Ah'd save de text for you': Recontextualizing the Sermon to Tell Her(story) in Zora Neale Hurston's *Their Eyes Were Watching God.*" *African American Review* 27:2 (1993): 167–78.

Hughes, Carl Milton (pseud. Hughes, John Milton Charles). *The Negro Novelist: A Discussion of the Writings of American Negro Novelists, 1940–1950.* New York: Citadel Press, 1953.

Hughes, Langston. *The Big Sea: An Autobiography.* New York: Hill and Wang, 1940.

Hughes, Langston, and Arna Bontemps, eds. *The Book of Negro Folklore.* New York: Dodd, Mead and Co., 1959.

Huggins, Nathan. *Harlem Renaissance.* New York: Oxford University Press, 1971.

Huie, William Bradford. *Ruby McCollum: Woman in the Suwanee Jail.* New York: E. P. Dutton, 1956.

Hurst, Fannie. "Introduction" to *Jonah's Gourd Vine.* Philadelphia: J. B. Lippincott, 1934.

———. "Zora Hurston: A Personality Sketch." *Yale University Library Gazette* 35:1 (July 1961): 17–21.

Hurston, Zora Neale. "Bare Plot against Ruby." *Pittsburgh Courier,* November 29, 1952.

———. "Black Death." Unpublished short story. Charles S. Johnson Papers, Special Collections, Fisk University Library.

———. "Characteristics of Negro Expression." In *Negro: An Anthology,* edited by Nancy Cunard, pp. 39–46. Reprinted in *The Sanctified Church,* 41–78.

———. "The Chick with One Hen." Unpublished essay, James Weldon Johnson Memorial Collection, Beinecke Rare Book and Manuscript Library, Yale University.

———. "The Conscience of the Court." *Saturday Evening Post,* March 18, 1950, pp. 23, 112, 114, 116, 118, 120, 122.

———. "Crazy for This Democracy." *Negro Digest* 4 (December 1945): 45–48. Reprinted in *I Love Myself,* 165–68.

———. "Doctor's Threats, Tussle over Gun Led to Slaying." *Pittsburgh Courier,* January 10, 1953.

——. "Drenched in Light." *Opportunity* 2 (December 1924): 371–74. Reprinted as "Isis" in *Spunk,* 9–18.

——. *Dust Tracks on a Road.* Philadelphia: J. B. Lippincott, 1942. Second Edition, edited and with an introduction by Robert E. Hemenway, Urbana and Chicago: University of Illinois Press, 1984. Manuscript in JWJ.

——. "The Eatonville Anthology." In *I Love Myself,* 177–88.

——. "The Elusive Goal: Brotherhood of Man." Unpublished manuscript in HC.

——. "Fannie Hurst." *Saturday Review* 16 (October 9, 1937): 15–16.

——. "The Fiery Chariot." Unpublished manuscript in HC.

——. "The Fire and the Cloud." *Challenge* 1 (September 1934): 10–14.

——. "The Gilded Six-Bits." *Story* 3 (August 1933): 60–70. Reprinted in *Spunk,* 54–68.

——. "High John de Conquer." *American Mercury* 57 (October 1943): 37–40. Reprinted in *The Sanctified Church,* 69–78.

——. "How It Feels to Be Colored Me." *World Tomorrow* 11 (May 1928): 215–16. Reprinted in *I Love Myself,* 152–55.

——. *I Love Myself When I Am Laughing . . . And Then Again When I Am Looking Mean and Impressive: A Zora Neale Hurston Reader,* edited by Alice Walker. Old Westbury, N.Y.: The Feminist Press, 1979.

——. "I Saw Negro Votes Peddled." *American Legion Magazine* 49 (November 1950): 12–13, 54–57, 59–60.

——. *Jonah's Gourd Vine.* Philadelphia: J. B. Lippincott, 1934. Reprinted, with an introduction by Rita Dove, New York: Harper and Row, 1990.

——. "Just Like Us: An Analysis of the Hebrews and the Modern Jews as They Were and Are As Against Our Traditional Conceptions." Unpublished manuscript in SC.

——. *The Life Story of Mrs. Ruby J. McCollum. Pittsburgh Courier,* February 28, March 7, 14, 21, 28, April 4, 11, 18, 25, May 2, 1953.

——. "McCollum-Adams Trial Highlights." *Pittsburgh Courier,* December 27, 1952.

——. "Magnolia Flower." *The Spokesman,* July 1925, pp. 26–29.

——. *Moses, Man of the Mountain.* Philadelphia: J. B. Lippincott, 1942. Reprinted, with an introduction by Blyden Jackson. Urbana and Chicago: University of Illinois Press, 1984.

——. "Mourner's Bench, Communist Line: Why the Negro Won't Buy Communism." *American Legion Magazine* 50 (June 1951): 14–15, 55–60.

——. *Mules and Men.* Philadelphia: J. B. Lippincott, 1935. Reprinted, with an introduction by Robert E. Hemenway, Bloomington: Indiana University Press, 1978.

——. "Muttsy." *Opportunity* 4 (August 1926): 246–50. Reprinted in *Spunk,* 19–37.

——. "My Most Humiliating Experience." In *I Love Myself,* pp. 163–64.

———. "The Pet Negro System." *American Mercury* 56 (May 1943): 593–600. Reprinted in *I Love Myself,* 156–62.

———. "Ruby Bares Her Love." *Pittsburgh Courier,* January 3, 1953.

———. "Ruby McCollum Fights for Life." *Pittsburgh Courier,* November 22, 1952.

———. "Ruby Sane." *Pittsburgh Courier,* October 18, 1952.

———. "Ruby's Troubles Mount." *Pittsburgh Courier,* January 17, 1953.

———. *The Sanctified Church.* Berkeley: Turtle Island, 1983.

———. *Seraph on the Suwanee.* New York: Charles Scribner's Sons, 1948. Reprinted, with a foreward by Hazel V. Carby, New York: HarperCollins, 1991. Manuscript in HC.

———. "Spunk." *Opportunity* 3 (June 1925): 171–73. Reprinted in *Spunk,* 1–8.

———. *Spunk: The Selected Stories of Zora Neale Hurston.* Berkeley: Turtle Island Foundation, 1985.

———. "Stories of Conflict." *Saturday Review,* April 2, 1938, p. 32.

———. "Sweat." *Fire!!* 1 (November 1926): 40–45. Reprinted in *Spunk,* 38–53.

———. *Tell My Horse.* Philadelphia: J. B. Lippincott, 1939. Reprinted, with an introduction by Bob Callahan, Berkeley: Turtle Island, 1983.

———. *Their Eyes Were Watching God.* Philadelphia: J. B. Lippincott, 1937. Reprinted, with a foreword by Sherley Anne Williams. Urbana: University of Illinois Press, 1978. Manuscript in JWJ.

———. "Trial Highlights." *Pittsburgh Courier,* November 29, 1952.

———. "Victim of Fate." *Pittsburgh Courier,* October 11, 1952.

———. "What White Publishers Won't Print." *Negro Digest* 8 (April 1950): 85–89. Reprinted in *I Love Myself,* 169–73.

———. "Zora's Revealing Story of Ruby's First Day in Court." *Pittsburgh Courier,* October 11, 1952.

Hutchinson, Percy. "Led His People Free" [Review of *Moses, Man of the Mountain*]. *New York Times Book Review,* November 19, 1939, p. 21.

Ikonné, Chidi. *From Du Bois to Van Vechten: The Early New Negro Literature, 1903– 1926.* Westport, Conn.: Greenwood Press, 1981.

Jackson, Blyden. "Some Negroes in the Land of Goshen." *Tennessee Folklore Society Bulletin* 19:4 (December 1953): 103–7.

Jackson, Bruce, ed. *The Negro and His Folklore in Nineteenth-Century Periodicals.* Austin: University of Texas Press, 1967.

———. "Stagolee Stories: A Badman Goes Gentle." *Southern Folklore Quarterly* 29 (1965): 188–94.

———. "What Happened to Jody." *Journal of American Folklore* 80 (1967): 387–96.

Jelinek, Estelle C. *Women's Autobiography: Essays in Criticism.* Bloomington and London: Indiana University Press, 1980.

Johnson, Barbara. "Metaphor, Metonymy and Voice in *Their Eyes Were Watching*

God. In *Black Literature and Literary Theory,* edited by Henry Louis Gates, Jr. New York and London: Methuen, 1984.

——. "Thresholds of Difference: Structures of Address in Zora Neale Hurston." *Critical Inquiry* 12 (Autumn 1985): 278–89.

Johnson, Barbara, and Henry Louis Gates, Jr. "A Black and Idiomatic Free Indirect Discourse." In *Zora Neale Hurston's "Their Eyes Were Watching God,"* edited by Harold Bloom, pp. 73–86. New York, New Haven, and Philadelphia: Chelsea House Publishers, 1987.

Johnson, Charles S. *Shadow of the Plantation.* Chicago and London: University of Chicago Press, 1934.

Johnson, James Weldon. "The Dilemma of the Negro Author." *American Mercury* (December 1928): 477–81.

——. *God's Trombones: Seven Negro Sermons in Verse.* New York: Viking Press, 1964. (Originally published in 1927.)

Johnson, R. Brimley. *Popular English Ballads.* 4 vols. Freeport: Books for Libraries Press, 1971. (Originally published in 1894.)

Jones, Charles C. *Negro Myths from the Georgia Coast, Told in the Vernacular.* Columbia, S.C.: The State Company, 1925.

Jones, Kirkland C. "Folk Humor as Comic Relief in Hurston's *Jonah's Gourd Vine.*" *Zora Neale Hurston Forum* 1:1 (Fall 1986): 26–31.

Jordan, Jennifer. "Feminist Fantasies: Zora Neale Hurston's *Their Eyes Were Watching God.*" *Tulsa Studies in Women's Literature* 7:1 (Spring 1988): 105–17.

Josephus, Flavius. *The Life and Works of Flavius Josephus.* trans. by William Whiston. Philadelphia: John C. Winston Co. (n.d.)

Kalb, John D. "The Anthropological Narrator of Hurston's *Their Eyes Were Watching God.*" *Studies in American Fiction* 16:2 (1988): 169–80.

Kaplan, Carla. "The Erotics of Talk." *American Literature* 67:1 (1995): 115–42.

Kitch, Sally L. "Gender and Language: Dialect, Silence and the Disruption of Discourse." *Women's Studies* 14 (1987): 65–78.

Kochman, Thomas. *Rappin' and Stylin' Out: Communication in Urban Black America.* Urbana: University of Illinois Press, 1972.

——. "Toward an Ethnography of Black American Speech Behavior." In *Afro-American Anthropology: Contemporary Perspectives,* edited by Norman E. Whitten, Jr., and John F. Szwed, pp. 145–62. New York: Free Press, 1970.

Krasner, James. "The Life of Women: Zora Neale Hurston and Female Autobiography." *Black American Literature Forum* 23:1 (Spring 1989): 113–26.

Kubitschek, Missy Dehn. " 'Tuh de Horizon and Back': The Female Quest in *Their Eyes Were Watching God.*" *Black American Literature Forum* 17 (1983): 109–15.

Larsen, Nella. *Quicksand and Passing.* Edited and with an introduction by Deborah E. McDowell. New Brunswick, N.J.: Rutgers University Press, 1986.

Lester, Julius. *Black Folktales.* New York: Richard W. Baron, 1969.

Levecq, Christine. "'You Heard Her, You Ain't Blind': Subversive Shifts in Zora Neale Hurston's *Their Eyes Were Watching God.*" *Tulsa Studies in Women's Literature* 13:1 (1994): 87–111.

Levine, Lawrence. *Black Culture and Black Consciousness: Afro-American Folk Thought From Slavery to Freedom.* New York: Oxford University Press, 1977.

Lindroth, James R. "Generating the Vocabulary of Hoodoo: Zora Neale Hurston and Ishmael Reed." *The Zora Neale Hurston Forum* 2:1 (Fall 1987): 27–34.

Lionnet, Françoise. "Autoethnography: The An-Archic Style of *Dust Tracks on a Road.*" In *Autobiographical Voices: Race, Gender, Self-Portraiture.* Ithaca and London: Cornell University Press, 1989.

Locke, Alain. "Dry Fields and Green Pastures." *Opportunity* 18 (January 1940): 7.

———. "Review of Negro Books." *Opportunity* (January 1938): 8–11, 27.

———. "The Negro: 'New' of Newer." *Opportunity* 17 (February 1939): 38.

Lott, Eric. *Love and Theft: Blackface Minstrelsy and the American Working Class.* New York: Oxford University Press, 1993.

Lowe, John. *Jump at the Sun: Zora Neale Hurston's Cosmic Comedy.* Urbana and Chicago: University of Illinois Press, 1994.

Lupton, Mary Jane. "Zora Neale Hurston and the Survival of the Female." *Southern Literary Journal* 15 (1982): 45–54.

MacGowan, Gault. "Negro Folklore" [Review of *Mules and Men*], Schomburg. No publication information.

McCarthy, Kevin M. "Three Legal Entanglements of Zora Neale Hurston." In *Zora in Florida,* edited by Steve Glassman and Kathryn Lee Seidel, pp. 174–82. Orlando: University of Central Florida Press, 1991.

McCredie, Wendy J. "Authority and Authorization in *Their Eyes Were Watching God. Black American Literature Forum* 16 (1982): 25–28.

McDowell, Deborah E. "Boundaries: On Distant Relations and Close Kin." In *Afro-American Literary Study in the 1990s,* edited by Houston A. Baker, Jr., and Patricia Redmond, pp. 51–70. Chicago and London: University of Chicago Press, 1989.

———. "The Neglected Dimension of Jessie Fauset." In *Conjuring:Black Women, Fiction, and Tradition,* edited by Marjorie Pryse and Hortense Spillers, pp. 86–104. Bloomington: Indiana University Press, 1985.

———. "New Directions for Black Feminist Criticism." *Black American Literature Forum* 14:4 (Winter 1980): 153–58.

———. "On Face: The Masks of Identity in Jessie Fauset's *Plum Bun* or Getting Rich in the Harlem Renaissance." In *"The Changing Same": Black Women's Literature, Criticism, and Theory,* pp. 61–77. Bloomington and Indianapolis: Indiana University Press, 1995.

———. "Reading Family Matters." In *Changing Our Own Words:Essays on Criti-*

cism, Theory, and Writing by Black Women, edited by Cheryl A. Wall, pp. 75–97. New Brunswick and London: Rutgers University Press, 1989.

———. "'That nameless . . . shameful impulse': Sexuality in Nella Larsen's *Quicksand* and *Passing.*" In *Studies in Black American Literature, Vol. III: Black Feminist Criticism and Critical Theory,* edited by Joe Weixlmann and Houston A. Baker, Jr., pp. 139–67. Greenwood, Fla.: Penkevill Publishing Co., 1988.

Mackenzie, Donald A. *Egyptian Myth and Legend.* New York: Bell Publishing Co., 1978. (Originally published in 1907.)

Marks, Donald R. "Sex, Violence, and Organic Consciousness in Zora Neale Hurston's *Their Eyes Were Watching God. Black American Literature Forum* 19:4 (Winter 1985): 152–57.

Mead, Margaret. *An Anthropologist at Work: Writings of Ruth Benedict.* New York: Houghton Mifflin, 1966.

Mercatante, Anthony S. *Who's Who in Egyptian Mythology.* New York: Clarkson N. Potter, 1978.

Mikell, Gwendolyn. "The Anthropological Imagination of Zora Neale Hurston." *The Western Journal of Black Studies* 7:1 (1983): 27–34.

———. "When Horses Talk: Reflections of Zora Neale Hurston's Haitian Anthropology." *Phylon: The Atlanta University Review of Race and Culture* 43:3 (1982): 218–30.

Mitchell-Kernan, Claudia. "Signifying, Loud-Talking, and Marking." In *Rappin' and Stylin' Out: Communication in Urban Black America,* edited by Thomas Kochman, pp. 315–35. Urbana: University of Illinois Press, 1972.

———. "Signifying and Marking: Two Afro-American Speech Acts." In *Directions in Social Linguistics,* edited by John J. Gumperz and Dell Hymes, pp. 161–79. New York: Holt, Rinehart, and Winston, 1972.

Monroe, Barbara. "Courtship, Comedy, and African-American Expressive Culture in Zora Neale Hurston's Fiction." In *Look Who's Laughing: Gender and Comedy,* edited by Gail Finny. Langhorne, Pa.: Gordon and Breach, 1994.

Moon, Henry. "Big Old Lies" [Review of *Mules and Men*]. *New Republic* 85 (December 11, 1935): 142.

Moret, Alexandre. *The Nile and Egyptian Civilization.* London: Kegan Paul, Trench, Trubner and Co., 1927.

Naylor, Carolyn A. "Cross-Gender Significance of the Journey Motif in Selected Afro-American Fiction." *Colby Library Quarterly* 18:1 (March 1982): 26–38.

Neal, Larry. "Introduction" to *Jonah's Gourd Vine.* Phildaelphia: J. B. Lippincott, 1971.

Newson, Adele. "'The Fiery Chariot': A One-Act Play by Zora Neale Hurston." *The Zora Neale Hurston Forum* 1 (Fall 1986): 181–202.

Ogunyemi, Chikwenye Okonjo. "Womanism: The Dynamics of the Contemporary Black Female Novel in English." *Signs* 2:1 (1985): 63–80.

Ostendorf, Berndt. *Black Literature in White America*. Totowa, N.J.: Barnes and Noble, 1982.

Oster, Harry. "Negro Humor: John and Old Marster." *Journal of the Folklore Institute* 5 (1968): 42–57. Reprinted in Dundes, 549–60.

Perry, Margaret. *Silence to the Drums: A Survey of the Literature of the Harlem Renaissance*. Westport, Conn.: Greenwood Press, 1976.

Petrie, W. M. Flinders. *Egypt and Israel*. London: Society for Promoting Christian Knowledge, 1911.

——. *Egyptian Tales, Translated from the Papyri*. Second Edition. 2 vols. New York: Benjamin Blom, 1971. (Originally published in 1899).

——. *A History of Egypt*. 3 vols. 10th edition. London: Metheun, 1923.

——. *The Religion of Ancient Egypt*. London: Constable, 1906.

——. *Religion and Conscience in Ancient Egypt*. London: Methuen, 1898.

——. *Religious Life in Ancient Egypt*. London, Boston, and New York: Houghton Mifflin, 1924.

——. *Social Life in Ancient Egypt*. London: Constable and Co., 1924.

Pierson, William D. "Puttin' Down Ole Massa: African Satire in the New World." In *African Folklore in the New World,* edited by David J. Crowley, pp. 20–34. Austin and London: University of Texas Press, 1977.

Pinckney, Josephine. "A Pungent, Poetic Novel about Negroes" [Review of *Jonah's Gourd Vine*]. *New York Herald Tribune Books,* May 6, 1934.

Plant, Deborah G. *Every Tub Must Sit on Its Own Bottom: The Philosophy of Zora Neale Hurston*. Urbana and Chicago: University of Illinois Press, 1995.

——. "The Folk Preacher and Folk Sermon Form in Zora Neale Hurston's *Dust Tracks on a Road*." *Folklore Forum* 12:1 (1988): 3–19.

Plomer, William. Review of *Jonah's Gourd Vine*. *Spectator,* January 4, 1935, p. 25.

Pondrom, Cyrena N. "The Role of Myth in Hurston's *Their Eyes Were Watching God*." *American Literature* 38:2 (May 1986): 181–202.

Preece, Harold. "The Negro Folk Cult." *Crisis* 43 (1936): 364, 374. Reprinted in Dundes, pp. 34–39.

——. Review of *Dust Tracks on a Road*. *Tomorrow,* February 1943.

Preu, Dana McKinnon. "A Literary Reading of *Mules and Men, Part I*." In *Zora In Florida,* edited by Steve Glassman and Kathryn Lee Seidel, pp. 46–61. Orlando: University of Central Florida Press, 1991.

Puckett, Newbell Niles. *Folk Beliefs of the Southern Negro*. Chapel Hill: University of North Carolina Press, 1926.

Racine, Maria J. "Voice and Interiority in *Their Eyes Were Watching God*." *African American Review* 28:2 (1994): 283–92.

Rambeau, James. "The Fiction of Zora Neale Hurston." *Markham Review* 5 (1976): 61–64.

Rawlings, Marjorie Kinnan. *Cross Creek*. New York: Charles Scribner's Sons, 1942.

——. *The Yearling*. New York: Charles Scribner's Sons, 1938.

Raynaud, Claudine. "Autobiography as a 'Lying' Session: Zora Neale Hurston's *Dust Tracks on a Road.*" In *Studies in Black American Literature, Vol. III: Black Feminist Criticism and Critical Theory,* edited by Joe Weixlmann and Houston A. Baker, pp. 111–38. Greenwood, Fla.: Penkevill Publishing Co., 1988.

———. "'Rubbing a Paragraph with a Soft Cloth': Muted Voices and Editorial Constraints in *Dust Tracks on a Road.*" In *De/Colonizing the Subject: The Politics of Gender in Women's Autobiography,* edited by Sidonie Smith and Julia Watson, pp. 34–64. Minneapolis: University of Minnesota Press, 1992.

Rayson, Ann L. "*Dust Tracks on a Road:* Zora Neale Hurston and the Form of Black Autobiography." *Negro American Literature Forum* 7:2 (Summer 1973): 39–45.

———. "The Novels of Zora Neale Hurston." *Studies in Black Literature* 5 (Winter 1974): 1–11.

Redding, J. Saunders. "The Negro Author: His Public and His Purse." *Publisher's Weekly,* March 24, 1945, pp. 1284–88.

Reich, Alice. "Pheoby's Hungry Listening." *Women's Studies* 13 (1986): 163–69.

Review of *Dust Tracks on a Road. Booklist* 39 (December 1, 1942): 120.

Review of *Dust Tracks on a Road. New Yorker* 18 (November 14, 1942): 71.

Review of *Jonah's Gourd Vine. Boston Chronicle,* May 5, 1934.

Review of *Jonah's Gourd Vine. The Nation* 138 (June 13, 1934): 683–84.

Review of *Jonah's Gourd Vine. Times Literary Supplement,* October 18, 1934, pp. 716–17.

Richardson, Ethel Park, comp., and Sigmund Spaeth, arr. *American Mountain Songs.* New York: Greenburg Publishers, 1927.

Roberts, John. Review of *Mules and Men. Journal of American Folklore* 93: 370 (October–December 1980): 463–67.

Roberts, John W. *From Trickster to Badman: The Black Folk Hero in Slavery and Freedom.* Philadelphia: University of Pennsylvania Press, 1989.

Robey, Judith. "Generic Strategies in Zora Neale Hurston's *Dust Tracks on a Road.*" *Black American Literature Forum* 24:4 (Winter 1990): 667–82.

Rose, Ernestine. Review of *Dust Tracks on a Road. Library Journal* 67 (November 1, 1942): 950.

Rosenblatt, Rosen. "Eccentricities: *Their Eyes Were Watching God.*" In *Black Fiction,* pp. 84–90. Cambridge, Mass.: Harvard University Press.

Rourke, Constance. *The Roots of American Culture and Other Essays.* New York: Harcourt Brace, 1942.

Rugg, Winnifred King. Review of *Seraph on the Suwanee. Christian Science Monitor,* December 23, 1948, p. 11.

Sadoff, Diane. "Black Matrilineage: The Case of Alice Walker and Zora Neale Hurston." *Signs* 11 (1985): 4–26.

Sanchez-Eppler, Benigo. "Telling Anthropology: Zora Neale Hurston and Gilberto Freyre Disciplined in Their Field Home Work." *American Literary History* 4:3 (1992): 464–88.

Saunders, James Robert. "Womanism as the Key to Understanding Zora Neale Hurston's *Their Eyes Were Watching God* and Alice Walker's *The Color Purple*." *The Hollins Critic* 25:4 (October 1988): 1–11.

Schwalbenberg, Peter. "Time as Point of View in Zora Neale Hurston's *Their Eyes Were Watching God*." *Negro American Literature Forum* 10 (1976): 104–5, 107–8.

Scott, Emmett J. *Negro Migration During the War.* New York: Arno Press and *The New York Times,* 1969.

Seabrook, W. B. *The Magic Island.* New York: The Literary Guild of America, 1929.

Sheffey, Ruthe T. "Zora Neale Hurston's *Moses, Man of the Mountain:* A Fictionalized Manifesto on the Imperatives of Black Leadership." *College Language Association Journal* 29:2 (December 1985): 206–20.

Sherman, Beatrice. "Zora Hurston's Story" [Review of *Dust Tracks on a Road*]. *New York Times,* November 29, 1942, p. 44.

Silvertone, Elizabeth. *Marjorie Kinnan Rawlings: Sojourner at Cross Creek.* Woodstock, N.Y.: Overtone Press, 1988.

Slaughter, Frank G. "Freud in Turpentine" [Review of *Seraph on the Suwanee*]. *New York Times,* October 31, 1948, p. 24.

Slomovitz, Philip. "The Negro's Moses" [Review of *Moses, Man of the Mountain*]. *Christian Century* 56 (December 6, 1939): 1504.

Smith, Barbara. "Toward a Black Feminist Criticism." In *Within the Circle: An Anthology of African American Literary Criticism from the Harlem Renaissance to the Present,* edited by Angelyn Mitchell, pp. 410–27. Durham and London: Duke University Press, 1994.

Smith, Jeanne Rosier. *Writing Tricksters: Mythic Gambols in American Ethnic Literature.* Berkeley and London: University of California Press, 1997.

Smith, Valerie. "Black Feminist Theory and the Representation of the 'Other.'" In *Changing Our Own Words: Essays on Criticism, Theory, and Writing by Black Women,* edited by Cheryl A. Wall, pp. 38–57. New Brunswick and London: Rutgers University Press, 1989.

———. "Gender and Afro-American Literary Theory and Criticism." In *Within the Circle: An Anthology of African American Literary Criticism from the Harlem Renaissance to the Present,* edited by Angelyn Mitchell, pp. 482–98. Durham and London: Duke University Press, 1994.

Smitherman, Geneva. *Talkin' and Testifyin': The Language of Black America.* Boston: Houghton Mifflin, 1977.

Speisman, Barbara. "Voodoo as Symbol in *Jonah's Gourd Vine*." In *Zora in Florida,* edited by Steve Glassman and Kathryn Lee Seidel, pp. 86–93. Orlando: University of Central Florida Press, 1991.

Stanford, Ann Folwell. "Dynamics of Change: Men and Co-Feeling in the Fiction of Zora Neale Hurston and Alice Walker." In *Alice Walker and Zora*

Neale Hurston: The Common Bond, edited by Lillie P. Howard. Westport, Conn., and London: Greenwood Press, 1993.

Starke, Catherine Juanita. *Black Portraiture in American Fiction: Stock Characters, Archetypes, and Individuals.* New York and London: Basic Books, 1971.

Steady, Filomina Chioma. *The Black Woman Cross-Culturally.* Cambridge, Mass.: Schenkman, 1981.

Stepto, Robert B. *From Behind the Veil: A Study of Afro-American Narrative.* Urbana, Chicago, and London: University of Illinois Press, 1979.

Stevens, George. "Negroes By Themselves" [Review of *Their Eyes Were Watching God.*] *Saturday Review,* September 18, 1937, p. 3.

Stoney, Samuel Gaillard. "Wit, Wisdom, and Folklore" [Review of *Mules and Men*]. *Books,* October 13, 1935, p. 7.

Stong, Phil. "Zora Hurston Sums Up" [Review of *Dust Tracks on a Road*]. *Saturday Review* 25 (November 28, 1942): 6–7.

Sylvander, Carolyn Wedin. *Jessie Redmond Fauset, Black American Writer.* Troy, N.Y.: Whitson Publishing Co., 1981.

Talley, Thomas W. *Negro Folk Rhymes.* New York: Macmillan, 1922.

Thomas, H. Nigel. *From Folklore to Fiction: A Study of Folk Heroes and Rituals in the Black American Novel.* New York: Greenwood Press, 1988.

Thompson, Gordon E. "Projecting Gender: Personification in the Works of Zora Neale Hurston." *American Literature* 66:4 (1994): 737–63.

Thompson, Ralph. Review of *Their Eyes Were Watching God. New York Times,* October 6, 1937.

Thornton, Jerome E. "'Goin' on de Muck': The Paradoxical Journey of the Black American Hero." *College Language Association Journal* 31:3 (March 1988): 261–80.

Thurman, Wallace. *Infants of the Spring.* New York: Macaulay, 1932. Reprinted, Carbondale and Edwardsville: Southern Illinois University Press, 1979.

Tompkins, Lucy. Review of *Their Eyes Were Watching God. New York Times Book Review,* September 26, 1937.

Turner, Darwin. *In A Minor Chord: Three Afro-American Writers and Their Search for Identity.* Carbondale: Southern Illinois University Press, 1971.

Untermeyer, Louis. "Old Testament Voodoo" [Review of *Moses, Man of the Mountain*]. *Saturday Review of Literature* 21:11 (November 11, 1939): 11.

Wainwright, Mary Katherine. "Subversive Female Folk Tellers in *Mules and Men.*" In *Zora In Florida,* edited by Steve Glassman and Kathryn Lee Seidel, pp. 62–75. Orlando: University of Central Florida Press, 1991.

Wald, Priscilla. "Becoming 'Colored': The Self-Authorized Language of Difference in Zora Neale Hurston." *American Literary History* 2:1 (1990): 79–100.

Walker. Alice. *In Search of Our Mothers' Gardens: Womanist Prose.* San Diego, New York, and London: Harcourt Brace Jovanovich, 1983.

Walker, S. Jay. "Zora Neale Hurston's *Their Eyes Were Watching God:* Black Novel of Sexism." *Modern Fiction Studies* 29 (1974–75): 519–27.

Wall, Cheryl A., ed. *Changing Our Own Words: Essays on Criticism, Theory, and Writing by Black Women.* New Brunswick and London: Rutgers University Press, 1989.

———. *"Mules and Men* and Women: Zora Neale Hurston's Strategies of Narration and Visions of Female Empowerment." *Black American Literature Forum* 23:4 (Winter 1989): 661–80.

———. *Women of the Harlem Renaissance.* Bloomington and Indianapolis: Indiana University Press, 1995.

———. "Zora Neale Hurston: Changing Her Own Words." In *American Novelists Revisited: Essays in Feminist Criticism,* edited by Fritz Fleischmann, pp. 371–93. Boston: G. K. Hall, 1982.

Wallace, Margaret. "Real Negro People" [Review of *Jonah's Gourd Vine*]. *New York Times Book Review* 83 (May 6, 1934): 6–7.

Washington, Mary H. "The Black Woman's Search for Identity: Zora Neale Hurston's Work." *Black World* 21:10 (1972): 68–75.

———. *Invented Lives: Narratives of Black Women 1860–1960.* New York: Doubleday, 1987.

———. "Zora Neale Hurston: A Woman Half in Shadow." In *I Love Myself,* pp. 7–25.

Waters, Ethel (with Charles Samuels). *His Eye Is on the Sparrow.* Garden City, N.Y,: Doubleday and Co., 1950.

Weigall, Arthur. *The Glory of the Pharaohs.* New York and London: G. P. Putnam's Sons, 1923.

———. *A History of the Pharaohs.* 3 vols. New York: E. P. Dutton, 1925.

———. *The Paganism of Our Christianity.* London: Hutchinson and Co., 1928.

Weldon, Fred O. "Negro Folktale Heroes." *Publications of the Texas Folklore Society* 21 (1959): 170–89.

Wilentz, Gay. "Defeating the False God: Janie's Self-Determination in Zora Neale Hurston's *Their Eyes Were Watching God.*" In *Faith of a [Woman] Writer,* edited by Alice Kessler-Harris and William McBrien, pp. 286–91. New York: Greenwood Press, 1988.

———. "White Patron and Black Artist." *The Library Chronicle of the University of Texas at Austin.* New Series No. 35 (1986): 21–43.

Williams, Sherley Anne. "Some Implications of Womanist Theory." In *Reading Black, Reading Feminist: A Critical Anthology,* edited by Henry Louis Gates, Jr., pp. 68–75. New York: Meridian, 1990.

Willis, Susan. *Specifying: Black Women Writing the American Experience.* Madison: University of Wisconsin Press, 1987.

Wolff, Maria Tai. "Listening and Living: Reading and Experience in *Their Eyes Were Watching God.*" *Black American Literature Forum* 16 (1982): 29–33.

Woodson, Carter G. *A Century of Negro Migration.* New York: AMS Press, 1970. (Originally published in 1918.)

Woodward, C. Vann. *The Strange Career of Jim Crow.* 3rd revised edition. New York: Oxford University Press, 1974.

Wright, Richard. "Between Laughter and Tears." *New Masses* 5 (October 1937).

Index